Musigny Roumier | L'Extravagant de Doisy-[...]s du chenin, Patrick Baudouin | Screaming Eagle | C[...]gne Coche-Dury | Champagne Krug | Harlan Estate [...]elin Jean-Louis Chave | Penfold's Grange | Amaron[...]ork André Ostertag | Jéroboam Clos Windsbuhl, Olivier Humbrecht Sassicaia | Impériale Château Mouton-Rothschild | Magnum Château Le Pin | Montrachet, Ramonet | Richebourg, Henri Jayer | La Mouline, Marcel Guigal | Trockenbeerenauslese, Egon Müller Martha's Vineyard, Napa Valley | La Tâche | Magnum Château Lafleur | Magnum Château La Mission-Haut-Brion | Château Dassault | Barbaresco, Angelo Gaja | Hermitage La Chapelle, Jaboulet | Château l'Évangile | Château Lafite-Rothschild | Château Rayas | Grands Echezeaux, Leroy | Trockenbeerenauslese, Joh. Jos. Prüm | Brunello di Montalcino, Biondi-Santi | Château Musar Grasevina | Tokay de Hongrie Eszencia | Magnum Château Cheval Blanc | Magnum Château Lafleur | Château Trotanoy | Magnum Petrus | Château Haut-Brion | Magnum Château Mouton-Rothschild | Muscat de Massandra | Châteauneuf-du-Pape, Célestins, Henri Bonneau | Vega Sicilia Unico | Clos des Lambrays | La Grande Rue Muscat de Massandra | Cagore de Massandra | Chambertin, Armand Rousseau | Quinta do Noval, Nacional | Château Latour à Pomerol Salon blanc de blancs | Champagne Bollinger, V.V.F. | La Romanée Muscat de Magaratch | Maury Mas Amiel | Château Ausone Châteauneuf-du-Pape, Domaine Roger Sabon | Romanée-Conti Petrus | Armagnac Laberdolive | Tokay 6 puttonyos, Otto de Habsbourg | Magnum Château Margaux | Cognac Rémy Martin Louis XIII | Château Coutet | Château d'Arche | Château Suduiraut Château Latour | Lacrima Christi, Massandra | Château-Chalon, Bourdy | Vin de paille du Jura, Bouvret | Armagnac, Lamaëstre Red Port, Massandra | Massandra, The Honey of Altea Pastures Klein Constantia | Cognac Dudognon | Château Feytit-Clinet Grenache | Château Gruaud-Larose | Vin de Zucco, duc d'Aumale | Cognac Hine | Louis-Philippe d'Orléans | Vinaigre balsamique, Leonardi | Syracuse | Château Bel-Air Marquis d'Aligre - Marquis de Pommereu - 1848 Vin de Louise | Muscat de Lunel | Porto King's Port | Château Palmer | Commanderia de Chypre | Pedro Ximénez, Toro Albala | Madère de Massandra Madère Impérial, Nicolas | Marsala De Bartoli | Pommard Rugiens, Félix Clerget | Xérès, Nicolas | Château d'Yquem | Xérès de La Frontera, Trafalgar | Cognac Napoléon, Grande Fine Champagne Réserve d'Austerlitz | Malaga de la Marie-Thérèse Cognac | Porto Hunt's | Whisky MaCallan | Marie-Brizard du Titanic | Bénédictine début XXe siècle, collection Maurice Chevalier Rhum Lameth | Calvados Huet | Chartreuse | Gouttes de Malte

| Musigny Roumier | L'Extravagant de Doisy-Daëne | Les Sens du chenin, Patrick Baudouin | Screaming Eagle | Corton-Charlemagne, Coche-Dury | Champagne Krug | Harlan Estate | Ermitage Cathelin, Jean-Louis Chave | Penfold's Grange | Amarone, Quintarelli | Work, André Ostertag | Jéroboam Clos Windsbuhl, Olivier Humbrecht | Sassicaia | Impériale Château Mouton-Rothschild | Magnum Château Le Pin | Montrachet, Ramonet | Richebourg, Henri Jayer | La Mouline, Marcel Guigal | Trockenbeerenauslese, Egon Müfler | Martha's Vineyard, Napa Valley | La Tâche | Magnum Château Lafleur | Magnum Château La Mission-Haut-Brion | Château Dassault | Barbaresco, Angelo Gaja | Hermitage La Chapelle, Jaboulet | Château l'Evangile | Château Lafite-Rothschild | Château Rayas | Grands Echezeaux, Leroy | Trockenbeerenauslese, Joh. Jos. Prüm | Brunello di Montalcino, Biondi-Santi | Château Musar | Grasevina | Tokay de Hongrie Eszencia | Magnum Château Cheval Blanc | Magnum Château Lafleur | Château Trotanoy | Magnum Petrus | Château Haut-Brion | Magnum Château Mouton-Rothschild | Muscat de Massandra | Châteauneuf-du-Pape, Célestins, Henri Bonneau | Vega Sicilia Unico | Clos des Lambrays | La Grande Rue | Muscat de Massandra | Cagore de Massandra | Chambertin, Armand Rousseau | Quinta do Noval, Nacional | Château Latour à Pomerol | Salon blanc de blancs | Champagne Bollinger, V.V.F. | La Romanée | Muscat de Magaratch | Maury Mas Amiel | Château Ausone | Châteauneuf-du-Pape, Domaine Roger Sabon | Romanée-Conti | Petrus | Armagnac Laberdolive | Tokay 6 puttonyos, Otto de Habsbourg | Magnum Château Margaux | Cognac Rémy Martin Louis XIII | Château Coutet | Château d'Arche | Château Suduiraut | Château Latour | Lacrima Christi, Massandra | Château-Chalon, Bourdy | Vin de paille du Jura, Bouvret | Armagnac, Lamaëstre | Red Port, Massandra | Massandra, The Honey of Altea Pastures | Klein Constantia | Cognac Dudognon | Château Feytit-Clinet | Grenache | Château Gruaud-Larose | Vin de Zucco, duc d'Aumale | Cognac Hine | Louis-Philippe d'Orléans | Vinaigre balsamique, Leonardi | Syracuse | Château Bel-Air Marquis d'Aligre - Marquis de Pommereu - 1848 Vin de Louise | Muscat de Lunel | Porto King's Port | Château Palmer | Commanderia de Chypre | Pedro Ximénez, Toro Albala | Madère de Massandra | Madère Impérial, Nicolas | Marsala De Bartoli | Pommard Rugiens, Félix Clerget | Xérès, Nicolas | Château d'Yquem | Xérès de La Frontera, Trafalgar | Cognac Napoléon, Grande Fine Champagne Réserve d'Austerlitz | Malaga de la Marie-Thérèse | Cognac | Porto Hunt's | Whisky MaCallan | Marie-Brizard du Titanic | Bénédictine début XXᵉ siècle, collection Maurice Chevalier | Rhum Lameth | Calvados Huet | Chartreuse | Gouttes de Malte

MICHEL-JACK CHASSEUIL

100 VINTAGE TREASURES
FROM THE WORLD'S FINEST WINE CELLAR

Photography
JACQUES CAILLAUT

Text written in collaboration with
Gilles du Pontavice

TECTUM
PUBLISHERS

English Edition
100 Vintage treasures from the world's finest wine cellar
© 2011 Tectum Publishers
Godefriduskaai 22
2000 Antwerp
Belgium
+32 3 226 66 73
info@tectum.be
www.tectum.be

ISBN: 978-90-79761-95-1
WD: 2011/9021/31
(149)

Original edition:
100 Bouteilles extraordinaires de la plus belle cave du monde
© 2010 Editions Glénat, All rights reserved
Graphic design and layout: Isabelle Chemin
Prepress and production: Glénat Production

Watercolours produced by Marc de Kester:
© Château d'Ampuis Guigal, page 61; © Château Lafite-Rotschild, page 81;
© Château Haut-Brion, page 105: © Château Margaux, page 151

This book is dedicated to my parents, René and Gisèle, who supported me financially and had the kindness to accept dozens of cases of wine delivered in my absence.

This book is dedicated to my son, who assisted me in this crusade and of whom I am proud. Today he produces Feytit-Clinet with brio and merits a place among the best producers in my book.

This book is dedicated to the winemakers around the world!

Here is the most extraordinary collection of great wines that I have had the opportunity to admire and I have been visiting exceptional cellars for a long time. This one is unique! Like Aladdin's cave, my old friend Michel-Jack Chasseuil's wine cellar is enchanted. I no longer remember our first encounter – I believe it was just after the publication of my 'magnum' book *The Great Vintage Wine Book* – but I know that his reputation as a connoisseur preceded him. The first time I went to Fonfolet Manor, his collection was already a treasure, and at every subsequent visit I noticed that the cellar had been expanded to accommodate new bottles.

Clearly, Michel-Jack Chasseuil is both an aficionado and a fine connoisseur of the rarest wines and spirits. He can be proud of his accomplishment, this incomparable 'assembly'. It is also entirely in keeping with his character that he has the desire to reveal to his readers the secrets of his masterpiece.

I pay tribute to Michel-Jack Chasseuil, and through him to the great producers and the great lovers of wine, and wish to all that they may continue to appreciate the world's finest beverage for many years.

MICHAEL BROADBENT
Christie's London

Good wine is not lacking on this planet. The great ones are much rarer, but more than the superiority of their taste (taste is, after all, subjective), it is their ability to inspire dreams that sets them apart. One can imagine that Michel-Jack Chasseuil must have spent a long time dreaming of great names or great labels, before inspiring others to dream in turn, accumulating in his cellar the rarest, the most famous vintages, in their most sought-after years. I have known Michel for more than twenty-five years. I was a *degustation* professor at the *Académie du vin*, the school founded in Paris by Steven Spurrier, I had brought together the students of my first class in a friendly and informal club. We met regularly to taste our most exquisite bottles in the continuation of the atmosphere of that first class, which had meant so much to them, as it had to me. Michel Chasseuil joined our group right away. He was at the time an engineer at Dassault, who had no idea that he would one day inherit, under fantastic circumstances, a beautiful vineyard in Pomerol, and even less the rest of his destiny. We immediately recognised and admired his strength of will and his ability to make his wildest dreams come true despite all obstacles. With a perseverance that none of us could have equalled, he contacted one by one all of the great wine producers on the planet and persuaded them to hand over to him bottles of all the remarkable vintages, old or young, so as to include them in a museum-cellar where they would all be assembled with the idea of making them visible to the public. You might say that 'visible' is a poor destiny for a wine, and that 'consumable' would be more appropriate; however, before being savoured it must first be seen, indexed, memorised, desired. Everything in its time. The incredible collection that we can admire today at Fonfolet Manor, in the region of Deux-Sèvres, is a veritable national treasure that deserves to be overseen by a foundation worthy of it, in what would become an international museum of *haute viticulture* savoir-faire. It is in this setting, and only in this setting, that official tastings would allow experts from all over, but always hand-picked, to assess the evolution of these grand vintages and to enlighten the public. A long life to this collection, to its perpetual enrichment, and to the tenacity of civilisation that has allowed it to acquire such a scope and such universality!

MICHEL BETTANE
President of the Wine Press Association
Member of the Wine Academy of France and the International Wine Academy (Geneva)

'The most beautiful
wine cellar in the world...'

I live in the French countryside, in my grandmother's house, in La Chapelle-Bâton, a small village in the region of Deux-Sèvres. This is where I was born on the 5th of December 1941 and where I grew up. And I came back. I bought my grandmother's café, as well as the other café in the village. Here I have a park, with deer, sheep, and birds: hens to lay eggs, geese as guardians, and many more, a multi-coloured peacock, my barnyard Pétrus (we call a wine that offers a multitude of aromas and flavours a peacock tail), a dove-grey drake and its albino mate, my barnyard Musigny blanc. Those who want to visit the most beautiful wine cellar in the world must come here, to La Chapelle-Bâton. In 2000 I had already built several cellars under the house, but I wanted to assemble my most beautiful bottles in a space that would be worthy of them and that would offer protection against the risk of fire. To reach it one must cross my old cellars, then go down a long, narrow underground passage. The room that I dug out is a drawn-out cul-de-sac. It's a wine cellar of course, already well stocked, but also a conservatory and even a museum: I took care in the design of the lighting and installed showcases to present the rarest bottles that are paired with related objects, like Napoleon Brandy 1805 and two letters signed by the Emperor. Sometimes I play Gregorian chants to 'tend' my bottles. The insulation is provided by the mass of earth, and the air circulation assures good hygrometry. I didn't need to install air conditioning, and if the temperature varies slightly from season to season, so much the better: wine is a living thing, it must breathe.

There, I brought together all of the world's great wines; it's a unique collection. I chose to present one hundred of them in this book, but the selection was not easy. I have tried to satisfy as many readers as possible by choosing wines from all of the great vineyards, and of the best vintages. As Jean Kressman, a native of Bordeaux, wrote: 'There is more history than geography in a bottle of wine.' From America to Australia, from Lebanon to Germany, I kept wines from the best vineyards. From 2005 to 1735, I invite you to discover rare wines through the work of winemakers.

People often ask me how much my wine cellar is worth. I'm not very concerned about that question, because my collection is not for sale. Some bottles are unique: one can try to estimate their value, but their true price would only be known if I were to sell them. However I don't sell them, or else I sell duplicates in order to buy other bottles. The greatest wines I would not be able to find today, because they are ever rarer and because they are running out. And also because they are more and more expensive. Fifty years ago, a Second Growth Médoc like Château Cos d'Estournel was worth hardly more than a minor Bordeaux; today it is worth thirty times more. With a month's salary from Dassault, I could buy two cases of Pétrus 1982; with the same salary, I could buy one, perhaps two bottles of Pétrus 2005. The price of great wines has soared, especially since Robert Parker's notes. Then the *nouveaux riches* arrived, like the Russians and Chinese. Common connoisseurs can no longer buy great wines, and it's a pity.

I have been a collector since I was young: stamps, minerals, birds... At twenty, I started collecting wines from my father. He was a postman in La Chapelle-Bâton, and my mother worked at the village post office as well. I owe my first experiences with wine to my grandfathers: one, who was a livestock trader, sold cows and brought back wine in casks that he then bottled. The other had a café in the village. So I began tasting wine as a teenager, and they taught me to respect it.

My taste for collecting developed my curiosity, and helped me a lot in my career. In 1955 I earned my *certificate d'études*. In 1960, a certificate in boiler making and a technical diploma in aeronautics. Then, in 1961, I left to do my military service in Strasburg, in the 1ˢᵗ engineering regiment. I was thin, almost scrawny, and endured my share of teasing… at first. But I won the first running contest, then the shooting contest, then the assault course… I was promoted to sergeant after eight months, then to training instructor for the young soldiers who were leaving for the war in Algeria. I was also the 'town writer' for soldiers from the French territories in the Caribbean who couldn't write, and who paid me in bottles of rum. After my service, I remained in the reserves, and after several training sessions I was promoted to reserve captain. The Ministry of Defence decorated me *Chevalier de l'ordre national du Mérite* by decision of François Mitterrand. That was useful later at Dassault, since they hired many former soldiers.

In 1963, I started at Établissements Dassault.

Back from the Army, I had time between two trains and went to introduce myself. At that time it was easy to find work. I wanted to work in a research facility, but I was only twenty-two, and they took me on as a worker in the boiler prototype workshop. We designed aluminium fuselage parts by hand, with a mallet and a planishing stake: artistic work. The prototype workers were an elite group. Marcel Dassault was generous. He offered eight vacation days more than the other employers. Factory workers retired at sixty-five and died one month later!

Right away I wanted to trade in my blue collar for a white one. I requested a promotion, but my shop foreman didn't want to let me leave: 'Chasseuil, you're fine here, you're lucky, a good job and a good salary for someone your age.' Good with my hands, I had become one of his best workers. So, during breaks, I would go up to the research department. In the lift, I would change out of my blue uniform and into white overalls, and I would go to see the bosses. Then, to save time, I started coming to work in grey overalls. My boss was not happy, he who had been coming to work in the traditional blue worker's uniform since the age of twelve. But he gave in: I was the only one in the workshop to work in grey overalls. My co-workers called me 'the grocer' or 'the urbane boilermaker'. At the end of the day, there were the workers in blue, the research technicians in white, and me, in the middle, in grey!

Michel-Jack Chasseuil with Marcel Dassault.

At the same time, I was taking courses at the Conservatory of Arts and Trades, playing tennis and skiing, rich sports at the time, which allowed me to meet important executives of the company, thereby encouraging my professional ascent. I was also learning to fly; I earned my first-degree pilot's license and flew Jodels. Thanks to an encounter on the ski slope, an engineer became interested in me, and I was finally able to move up to the research department as a draughtsman. But looking ahead to the common market and following the wishes of General de Gaulle, I realized that it would become indispensable to master English.

So in 1967, I took a period of unpaid leave and left to work in South Africa for the Atlas Aircraft Corporation as an immigrant draughtsman. At that time, it was quite an opportunity: that country offered a double salary, a house, and more than anything I dreamt of seeing Africa's wild animals. I learned English and lived an unforgettable experience: drinking 50-year-old pastis in an isolated bistro in the Karoo desert, and in a cordial glass; impossible to add water! As for wine, at that time there were very few vineyards in that country, even though in the past it had been a major producer.

Back at Dassault in 1970, I returned to my job as a draughtsman in the prototype office. A month later, my mastery of English led to my being transferred to a management position in international sales for the Mirage. In 1975, I was promoted to 4th echelon chief technical agent for maintenance of the Mirage abroad. That same year I got divorced and won custody of my four-year-old son Jérémy after a fierce legal battle.

Always a go-getter, I wanted to move up in the company and gave myself the means, be it through work, sports or networking. Everything started at the age of ten, when I began my stamp collection. A relentless collector, I went on to become president of the philately section of the Dassault works council. At a time when everyone was talking about aerospace and the Concorde, I had the idea for a postage stamp with a Dassault aeroplane. In 1981, after many exchanges with the Postal and Telecommunications Ministry, a stamp representing the Mirage 2000 was printed. Marcel Dassault received me to offer his congratulations: 'I've heard that, thanks to you, a postage stamp with one of our planes is going to appear. It's wonderful! And during the Paris Air Show! Envelopes for the whole world will be stamped and cancelled with a Mirage, what a great advertisement! You have carte blanche to decorate the air show post office with models of all the company's aeroplanes, and you will have a VIP badge giving you access to the presidential booth. Bravo!'

Later, in 1987, Serge Dassault entrusted me to oversee the commemorative stamp issued on the occasion of his father's death. A year later, Madame Dassault requested that I supervise the production by the Hôtel des Monnaies of a bronze medallion with the image of her husband. Of the five vermeil medallions produced, she gave number 1 to her son Serge, and number 2 to me.

After the death of Marcel Dassault, there were layoffs. The Rafale was not selling well, not one was sold abroad and there wasn't even the same ambiance anymore. So I volunteered to take early retirement at forty-seven, with a five hundred thousand franc indemnity. It wasn't until the age of sixty-five that I truly retired from aeronautics, but then I devoted myself to my collection of great wines, either buying them or trading them for cases of my Pomerol, le Château Feytit-Clinet.

I had in fact inherited half of Feytit-Clinet, a vineyard belonging to Madame Mary Domergue, whom I met in 1979 at the request of her family. At the time she was des-

titute, living under the tutelage of her guardian, the mayor of Pomerol, who was indifferent to the conditions in which this poor woman was living. After an inheritance battle with her brother-in-law, she was ruined and owed two million francs, the value of the vineyard at the time, to the state. I paid the estate tax by taking out a loan, took care of her, brought her to Paris and let her keep her vineyard, which otherwise would have been sold at public auction. To thank me, Mary, who had no children, left me her share of Feytit-Clinet. But I had to take out another loan for seven hundred and eighty thousand francs to pay the estate tax. The other half of Feytit-Clinet went to her brother-in-law René who gave it to the city of Bordeaux. The chateau being leased out for tenant farming, every year I received my share in kind, four hundred twelve-bottle cases that I sold or exchanged.

Then my son Jérémy, after graduating as an oenologist from the University of Bordeaux in 1995 and working afterwards at the Chateau La Dominique, was able to buy back the second half and resume its operation in 2000. We now form an agricultural land group under the name of Jérémy Michel Chasseuil, half mine, half his. We have changed the label, which used to be black, while keeping the golden coat of arms liberally inspired by that of the Feytit-Clinet.

city of Bordeaux. The vineyards of the plateau boast a gravelly clay soil. Our vineyard, at the west end of the village, has merely a sandy soil with high iron-oxide content, which does not allow for such strong wines, however it produces finer and more complex ones. This year, we planted a plot that had never been planted because of the humidity of the soil: we had to drain the plot and bring back, little by little, soil accumulated at the end of our rows of vines, because here you can only bring in your own soil. We also plan to replant a plot with low-yield clones. Jérémy does fine work; we are doing all we can to raise Feytit-Clinet to the level of the greatest Pomerol wines, and we are becoming known: we receive very good reviews in the journals, and the wine sells well en primeur... which is very useful for pursuing my collection.

This collection is my vocation. I devote my entire life to it. Friends call me 'the monk'. My goal is to bring together all the great vintages of the great wines of France, and the best of the world at large. In 2008, I had collected the best wines of Robert Parker's book *156 Greatest Wines of the World*. I look for all the wines mentioned in books devoted to the world's best wines, the books of Faure-Brac, Cobbold, Vrinat, Mastrojanni, Goulaine... This last put me on the path of the Romanian Cotnari, of which I'm looking for a bottle from before the war. I take note of the comments in the press on the best wines. For example, if I read that the Bortoli Marsala is nearly extinct, I tell myself, 'I need some Bortoli!' and I phone Bortoli, who sends me some 1830 and some 1860. For each rare vintage, I need to find the purveyor, or go to the estate. If I have to go ten times, I go ten times. If I have to beg, I beg. After a lot of hard work and perseverance, many people have respect for what I do, and they are often happy to have their wine as part of my collection, the reference. I am missing a bottle of Yquem 1847, which I hope to find one day. The oldest existing Chartreuse, which is included in this book, took me twenty-eight years of waiting: it is an 1853, the oldest one produced after the elusive 1840! I also collect what is no longer exactly wine, like Patrick Baudouin's 'Layon' which has an alcohol content of a mere 0.9° and 700g of residual sugar. Or the balsamic vinegar of Modena, of which only a few one-hundred-fifty-year-old bottles are left.

In 1980, I already had a half century of Yquem, forty years of Pétrus, Romanée-Conti 1905, 1921, 1929, all the great wines of France bought for peanuts. In 2009, I have one hundred years of Yquem and eighty of Petrus (the breakdown appears at the end of this book, with the other great wines of the best estates). After French wines, I decided to open my collection to foreign wines, with the help of the book *Guide to the Wines of the World* from Slow Food Editions, and the advice of Hugh Johnson and Michaël Broadbent. I started with Spain, Italy, Australia, South Africa, and Austria. Twenty-five years later, my collection of foreign wines is larger than my collection of French wines.

I bought before the crowds, before people were interested. In that, I followed the advice of Marcel Dassault: 'Only buy what's rare, what you won't find later.' I also bought at a time when there were no counterfeits: my bottles are authentic, while we see today a lot of suspicious bottles. The world of connoisseurs and rare wine merchants is small, I know who does what... and there are a lot of naïve and wealthy buyers. But billions alone are not enough to build an exceptional collection.

Sometimes people tell me that there is no point in conserving bottles that will never be drunk. Keeping a full bottle that is more than one hundred years old seems ridiculous, agreed. However, the great ranked vintages are in the same position in their wine-libraries: At the Chateau Lafite estate, there is still wine from 1797 and in Yquem there is wine from 1811; when it no longer tastes good, it becomes a relic.
Even I wonder sometimes, lying in the grass, if I should stop living like a monk. A year ago, I said to myself: I've had enough, that's it! Having all of these wines, it's an interesting legacy, but it's exhausting to oversee the crème de la crème of the two hundred fifty best producers of the world, and always broke! Moreover, all other collections end up being sold at auction: out of one hundred collectors, ninety-nine drink or sell their collection. And when I am dead, I am not going to take my collection with me. Why not take advantage of it now, go around the world, eat and drink like a king... Then, the next day, I said to myself: after travelling around the world, when I go back to the producers to buy wine, they will tell me, 'But Monsieur Chasseuil, we haven't seen you for a long time, we have no more wine for you', because I will no longer be their client. Privilege and priority won through many years of personal relations. And I will miss it, like those artists or tennis players who try to return to their passion. So I decide to continue, but on the condition that this collection serve a purpose, and that it continue after I am gone. I

will teach all of this to my grandchildren, because, in the end, a wine cellar is meant to be shared.

Keeping my wines is my right and my choice.

If I feel like opening a great and unique bottle with my son and my grandchildren, I do so. And if I live an ascetic lifestyle so I can save up to buy even more wines, I can afford to, because I have tasted them all, at least all the major bottles. I know the qualities of the good vintages; I can deduce the value of others.

In 1994, I created the International Academy of Rare Wines and Spirits, registered on 18 July. The mission of this association is to help people to discover, know, taste and promote rare wines from around the world. To circulate and protect the spirit, history and culture of wines and spirits in France and abroad. It serves to promote cultural exchanges; encounters among professionals, connoisseurs, students; as well as to organise trips, conferences, seminars and the exchange of information centred around the art of wine.

I have kept files of ten years of *dégustation*, performed in small private groups of twelve. We tasted so many great wines! For example: some thirty vintages of Haut-Brion, including 1945, 1928, 1899. We drank La Tâche 1959 and 1955, Romanée-Conti 1929 and 1937, La Mouline 1978 and 1976, Yquem 1921, 1967, 1947, 1874, Lafite 1875, Palmer

1929 and 1878, La Mission 1961 and 1959... I have drunk Yquem 1937 three times, that's enough. I have drunk all the Latour of the century with Robuchon. I've drunk Mouton 1945 five times, at the price of one thousand francs per bottle in 1980. I still have three bottles and a magnum. They are worth five thousand euros each, but I choose to keep them in my collection. For my grandchildren, but also as relics for later. And yet my cellar is a living thing: wines come in and out as the selection becomes more and more draconian.

There are wines that I cannot sell. My notoriety comes from my collection, like the gold in the national bank guarantees the currency. My Noval Nacional Port 1931 is perhaps the only perfect bottle left in the world; I would not trade it for the Mona Lisa. What I do is a money pit today... but people will talk about it in the future. Fortunately our ancestors kept marsalas from 1830 or madeiras from 1870; they are still so good! The philosophy of passing wine cellars on within families is lost. The children move and the cellars don't follow, whereas three generations are necessary for a liquor to become rare. In less than twenty years, old wines will have become impossible to find. And in twenty years, many new wines will no longer be good; people today make wine to be drunk immediately, easy, flattering, fashionable. Grape stems are no longer left in the wine. Then again, who has the means and the inclination to bottle a wine to be drunk in fifty years? I created my conservatory so that

Age alters the colour of Yquem: the older it gets, the darker it becomes.

great wines would remain traceable, so that there would be at least one bottle of the greatest wines ever produced, one authentic bottle in good condition. Because the climate is changing. Already, in Australia, grape vines are being removed because of chronic drought. I keep testimony of lost vineyards. Other vineyards, active today, will disappear. I will keep archives of them.

Not a mausoleum, but more than a collection, my cellar is a conservatory. My bottles are ready to drink; we could open one every thirty years. I am the curator, I maintain and conserve. My objective is to register my entire collection in Saint-Émilion, a UNESCO world heritage site, in the form of a foundation. My collection would be the nucleus, its gravity would attract other old wines, *dégustations* would be organised, as well as annual gala dinners to benefit charities. There will be a steering committee composed of seven members from different countries, responsible, along with my son Jérémy, for operating the foundation. My grandchildren, if they wish, can take over from him.

I am not thinking merely of myself. I am thinking of humanity. In Greenland, thirty million seeds from around the world have been buried so as to remain traceable. But no one has thought about wine. In wine, there is every mineral in nature. It is the world's memory: there is wine from before the phylloxera outbreak and wine from after. There is wine from before Hiroshima, and wine from after; they are distinguishable. If one day there is a great disaster, my cellar will remain. Imagine that in 2190, fifty scientists start to study an Yquem 1811, collected and conserved by the son of a postman in La Chapelle-Bâton! They will have before them the traceability of the planet Earth, the history of its climate. This alone justifies my choice to conserve these wines. But there is also the conservation of our heritage. Wine is a treasure. In Portugal, everyone talks about port. At the invitation of the Spanish Ministry of Culture, I went to Jerez to participate in a meal accompanied exclusively by Spanish sherry. In France, almost no one knows Spanish sherry. As for our own wines, we neglect them while France should be proud of them. We have an inestimable natural heritage. Along with our wealth, the unique variety of our regions, our gastronomy, we have our wines, which are works of art. And every year the fruit of hard work. In March we hope that it won't freeze, when the vines blossom, we hope that it won't rain, then that it won't hail, that it won't be too hot; at the grape harvest, we hope

that it won't rain, and likewise for vinification, for the barrels, the bacteria... And when, by chance, as in 2005, we produce an exceptional bottle, they tell us that we mustn't drink if we want to live a long life. When will we finally react, to promote the art, the spirit, the fabulous wealth of wines and spirits? I hosted Japanese visitors in Pomerol; it was a magnificent moment for them. They tasted some petrus and left with the empty bottle that they religiously placed on their mantelpiece, and they are proud of having drunk it.

I teach my grandchildren about wine, I teach them to taste it and to respect it. Instead of disparaging wine, we should teach young people to love it; we should teach them this delicate art that is an integral part of our culture. I even believe that there should be an oenological test in the baccalaureate and that the students of the most famous universities should have a class in a great vineyard. I defend a civilisation: over five thousand years, starting with a few wild vines, men have created some five thousand vintages. It is an art. Good wine does not produce alcoholics. Louis Pasteur even wrote that 'wine is the most hygienic of beverages'. For someone who drinks wine every day and who tastes good old liquors, that observation cheers me up.

My son Jérémy and my grandchildren, Adrien and Étienne.

I hope to have a wonderful degustation in 2041 to celebrate my one-hundredth birthday. Resveratrols, polyphenols and minerals consolidate my organism, and wine is my motor oil!

There is so much to discover and to share! Who knows Romanian Cotnari or Crimean Aleatiko? In 1997, I discovered the cellars of Massandra in Crimea. Since then, I regularly return, like a pilgrimage, and I have the pride and the pleasure to be a guest of honour and to taste dozens of unknown wines. Massandra is a second world of wine, where they do the same things that we do here. A second world, where sauternes, tokaji, sherry, port, madeira, malaga, and great Muscats that are completely unknown to us are produced. They made Marsala in 1920, 1930, 1940, when there was no more in Marsala. They make port with cabernet grapes! They have the five thousand wine cultivars from around the world, one hundred feet of each variety. Most of the great wines collected in that million-bottle cave of dessert wines are in my collection. As for the dry red wines, they are not the best. But I have all of their great dessert wines, and I hope to bring home more. Out of six hundred fifty wines referenced in Massandra, I have fifty of the best vintages, including seventeen of the sixty-one remaining bottles stamped with the coat of arms of Czar Nicholas II.

It is thanks to a story about Massandra on French television that my collection became known and that the idea of a book about my finest bottles was born. I could have included two or three hundred, but one has to stop somewhere. I had to make choices to establish lists that would include award-winning wines, like the list of the twelve best wines of the 20ᵗʰ century published by *Wine Spectator*. I found a few bottles that I had been missing, but they have become very expensive and I can't afford to buy everything.

The wines in this book are not an ideal compilation brought together simply for a photo shoot, but rather a selection of the bottles that lay in my cellar. The great mythical wines that are known everywhere and that I have been able to acquire. And others that, although unknown, are equally great wines. Some choices may seem surprising, like the magnum L'Extravagant in memory of Lady Diana, or an old grenache from 1868 of unknown origin that figures along with the greatest wines of the world, in memory of my grandparents from La Chapelle-Bâton. But this book is not merely another book about great wines. This is the book of the most beautiful collection in the world. Andreas Larsson, currently the greatest sommelier in the world, came to see me in December 2009, and like most of the personalities of the viticultural world, he left a reminder of his visit in the parchment guest book in my *cave*: 'You have an immense collection, the most beautiful wine cellar in the world'. For those who will never have the chance to visit it, here is the story of one hundred of my most beautiful bottles. It is the book of my life as a collector.

CONTI
DOM
CONTI
ROMANÉ

The estate of Chambolle, founded in 1924 by Georges Roumier, remains one of the best of the Côte de Nuits. His grandson Christophe manages it today, but the labels continue to carry the name of Domaine Georges Roumier. The cultivation is traditional, without fertilizer or herbicide. The grapes are harvested at maturity, sorted, and partially destemmed depending on the year. The wine-making process begins with prefermentary maceration to promote the development of indigenous yeasts. The use of new casks is moderate, and the wines age for twelve to fifteen months on their dregs. They are bottled as late as possible, and are not filtered. It is precise work, like *haute couture*, to dress every wine with great finesse. The estate extends for some fifteen hectares, including the first Chambolle vintages: Les Cras and Les Amoureuses, 40 ares, worth the great vintages; 3 ares of Clos Vougeot and 2 of Corton-Charlemagne; 1.5 hectares of Bonnes-Mares, over two plots, one of red earth and the other of white earth. And the Musigny: a wine that barely exists, an essence of Burgundy, the few bottles that are produced, fly off every year to well-hidden cellars. Its value at auction? For the best vintages, 1,000 to 2,000 euros. On the world market? Nothing less than 1000 euros, drop by drop, two bottles of 1990 for 4000 euros, four 1985 between 5,000 and 10,000, one 1978 for 7,000. One does not find a 2005 for sale. It is the youngest vintage in my selection of extraordinary bottles, because it is inaccessible. I met Christophe Roumier around 1985. Since then, every year he sells me a dozen bottles of Bonnes-Mares. 1989 and 1990 are great vintages, as are 1995 and 1996. But I have never been able to get from him a bottle of Musigny: he produces a mere three hundred per year! I was able to acquire a 1998, a 2004, and a 2006, only by begging a wine merchant! 'Musigny is to reds what Montrachet is to whites: pure melody.' (Jean-François Bazin). A poor soil, clayey rather than calcareous, ever coveted. Christophe Roumier's Musigny is a rare pearl, with aromas of alpine berries: cherry, raspberry, blueberry, wild strawberry... with an extravagant femininity, a bewitching complexity that make it the finest and most delicate wine of the Côte de Nuits. And the bottle that I chose is from 2005, a perfect year, which Christophe Roumier was finally able to sell me shortly before Christmas 2009. My bottle represents 0.33 % of the production.

> 'Christophe Roumier's Musigny is a rare pearl, with aromas of alpine berries: cherry, raspberry, blueberry, wild strawberry... with an extravagant femininity, a bewitching complexity that makes it the finest and most delicate wine of the Côte de Nuits.'

Musigny, Roumier 2005

Appellation: Musigny, grand cru, Burgundy, France.

Vineyard area: 13 hectares, including 996 m² in Musigny.

Variety: pinot noir.

Age of vines: 40 years.

Average production: 300 bottles.

Best vintages: 1978, 1990, 2005.

Silver tasting cup from the 18th century.

Château-Doisy-Daëne is a Barsac vintage registered in 1855, close to Climens, and which deserves the rank of premier vintage, so enchanting is its consistent quality, even in non-exceptional years. The Dubourdieu family has owned it since 1924: Pierre, the patriarch, a perfectionist and relentless worker, and his son Denis, the infamous agronomist, professor at the Institut d'oenologie of Bordeaux. I have known this family since my beginnings as a collector, and I enjoyed going to their estate to taste the 'bourru', just harvested, with its flavour of ripe pineapple. Pierre would never let me leave without uncorking an old vintage. The 1924, tasted in 2007, is a miracle of complexity, still fruity and long in the mouth. But the wine that most impressed me is the micro vintage L'Extravagant, a nectar of passion fruit, a delicacy in its own right, to drink to intoxication without batting an eyelid! This vintage, usually of pure sauvignon, but occasionally of pure sémillon as in 1997, has been elaborated only in the great vintages since

1990. These few casks of long fermentation are bottled in 0.25-litre bottles.

Pierre Dubourdieu has engaged in endless audacious experiments, such as high fermentation temperature or one-time-only production of a late-vintage 'Christmas wine'. Denis invented L'Extravagant, rich in alcohol and richer still in liqueur. To commemorate the death of Lady Diana, I decided to place in my *cave* a unique wine from 1997 that reflects her personality. A great dessert wine seemed appropriate, but which one? It had to be the best in the world.

smooth aromas of candied tropical fruits. This vintage is a veritable tour de force in wine making (with the genius Dubourdieu, one reaches the apex). It will age perfectly for fifty to a hundred years.'

I wanted an eternal bottle. I had a special magnum made incorporating an engraved royal crown gilded with fine gold. But I would need a miracle! Would Pierre Dubourdieu make an exception for me? 'As you know, Monsieur Chasseuil, this wine is very rare, and we only sell small emblazoned Bohemian crystal bottles. And you ask me

'A nectar of passion fruit, a delicacy in its own right, to drink to intoxication without batting an eyelid!'

L'Extravagant is as gracious, as unique and extravagant as Diana. This wine was graded 99/100 by Parker, far ahead of its neighbour Climens, and even ahead of Yquem, which ranked a mere 96. Parker described it thus: 'A prestigious vintage, spectacular, truly formidable in the mouth, raising

for a litre and a half for a single bottle! My wife and I will have to think this over.'

Two years later, I get a phone call: 'Monsieur Chasseuil, come by and see us, I have something for you.' It was the famous magnum, one-of-a-kind, filled to the brim and sealed with wax. It will age at least three hundred years! Monsieur Dubourdieu added: 'Since we have such admiration for your collection, my wife and I give you as well a bottle of 1924, the year we became proprietors of the vineyard!' I had tears in my eyes, and left with these two relics for my sanctuary; I was happy.

Magnum L'Extravagant de Doisy-Daëne 1997

Appellation: selection of the vineyard of Château Doisy-Daëne, appellation Sauternes, second cru classé, Bordeaux, France.

Vineyard area: 15 hectares.

Varieties: sémillon and sauvignon.

Age of vines: 40 years.

Average production: 30,000 bottles.

Best vintages: 1924, 1929, 1937, 1947, 1959, 1967, 1983, 1990, 1996, 1997, 2001, 2003, 2005.

les sens
du
Chenin

250 ml · 0.9%

Patrick Baudouin

1997

I met Patrick Baudouin in 1990, at a tasting of great Coteaux-du-Layon 1989. The vineyard was in full renewal, thanks to a generation of winemakers like Jo Pithon and their low-yield vintages. Since then, I have of course placed in my cave the best dessert wines of the Loire. My best memory of tasting Coteaux-du-Layon is the Château-de-Fesles 1929, then 1947 and 1990.

But I was not with Patrick Baudouin on that 19th of September 1997 when, on his way to the laboratory, he stopped a moment in a plot and got a shock: while the harvest had not been pressed, (1997 is an exceptional year with liqueur rates never before seen), each bunch of chenin grapes had a

'A 'wine' of an extraordinary smoothness, almost like honey, extravagantly long in the mouth with a mixture of notes of candied apricot, dulce de membrillo, passion fruit...'

Glass grapes showing the colour of the grapes candied by the botrytis.

few that were entirely crystallized, nearly dried out. The taste was candy-like, but also with the indispensable acidity. He had to obtain a dispensation of the harvesting ban, gather a team of eight grape-pickers, for four days, harvest grape by grape enough to make a half-cask, or rather try: 'After an hour, one drop falls into the three hectolitre vat... After analysis, we had to pinch ourselves: more than 700 grams of sugar per litre, 14 of acidity, and the signs of botrytis.'

The fermentation was done in 15-litre demijohns, the bottling seven years later. The yeast was able to produce merely 0.9 % alcohol, bogged down in 690 grams of residual sugar! An essence of chenin with the sweetness balanced by an extraordinary acidity.

I discovered this nectar in 2006, in Jerez de la Frontera, at the wine fair, the international gathering for dessert wines. 'Michel! I managed to get the essence of chenin, the wine of a lifetime!' called out Patrick Baudouin.

And I did in fact discover a 'wine' of an extraordinary smoothness, almost like honey, extravagantly long in the mouth with a mixture of notes of candied apricot, dulce de membrillo, passion fruit... How could I taste another wine after this flavour explosion, at least not before swallowing a big glass of sparkling water?

This rare wine, the fruit of an exceptional year and of a winemaker's audacity, was bottled in 25-centilitre bottles. But for my collection, Patrick was willing to fill up a 75-centilitre bottle. This wine should age more than a hundred years. Of course, I will not drink it; it is here as a testimony for posterity.

Les Sens du chenin, Patrick Baudouin 1997

Appellation: No appellation, product of the Coteaux du Layon, Loire, France.

Vineyard area: 15 hectares.

Variety: chenin blanc.

Average age of vines: 40 years.

Best vintages: 1989, 1990, 1997, 2003, 2005.

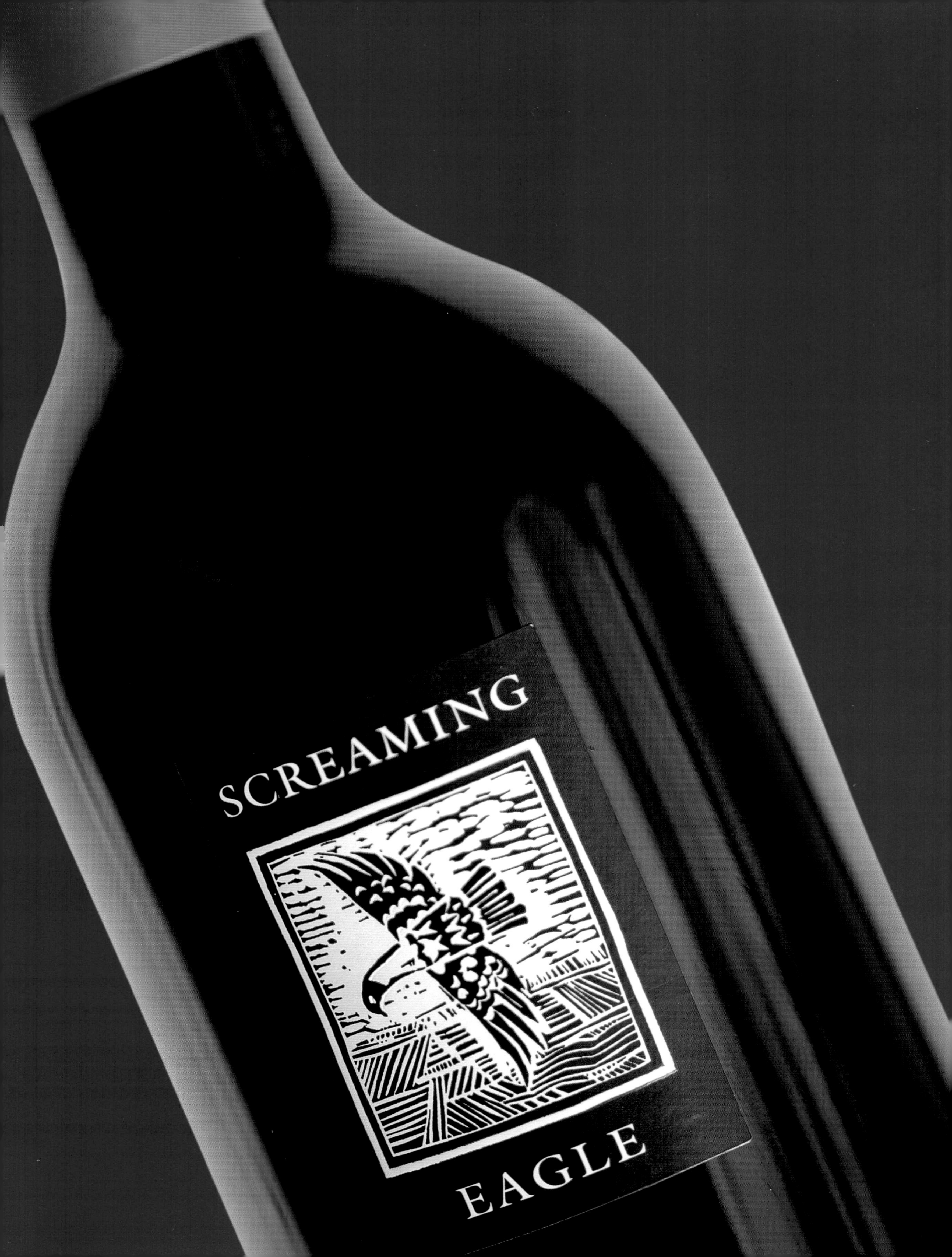
SCREAMING
EAGLE

'A rare wine, of which a mere four hundred cases are sold around the world every year – and 3-bottle cases at that!'

Screaming Eagle 1997

Appellation: Napa Valley, California, United-States.

Vineyard area: 23 hectares.

Variety: cabernet sauvignon.

Production of this vintage: 1,200 to 1,500 bottles per year.

Best vintages: 1992, 1995, 1997, 2002, 2005, 2007.

One day, Denis Wilson, an Englishman who owns a small house not far from me in La Chapelle-Bâton, gave me an article to read entitled 'Getting the Bird' which questioned why rich Californians were rushing for the chance to acquire a bottle from 1996 for 750 dollars. It was Screaming Eagle, and the article specified the necessary criteria for a cult wine: very limited production; a famous winemaker, good grades and eulogistic, extravagant reviews. I immediately set out on a quest for a bottle – at least one – of this famous Californian 'cult' wine. Mission impossible: I even met the head of the International Wine Office for the United States: 'I haven't been able to get one either. It's reserved for billionaires!' This estate in the Napa Valley only dates back to 1989, and its first wine to 1992. The wine is a selection of cabernet sauvignon, dark, very concentrated. The 1997 is a perfect wine.

Never discouraged, I contacted Michel Rolland, reputed oenologist, consultant for prestigious Napa Valley wineries like Har-lan, Bryant Family, etc. He confirmed for the rarity of this wine, of which a mere four hundred cases are sold around the world every year – and 3-bottle cases at that! The waiting list of five thousand names would keep me waiting for years. So be it. In 2000, I send a fax anyway to the proprietor Mrs. Jean Phillips in Oakland. With all the passion I can muster, and attaching a comment by Michael Broadbent, who had visited my wine cellar: 'The happy owner of the greatest wines, of the greatest vintages.' The Englishman Broadbent is the most renowned expert in the world, along with Robert Parker, and the first to have appraised the oldest wines.

And, as if by miracle, I was lucky enough to receive, sometime later, an order slip for three bottles of 1997 for 400 dollars, along with a letter pointing out that a 6-litre imperial bottle had sold for 500 000 dollars at auction in 2002, and that a double magnum of 1997 had reached 85,000 dollars (the proprietor offers these large bottles to charities, and billionaires buy them). While visiting the Parisian wine cellar of Chase Bailey, an American collector, before a tasting of fifteen great Bordeaux from 1947, I am surprised to discover, upright, that famous 500,000-dollar imperial, with its small label, a wooden engraving of an eagle flying over the vineyard. Bailey tells me that Mrs. Phillips is a good friend and that he will speak to her about my collection. Since then, every year, I receive my little case of Screaming Eagle. The 1997 is ranked 100/100 by Parker. It is worth 3,000 dollars per bottle. In 2009, during a *degustation* organized by Bailey for his birthday, Screaming Eagle finished first among the fifteen best California wines of 1997. I had already tasted the vintages 1995 and 2001, perfect as well. Robert Parker writes this of the 1997:

'There is nothing better than the 1997 Screaming Eagle, a perfect wine'.

The two tenors of Burgundy, red and white, given the miniscule quantities of the bottles they produce, of exceptional quality, are of course Jean-François Coche-Dury and Christophe Roumier. The first for his Corton-Charlemagne, the second for his Musigny. Jean-François Coche-Dury, a large man, humble and discreet, is a true *vigneron* who excels in his every task, from his vines to his chai, a legendary winemaker like Henri Jayer was for red wines. He preaches mouth, it gives mineral flavours, lemon, ginger, apple, fresh hazelnut, orange. Practically impossible to find on the market, this Corton-Charlemagne reaches prices twenty times higher than the price at the estate, and it is not rare on Highway 74, close to the Coche estate, to see a Mercedes with an epicurean driver ready to hand over two 500-euro notes in hope of going home with a bottle of Corton! I met Coche some fifteen years ago. He provided me with two bottles of Meursault, deserve these, they're a gift. This is a sample of the best my cellar has to offer.' However the contents of this case, which I religiously placed in the paradise of my cellar, my Coche-Dury collection, must remain secret, out of respect for the mysticism of wine. 'And every year you will get a bottle of Corton-Charlemagne.' For me that was the cherry on the cake – even if it takes me twelve years to accumulate a full case, a privilege usually reserved for billionaires.

'Practically impossible to find on the market, this Corton-Charlemagne reaches prices twenty times higher than the price at the estate.'

the importance of working with the vine, which must produce a harvest fit for a great wine. His vines produce a small yield – 35 to 45 hectolitres per hectare – particularly because of the cordon de royat pruning system. All of his wines are of excellent quality, but the Corton-Charlemagne earned him his reputation, as did the Meursault-Perrières, of which only three thousand bottles are produced. The young Corton gives off aromas of melon, acacia, pear, spices, vineyard peach, exotic fruit. In the which more than satisfied me. Then, the following years, a Perrières and two Rougeots. Thanks to my persuasive abilities, in the 2000s I was entitled to six bottles, I was privileged! With the help of his wife, I succeeded in bringing him down to my wine cellar. This is a man who rarely laughs, but that day he was smiling from ear to ear as he congratulated me, and upon my next visit to his cellar, I had the surprise of receiving, in addition to my annual quota, a case of six other bottles: 'Here, you

Pewter grapes: the sign of a distinguished sommelier.

Corton-Charlemagne, Coche-Dury 1996

Appellation: Corton-Charlemagne, grand cru, Burgundy, France.

Vineyard area: 1 hectare.

Variety: chardonnay.

Age of vines: 30 to 50 years.

Average production: 1,500 bottles.

Best vintages: 1986, 1989, 1992, 1995, 1996, 2001, 2005, 2006.

Krug is a superlative! Champagne for billionaires, the king of champagnes, a piece of world heritage. Extravagance and rarity can describe this estate founded in 1843 by Johann-Joseph Krug. All the wines produced are of very high quality, starting with the Grande Cuvée, the 'yearless Brut' that is the base of all champagne: an assembly including around 50 % pinot noir from eight to ten different vintages and more than twenty villages. It is the archetype of the Krug style, intense, straight and full-bodied. The Krug rosé has been produced since 1983. It has a light copper colour, like an onion peel. The acidity is perceptible and identifies a *vin de garde*. It is perfect for accompanying lobster.

The rare Clos-du-Mesnil comes from a single plot of 1.97 hectares in the heart of the village of Mesnil-sur-Ogeret, known since 1698. Like Salon, it is a mono-cru of a single variety, a Chardonnay blanc de blancs, the 'Romanée-Conti' of champagne. For Richard Juhlin, author of the book 4,000 *Champagnes*, the Krug Clos-du-Mesnil is the best wine in the world. Its first year was 1979. Only fifteen thousand bottles are produced, silky and voluptuous with intense flavours. The Krug Millésimé is only produced in great years.

The Clos-d'Ambonnay, a new rare pearl of Krug, has only been produced since 1995, and was put on the market in 2008. I was lucky enough to be invited to the inauguration and the exposition of this exceptional champagne (which sells for 3,000 euros per bottle for the one thousand five hundred bottles produced), and I could not resist the temptation of buying the rare mahogany case of six bottles, sold only that day and at a 'friendly' price. A bit of madness for a crazy day: staying at the Hôtel des Crayères, the stroll through the vineyards, the *degustation* of the great vintages of Krug, and that delicate and sumptuous lunch at the Clos d'Ambonnay, accompanied by Yquem 1995, Margaux 1995, with of course Clos-d'Ambonnay 1995.

The Krug estate is the only one to practise fermentation in small 205-litre oaken casks, which gives the wine its unique solidity and longevity. Malo-lactic fermentation is avoided, and so the wines retain an acidity that reinforces their aging qualities. Keeping the wine in a cellar for seven or eight years gives it its complexity. The smell is miraculously fresh, intense, evolving with age into notes of nuts, apricot, plum, gingerbread, caramel, coffee, even mushroom for the oldest wines. I have known Henri Krug since 1980, and I have been lucky enough to exchange a few bottles of Clos-du-Mesnil 1982 and 1983 with him for some Feytit-Clinet. I have conserved these precious bottles their little wooden case, in a special corner of my wine cellar, next to the rare vintages: 1985, 1990, 1995, and 1996.

'The smell is miraculously fresh, intense, evolving with aging into notes of nuts, apricot, plum, gingerbread, caramel, coffee, even mushroom for the oldest wines.'

Champagne Krug Clos d'Ambonnay 1995

Appellation: Champagne, France.

Vineyard area: 20 hectares, plus purchase of grapes.

Varieties: pinot noir, pinot meunier, chardonnay.

Age of vines: 20 years.

Average production of all vintages: 500,000 bottles.

Best vintages: 1928, 1947, 1959, 1961, 1975, 1982, 1985, 1990, 1995, 1996.

Harlan is one of about ten California cult wines. In my opinion, it belongs in the top three along with Screaming Eagle and Bryant Family. In any case, it is the only wine to have received the grade of 100/100 from Robert Parker five times in the last fifteen years. Among other wines, only the famous Mouline of Guigal can make such a claim. Personally, I have only tasted it twice, and I was lucky

'It is the only wine to have received the grade of 100/100 from Robert Parker five times in the last fifteen years.'

enough to taste the 1997, graded 100, memorable: like a great Château-Latour, only more supple and stronger at the same time! The proportion of grape varieties of this wine is like that of Médoc, and Michel Rolland recommended the process. This 1997 was in competition with the greatest California wines of the year, an organisational *tour de force* performed by my friend Chase Bailey to celebrate his fiftieth birthday. Drinking all these wines in a grand year was an unheard-of experience. Chase let me take the empty bottles home and I am proud to have lined them up in my cellar, as a reminder of that fabulous tasting. Of all of them, I preferred Harlan, the equal of Screaming Eagle.

I had to wait ten years before I was able to buy it en *primeur* at the estate, in the appropriately named city of Oakville. I wrote every year, with my usual arguments, or should I say my prayers. And the miracle happened in 2008: I was finally able to buy six bottles and a magnum of 2006. I have an original case of six bottles from 1994, bought in 1998. At that time, American 'cult wines' were not very well known and not too difficult to find, via Great Britain. This one was also graded 100, and probably the best. Who could I quote besides Robert Parker? Here is what he wrote in his book *The Greatest Wine Estates of the World*: 'The 1994 satisfied all of my expectations of perfection. Spectacular aromas of blackberry, minerals, cedar wood, coffee, toast, accompany the opaque violet colour. In the mouth, it reveals exquisite levels of phenomenally pure and rich fruit followed by a finish of more than forty seconds. An ample wine of dazzling aromas, with flavours of prodigious depth. Close to immortality.'

I just acquired the 2007, which is going to break all records.

Harlan Estate 1994

Appellation: Napa Valley, California, United States.

Vineyard area: 15 hectares.

Varieties: cabernet sauvignon 70 % (but often more in the assembly of the great wine), merlot 20 %, cabernet franc 8 %, petit verdot 2 %.

Age of vines: 15 years.

Average production: 20,000 bottles.

Best vintages: 1991, 1993, 1994, 1995, 1996, 1997, 2001, 2002, 2005, 2007.

I discovered this confidential vintage in a Parisian art gallery. Of course I knew the great Hermitages of Gérard Chave, whose family has been producing wine for more than five hundred years, and from whom I used to buy two cases every year. I'm happy to still be entitled to six bottles, because his wines sell abroad at light speed and the waiting list is long. His Hermitages have an extraordinary concentration, with magnificent substance. Assemblies representative of the best quarters of the vineyard, they come particularly from one plot of three very old vines, Les Rocoules, and

'Its smooth and viscous texture offers flavours of liquorice, caramel, blackcurrant, truffle, candied prune, blackberry jam.'

from one other whose vines are eighty years old, Les Bessards.

That day, as I was delivering a few cases of my Feytit-Clinet to Monsieur Lebouc in his gallery of masterpiece paintings, this epicurean gentleman, showing me a superb canvas, said, 'I bet you don't have any Cathelin. I'm the one who sells his paintings; Bernard Cathelin is a great friend of Gérard Chave, who asked him to paint the label of that prestigious vintage.' You learn something every day! Afterwards, I was able to buy the first three vintages: 1990, 1991 and 1995, and at my insistence Jean-Louis Chave was kind enough to reserve for me a bottle of 1998, then 2000 and 2003. The 1990, of which I have a beautiful three-bottle case, is of such extraordinary quality that after the death of Bernard Cathelin in 2004, I decided to weave a little story around that mythical bottle. I went to see his wife, who quite courteously received me, and after my impassioned explanations, gave me a brush, a palate and a tube

of red paint, the painter's favourite colour, as well as a few catalogues of his work to display in my showcase. Red evidently dominated the label of this vintage. The spelling of 'Ermitage', without H, is rarely used but completely legitimate: the appellation decree is labelled as follows: 'appellation d'origine controlee Hermitage or l'Hermitage with or without H'. In fact, the name comes from a hermitage built in the 13th century by a crusader, the Knight of Stérimberg. The wine's reputation has always been illustrious. If Lafite 1795 was so good, it is because it was reinforced at the hermitage!

The 2003, another great year – only one hundred twenty-five cases – resembles a port. It is one of the most monumental wines ever produced in France. Its smooth and viscous texture offers flavours of liquorice, caramel, blackcurrant, truffle, candied prune, blackberry jam. It should still be perfect in 2075! I also very much appreciated the Hermitages 1978 and 1985.

Ermitage Cathelin, Jean-Louis Chave 1990

Appellation: Hermitage, Rhône, France. Selection of syrah over the 10 hectares of the vineyard, mainly in the plot of Les Bessards.

Variety: syrah.

Average age of vines: 50 years.

Average production: 2,500 bottles.

Years produced: 1990, 1991, 1995, 1998, 2000, 2003.

Tools of the painter Cathelin offered by his wife.

This estate dates from 1844, when Doctor Christofer Penfold, having come from Sussex, planted European varieties in Grange Cottage, now a suburb of Adelaide, with the goal of producing fortified wines. His descendants bought vines from all over southern Australia. But fame only arrived with the Grange-Hermitage, a syrah selection elaborated by the

'Grange is Penfold's Petrus, reserved for the enlightened few.'

winemaker Max Schubert, whose first year, confidential, is 1951. Recognisable by his famous nose, as big as a 200-gram truffle, he raised the Grange-Hermitage to the top of syrah wines in the Southern Hemisphere. The Grange lost the name of Hermitage in 1990, after a legal battle with that French AOC. Max Schubert passed away in 1994, and the oenologist Peter Gago now produces the wine.

I became interested in Australian wines in 1985, particularly in the Grange-Hermitage of the Penfold's firm. I bought them in England, since at that time virtually no one in France was interested in foreign wines. Even the Côte-Rôtie and the Hermitages of the Rhône Valley were only known in a few great restaurants! Then, at Vinexpo, I was able to taste a little bit of Grange, discreetly because there was only one bottle for the week. Penfold's is a large estate that produces wine throughout Australia and offers a very large selection of wines. Grange is Penfold's Petrus, reserved for the enlightened few. Surprised to see a Frenchman interested, the English became more pleasant at each Vinexpo. My reputation as a 'froggy', as they called me, offered me the privilege of a twelve-bottle case every year (at this point I must have a hundred), including the famous 1998. I am looking for the 1955. Aged twenty months in casks of American oak, this world-renowned cult wine is for Australia what Vega Sicilia is for Spain. It has become mythical since its first grade of 100/100 by Parker for the 1976. Certain one hundred twenty-year-old Shiraz vines are used in the elaboration of grange to produce a superbly aging wine. With a ruby colour as intense as ink, this nectar becomes tuilé, brick-coloured with age. It gives off aromas of coffee, chocolate, blackberry jam; when young, the wine smells of blackcurrant, cherry, hawthorn, plum. The wine is thick, smooth, bold, rich, with an extreme concentration, infinitely long in the mouth. A veritable legend in the vintages 1971, 1976, 1986 and 1998. In the mouth, the 1990 is like fireworks, with smoky and mentholated notes and complex spices.

Penfold's Grange 1990

Appellation: South Australia.

Vineyard area: selection of the 400-hectare Penfold's vineyard.

Variety: only syrah (shiraz).

Age of vines: 60 years.

Annual production: 60,000 bottles.

Best vintages: 1952, 1955, 1971, 1976, 1986, 1990, 1998, 2001, 2002, 2005.

Giuseppe Quintarelli is an eccentric character that I rank among 'true' winemakers, just like Henri Bonneau or the late Jacques Reynaud of Châteauneuf-du-Pape. Rare are those who have been lucky enough to meet them or to be able to bring together in their wine cellar the bacchic works of these three *vignerons*. Giuseppe, extravagant but simple, is the most discreet of the three. He is the pope of Venetia, along with Romano dal Forno, whose sumptuous Amarone is extraordinary and inimitable.

Amarone is a wine from grapes harvested late and dried until March, then pressed. The juice is placed in old tuns for at least three years. This highly concentrated wine, built to age, has an extraordinary complexity and richness; it can reach up to 18° of alcohol content.

Jean Solis, one of the most reputed Swiss tasters, laughed when he offered me two bottles of 1990: 'This wine can age until 2040, but you'll be dead!' I answered as quick as a flash, 'These days, a hundred years isn't rare. In 2040, I'll only be ninety-nine. Since life expectancy increases by one year every four years, you could even say that by 2050 I will have gained ten more years. Next time, find me an Amarone that can age until 2050!'

Amarone, with a sombre garnet-red colour, is usually drunk in winter, for example to accompany hare *à la royale*. Juicy and plump, it gives off aromas of truffle, prune, blackberry, wild blueberry, liquorice, spices. I have drunk Amarone some ten times, thanks to my friend Carlos Dossi, but Quintarelli only twice, since I only have twelve bottles. In the future these will be wines fit for an anthology.

> 'Amarone is a wine from grapes harvested late and dried until March, then pressed. The juice is placed in old tuns for at least three years.'

Amarone, Quintarelli 1990

Appellation: Amarone della Valpolicella, Venetia, Italy.

Varieties: corvina, corvinone, rondinella, molinara.

Production : 1,000 bottles.

Best vintages: 1985, 1990, 1995, 1997, 2004.

I met the Ostertag family during the period of the great vintages 1988, 1989 and 1990, including the *Sélections de grains nobles*, which are perfect, especially the 1989. André Ostertag communes with the earth, his land, which he works for the good of his grapes. He thinks, reflects, as an artist, on how to obtain wines of great quality while still leaving them their uniqueness, their soul, the stamp of their land. In his chai, his soul mixes with the soul of the wine. He writes: 'Between the cask and me there has always been a very personal relationship.' One is convinced of the truth of this statement by seeing his Work 1989, where inspiration reigns above all.

What is Work? Entitled in 1989 '*Terre à vins*', it describes in flavours and in colours three types of earth and three types of wine. It is a black wood box, numbered (1 to 400), containing six half-bottles of *Sélections de grains nobles* of 1989, plus three pebbles and a booklet. Each of the three wines has a label and a capsule made from its own earth, a 'soil mush'. The design of the label is by the famous jazz musician Daniel Humair. The three wines and the pebble that accompany them are:

- Grand Cru Muenchberg, Riesling variety, pink sandstone pebble;
- Grand Cru Muenchberg, pinot gris variety, limestone pebble;
- Grand Cru Fronholz, gewürztraminer variety, quartz pebble.

These three wines are *Sélections de grains nobles*: Only the berries affected by noble rot were conserved during pressing, under the surveillance of a sworn agent. The natural sugar content of the mash was 256 to 279 grams per litre.

The pinot gris, harvested on 31 October 1989 at 26° alcohol potential, even offers 287 grams of residual sugar. Matured in new casks, it has the thickness of honey, an incredible viscosity, and should keep more than fifty years.

André Ostertag writes in *La lettre du vigneron*: 'The Work 1989 is for me a strong desire for liberty that is expressed through an opening up of creation, a uniting of energies and a mixing of influences for more intensity, more emotion, more vibrations.' The tasting of these three nectars should bring us all of these sensations, and I am happy to have selected his mythical wine among my extraordinary bottles!

'Matured in new casks, it has the thickness of honey, an incredible viscosity, and should keep more than fifty years.'

Work, André Ostertag 1989

Appellation: Alsace, France.

Vineyard area: 13 hectares, bio-dynamically grown since 1998.

Varieties grown: sylvaner, muscat, pinot gris, riesling, gewurztraminer.

Production of Work 1989: 400 boxes of 6 half-bottles.

Best vintages: 1971, 1983, 1989, 1990, 1994, 2001, 2005.

These pebbles come from the vines of Muenchberg riesling, Muenchberg pinot gris and Fronholz gewurztraminer. They were crushed and used on the labels and the capsules of the bottles.

ALSACE

Clos Windsbühl
HUNAWIHR
Appellation Alsace Contrôlée

GEWURZTRAMINER 1989
DOMAINE ZIND HUMBRECHT

Léonard et Olivier HUMBRECHT - WINTZENHEIM (Haut-Rhin) FRANCE

3000 ml

DOMAINE ZIND HUMBRECHT

The Zind-Humbrecht estate can be considered the most beautiful and reputed of Alsace. Thanks to Michel Bettane, I met Léonard Humbrecht in the 90s. His *Sélections de grains nobles* left an indelible memory, and all of the 1989 varieties left me speechless. However, it's hard to obtain the best wines, unless you are a long-time client. Olivier Humbrecht (Master of Wine and perhaps the greatest winemaker, according to Parker), heir of three centuries of winemakers, pursues the task begun by his father in 1959: to produce the best local wines, with the smallest yields of the regions, and biodynamically *s'il vous plaît!*

Let us enumerate these grand terrains, from south to north: the Grand Cru Rangen de Thann in Clos Saint-Urbain, 5-hectare monopoly of breathtaking hills that in the best years produce magnificent *Sélections de grains nobles*; the Grand Cru Goldert in Gueberschwihr, where gewürztraminer and muscat grow happily in very chalky soil; Hengst where the gewurztraminer offers late harvests with superb ageing capacity; the Riesling du Clos Haüserer and the Pinot gris of Rotenberg in Wintzenheim; the vineyards of Turkheim: the Grand Cru Brand and its Riesling with full southern exposure, mature and full of elegance, the Clos Jebsal pinot gris that often botrytises, the Heimbourg and the Herrenweg; and finally that Clos du Windsbuhl in Hunawihr, purchased in 1987, and from which I have this Jéroboam of gewürztraminer 1989. Its high altitude of 350 metres offers late harvested wines, but wines that age very well thanks to their acidity.

The wines of the Zind-Humbrecht estate have a breathtaking aromatic richness; they abound with incomparable and persistent aromas like grapefruit, acacia, lime, hawthorn, white peach, rose, tea. The late harvests and the *grains nobles* evolve into flavours of pineapple, dulce de membrillo, apricot jam, candied orange, litchi, honey, caramel. The wines then develop an oily texture, extremely dense. The *Sélections de grains nobles* are prodigious. The main thing is to find them!

'The late harvests and the *grains nobles* evolve into flavours of pineapple, dulce de membrillo, apricot jam, candied orange, litchi, honey, caramel…'

Jéroboam Clos Windsbuhl, Olivier Humbrecht 1989

Appellation: Alsace, France.

Vineyard area: 40 hectares; du Clos: 4.5 hectares.

Varieties grown: 30 % riesling, 30 % gewürztraminer, 30 % pinot gris, the other 10 % are composed of chardonnay, muscat, pinot blanc, auxerrois and pinot noir.

Best vintages: 1961, 1966, 1971, 1976, 1985, 1988, 1989, 1990, 1994, 1995, 1998, 2001, 2002, 2005, 2007.

The San Guido estate produces Sassicaia, one of the greatest wines in Tuscany, you could even say one of the most reputed of all Italy. The proprietor, Marchese Nicolo Incisadella Rochetta, creates this wine from cabernet varieties, and it rivals the immense redigaffi of Tua Rita or the masseto of Ornellaia of the merlot variety. Because in the sangiovese homeland that is Tuscany, many great winemakers have chosen Bordeaux varieties for their prestigious vintages, declaring themselves *vini da tavola*, today IGT Toscana, while at the same time acquiring the status of 'Super Tuscans' that has opened the luxury wine market to them. Sassicaia has been given the privilege of a personal DOCG appellation, Bolgheri Sassicaia, which confirms the use of *cabernet*. Sassicaia is an exceptional wine that develops aromas of blackcurrant, raspberry, blackberry, truffle, with well blended tannins. The wine is dense, concentrated, multidimensional, savoury, elegant, with a good acidity that permits it to age well. The 1985 should still be delicious in 2040. Its reputation is such that it is difficult to find a single bottle outside of billionaires' wine cellars.

I was lucky enough to acquire three bottles thanks to Monsieur Carlo Dossi, a famous Italian bon-vivant who lives in Paris and runs his wine boutique *Idea Vino* in the 11th arrondissement. If you read the book published in his honour in 2005, you will realize that he is not merely a great wine connoisseur, but a noted gastronome. A passion instilled in him by his father and grandfather, ham specialists. This magician can appraise, in a few seconds using his 'sounding bone' made of dried horse tendons, the flavour of a ham.

Every year since 1988 I have bought a case or two of Sassicaia. I missed the 1985, but I knew that there was a six-bottle case left among the five hundred references that he proposed. For many years, he would laugh and say to me: 'I am saving this case for my grandchildren – you don't have it in your collection!' And then one day, as the year 2000 was approaching, he invited me into the basement of his boutique and, par-

Sassicaia 1985

Appellation: Vino da Tavola, today Bolgheri Sassicaia, Tuscany, Italy.

Vineyard area: 50 hectares.

Varieties: cabernet sauvignon 85 %, cabernet franc 15 %.

Average age of vines: 30 years.

Average production: 180,000 bottles.

Best vintages: 1975, 1985, 1990, 1995, 2000, 2004, 2006.

'The wine is dense, concentrated, multidimensional, savoury, elegant, with a good acidity that permits it to age well. The 1985 should still be delicious in 2040.'

odying an Italian proverb, said: 'A barrel of Sassicaia 1985 can perform more miracles than a church full of saints. Take these three bottles, they are a gift, this 1985 is too rare, it's not for sale, it must be drunk or given to friends. I know your passion for wine, and this way you will have good luck as you approach the year 2000.' 1985 is the year that elevated Sassicaia to stand among the great wines, after a tasting by the European jury where it won first prize, ahead of the premier Bordeaux Grands Crus classes 1855.

When I had tastings with Carlos, I particularly appreciated the 1988, 1990, 2000, 2004 and 2006. It's true that since the 2004, 2005 and 2006, the quality is getting even better.

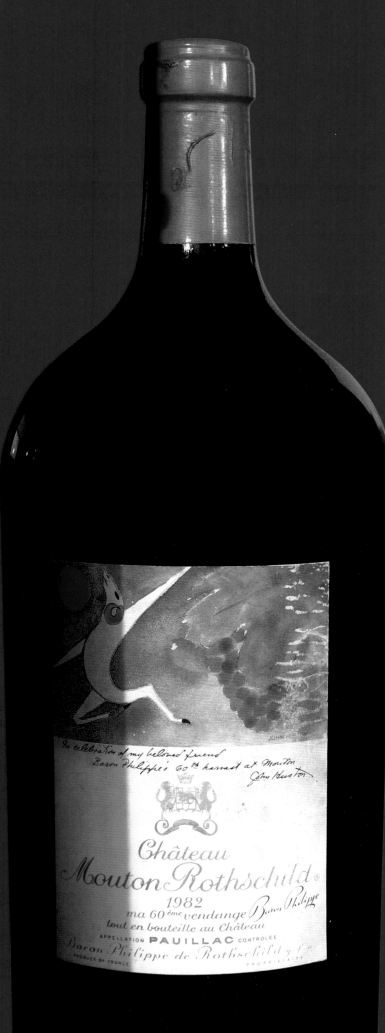

> 'A grand wine that will keep at least fifty years, the best of the chateau along with the mythical 1945.'

Sometimes you have to pounce when an opportunity presents itself. It was mid-day sometime in 1987; I was still working at Dassault in Vélizy. The phone rings, My friend Pierre Villard, a photographer at the Sipa-Presse agency and a lover of great wine, declares: 'I have a big one for you! A Mouton 1982, an imperial, in its original case!'

They say it is the greatest Médoc of the year, and one of the greatest Mouton-Rothschild. The label, by John Huston, represents a white sheep frolicking in a fresh countryside. A grand wine that will keep at least fifty years, the best of the chateau along with the mythical 1945. But there's one problem: 'I need four thousand francs before 2:00 PM. We'll meet at the Place de l'Étoile!'

Two hours is not a long time and I only have a thousand francs in my bank account. So I borrow from a friend, I empty my son's piggy bank; I hastily sell my pair of Victoire de Samothrace stamps to a philatelist friend. The green 30-centime and the red 55-centime, only one thousand five hundred in circulation! No time for lunch, I jump into my car and I dash to the Place de l'Étoile. Pierre is there with the beautiful baby. Another one that I bought with pure energy, with pure luck. But I have no regrets!

Large bottles like the imperial are more and more coveted because they are rare and they increase in value. The proprietors of vineyards make fewer and fewer, since the fragility of the glass, incredibly thin in some places, often breaks during bottling.

Imperial Château Mouton-Rothschild 1982

Appellation: Pauillac, second cru classé in 1855, premier cru since 1973, Bordeaux, France.

Vineyard area: 80 hectares.

Varieties: cabernet sauvignon 77 %, merlot 11 %, cabernet franc 10 %, petit verdot 2 %.

Average age of vines: 48 years.

Average production: 300,000 bottles.

I was late in developing an interest in the Château Le Pin, in Pomerol: when 'garage wines' were in style, a precise classification was made of them, and the Le-Pin became a sought-after wine. They are called 'garage wines' because certain winemakers who only owned very small plots made a few barrels, in their garage or an outbuilding, in order to produce a mere two or three thousand bottles. Others chose the best plot, pruned the vines short and thinned them; five to seven bunches per

most legendary cru of Bordeaux, along with Petrus. First of all because it is located in Pomerol, a small appellation of merely 780 hectares for some two hundred fifty proprietors, world renowned, where the dominant merlot variety offers all its qualities. Also because Robert Parker gave a 100/100 to the 1982.

In 1988, I spoke to the proprietor Jacques Thienpont, who let me know that the wine was reserved each year en primeur, and that he did not have a waiting list for new

to pick up his case, I thought of you. It's a case of six magnums of 1989, you're starting well here', he said with a smile. Since then, I have gone every year to pick up my case, and two or three times to his chai to maintain our good relations. And then with the year 2000 approaching, as we were preparing to celebrate the 100th anniversary of Pomerol, I said to Jacques Thienpont:

'To commemorate this great day, I know we are going to drink Petrus and Le-Pin. But could you possibly sell me your best vintage, the 1982?'

'I haven't had any myself since a long time ago. In any case it would be very expensive!'

But when the day arrived, I saw Thienpont arrive with a package under his arm. It was a beautiful magnum of 1982 that a client of his who was having financial problems had wanted to sell. For me that was an unforgettable 100th anniversary of Pomerol: we were able to taste some thirty of the best Pomerols, and I brought home the rarest of all, a Le-Pin 1982. A wine that is now impossible to find and that can run to 5,000 euros per bottle. In his June 2009 edition of *Wine Advocate*, Parker reconfirmed it at 100 points with this remark: 'flamboyant, exotic, concentrated, dense, caramel, chocolate, plum, fig, powerful'.

> **'With the unique characteristics of its homogeneous soil, offering flavours of coffee, chocolate, caramel, blackcurrant, it is the most legendary cru of Bordeaux, along with Petrus.'**

foot. They did a *saignée* of the vats to get a more concentrated wine that they matured in new oak casks in order to rival the greatest crus. And the garage was sufficient to stock the bottles.

Contrary to what certain people have written, the Château-le-Pin is not a garage wine. With the unique characteristics of its homogeneous soil, offering flavours of coffee, chocolate, caramel, blackcurrant, it is the

clients. Tirelessly, I went back to see him at his chai and in the vineyards at each vendange. One evening in 1992, I tried again, this time with the press-book of my 10,000-bottle wine cellar, to show off my Mouton 1945, my Cheval-Blanc 1947... And thanks to my persistence, I succeeded in getting him to take out the notebook in which he kept the names of his clients.

'You're lucky: one client hasn't come

Magnum Château Le Pin 1982

Appellation: Pomerol, Bordeaux, France.

Vineyard area: 2 hectares.

Variety: merlot.

Average age of vines: 30 years.

Average production: 6,000 bottles.

Best vintages: 1982, 1989, 1990, 1994, 1998, 2000, 2005.

POMEROL

The estate dates back to 1906, but more than anything it is Pierre Ramonet who gave it its reputation. It includes vines with the Villages appellation, premier crus, grands crus like the Bâtard-Montrachet and the Chevalier-Montrachet, and 26 ares of Grand-Montrachet.

Montrachet, the best dry white wine in the world, comes from in-between the villages of Chassagne and Puligny. The Ramonet plot is in Puligny, to the north of the Meursault road, one of the best soils.

The Ramonet estate produces vines of phenomenal concentration. Perfect mastery of woodiness makes an elegant, fine and generous Montrachet with an almost oily boldness. It acquires scents of pear, spices, honey, white flowers, anise, and as it ages, candied aromas of hazelnut, fig, coconut. It is often explosive in the mouth and eternally long. The fabulous 1959 still has a charming freshness. The 1978 vintages have an incomparable structure and have been purchased by all of the great restaurants. It is the first vintage produced. My 1979 is the second.

In 1983, I had the opportunity to exchange a few cases of Feytit-Clinet with Noël Ramonet for a half dozen Montrachet 1979, as well as some 1985 and some 1989. I realized that he was interested in all of the great wines of the world and that his wine cellar contained great wines of Bordeaux and the Rhône. My six bottles of Montrachet Ramonet are a testimony to the greatest white wines of Burgundy, and thus of the world. This 1979 remains one of the best Montrachets I have ever tasted, along with the one of the La Romanée-Conti estate. The two Ramonet brothers continue to produce great white ageing wines with the same passion, particularly the 2005 and 2006.

'Perfect mastery of woodiness makes an elegant, fine and generous Montrachet with an almost oily boldness.'

Montrachet, Ramonet 1979

Appellation: Montrachet, grand cru, Burgundy, France.

Vineyard area: 10 hectares, including 26 ares in the Montrachet appellation.

Variety: chardonnay.

Average age of vines: 40 years.

Best vintages: 1979, 1985, 1989, 1990, 1995, 1999, 2002, 2006.

Henri Jayer is a myth in Burgundy: the wizard of pinot noir. Born in 1922, retired in 1996, he left us in 2006. In his lifetime, this son of a modest factory worker revolutionised the production of Burgundy wines with a few simple precepts: small yields, healthy grapes 'the size of a pea', no stalks, low temperatures in the vat, new casks from the Tronçais Forest, no filtration, bottling by hand (his two-

> **'The Cros-Parantoux, which made Henri Jayer a legend, has a brilliant colour, a complex bouquet, a pronounced taste of fruit, a peacock finale, and always seems younger than the ten years declared on its label.'**

spouted 'goat' is famous, it avoids rushing the wine). Having come to winemaking by chance, he progressively developed a vineyard that is small in size but prestigious by climate: Echezeaux in grands crus, and Vosne-Romanée Les Beaumonts and Cros Parantoux in premiers. This last, 72 sloping ares wedged above the Richebourg, with eastern exposure, was brought into cultivation by Henri Jayer in the 1950s, removing the rocks with a wheelbarrow, he planted it and took it to the level of the most reputable localities among the three hundred in the Côte. The terrain is such that to plant vine stock one needs explosives! It

was his favourite wine in the great year of 1978, a wine about which Henri Jayer said that 'it is incontestably one of the finest of the century'.

The Cros-Parantoux has a brilliant colour, a complex bouquet, a pronounced taste of fruit, a peacock finale, and always seems younger than the ten years declared on its label.

These three thousand bottles were immediately desired by all connoisseurs, and their astronomic price has nothing to do with Henri Jayer, who is happy just to serve his loyal clients while keeping a waiting list that evolves as slowly as his wines. I missed one of my best opportunities in my purchases of rare wines: it was in 1993, Henri Jayer had miraculously reserved for me a case of Cros-Parantoux and one of Échezeaux, in the great 1990 vintage. At 300 francs per bottle, it came to 3 600 francs for a case of twelve. Unfortunately, I did not have the means to buy the two cases. I chose the grand cru, and left the premier cru. In 2000, one case of Cros Parantoux 1990 sold for 45,000 dollars in the United States. As I write these lines, it can be found for 5,700 euros for a bottle, the equivalent of 37,000 francs! As for the 1978, it is impossible to find. My best memory of Henri Jayer's wines is a Richebourg 1978 that he himself served in his wine cellar; an unlabeled bottle whose vintage I had to determine blind. It seemed so young that my son and I thought it was a 1990! This is the bottle I chose to include in this book, not as reputed as the Cros-Parentoux, but infinitely rarer and even better.

When I look at my case of Échezeaux 1990 in my cellar, I know that until my dying day I will regret not having it accompanied by the case of Cros-Parantoux. 1990 is also the year I met Jayer for the first time, on the recommendation of Michel Bettane, the man who led me to discover Burgundy. Eight years later, I was lucky enough to receive from Henri Jayer's hand his *Ode aux grands vins de Bourgogne* with a dedication to me. One more sentence to put my misjudgement into perspective: 'When my wines are young, one can guess their age, when they are old, one believes them young!'

Richebourg, Henri Jayer 1978

Appellation: Vosne-Romanée premier cru, Burgundy, France.

Vineyard area: 0.72 hectares.

Average age of vines: 45 years.

Average production: 3,000 bottles.

Best years: 1978, 1985, 1990, 1996.

I met the Guigal family during the period of the famous Mouline 1978, when Rhône wines, particularly the Côte-Rôtie, were unknown and sold cheaply: one could find Côte-Rôtie for 40 francs and the Châteauneuf for 15. Étienne Guigal, who worked at the Vidal-Fleury estate - which his son eventually purchased -, had founded his estate in 1946.

Marcel took it over in 1961 and developed an important commercial activity producing six million bottles per year. In 1970, he produced his first vintage of La-Mouline, from very old terrace-cultivated vines with a large percentage of the viognier variety. In 1975 his son Philippe was born, and Marcel planted La Landonne in Côte Brune, only syrah, of which the first vintage is 1978. In 1985 La Turque came out, an astounding quality for young vines. Robert Parker was not stingy with his 100/100 for these cult wines, the best of the 240 hectares of the appellation.

Marcel Guigal restored the image of the

> ‘A legendary wine, exceedingly rare today, which can age many years like a vintage port.’

Côte-Rôtie from the village of Ampuis. After Vidal-Fleury, he bought the chateaus of Ampuis, De Valouit, Grippat, Bonserine... A knight of the Legion of Honour since 1998, he was elected personality of the year for oenology in 2006.

This bottle of Mouline 1976 is a legendary wine, exceedingly rare today, which can age many years like a vintage port. Its colour is as dark as ink. It has aromas of Alpine berries, blackcurrant, blueberry, violet, exotic scents of barbecue; in the mouth it is round, fruity, the tannins are silky and melded; the concentration is extraordinary, the complexity extreme, the finish presents an infinite string of ‘caudalies’. I drank this wine three times with the Guigal family and I told Philippe that it was one of the greatest wines of my life, along with Cheval Blanc 1921, Petrus 1947, Latour 1961... This bottle was give to me by Marcel along with another rarity: the 1989 ‘Homage to Étienne Guigal’, produced in only six hundred samples from grapes of the La Pommières locality, eighty-year-old vines, the first that the young Marcel worked with, and that aged in an oak tun sculpted in the image of Étienne Guigal.

Guigal's château in Ampuis.

La Mouline, Marcel Guigal 1976

Appellation: Côte-Rôtie, Rhône, France.

Vineyard area: 1 hectare.

Variety: syrah 89 %, viognier 11 %.

Very old vines replanted after the phylloxera as of 1892 and renewed by complantation as the old vine stock died.

Aging: 42 months in new casks.

Average production: 5,000 bottles.

Best vintages: 1976, 1978, 1983, 1985, 1988, 1990, 1991, 1999, 2003, 2005.

In Moselle, German winemaker Egon Müller has one of the most beautiful vineyards in Germany: the Scharzhof estate in Wiltingen on the Sarre, which his family purchased in 1797 and has conserved ever since. He used to own the Sainte-Marie aux Martyrs de Trêves Monastery, nationalised by Napoleon before being sold as a national heritage site. This trockenbeerenauslese represents all that is best in German dessert wines, as its etymology attests: *auslese* is a selection of the best grapes in late harvest; *bereen* adds a selection of botrytised grapes; the prefix *trocken* the selection of only grapes botyrised and withered from over-maturity. On vertiginous slopes, with full southern exposure but in a cold and windswept region, riesling is challenged and only produces grapes of this quality from time to time. And when Egon Müller makes trockenbeerenauslese with his grapes, of which some date from before

> 'This trockenbeerenauslese represents all that is best in German dessert wines in, as its etymology attests: *auslese* is a selection of the best grapes in late harvest.'

phoned me from Germany, to tell me that he was going on vacation with his wife in La Rochelle, and to ask me if I could bring him a case of the best vintage of Feytit-Clinet. Of course, I proposed an exchange: several cases of my pomerol for one bottle of his nectar; if he wouldn't sell it, per-

the phylloxera, he makes minute quantities, some forty litres on average. This wine, rare and precious, hits records at auction. I tirelessly asked Egon Müller Sr., then Egon Müller Jr., to sell me at least one bottle. But he would tell me that I had but to come to Trêves on the day of the auction, since this wine is sold only there, and to the highest bidder!

In 2005, at Egon Müller's stand at Vinexpo, I met his wife. She let me know that her husband adored Pomerol wines. So I offered him a bottle of my Feytit-Clinet 2003, a grand vintage. Sometime later, Egon Müller

haps he would trade it. We tasted the 1975 vintage together, extraordinary. He left me a bottle, as well as the breathtaking 1994 and 2007, and an auselese 1959 from his personal collection But I will have to wait a bit longer to fill my six-bottle case.

Trockenbeerenauslese, Egon Müller 1975

Appellation: Scharzhofberg, Moselle-Sarre-Ruwer, Germany.

Variety: riesling.

Average age of vines: 50 years.

Production: 40 litres every 3 years on average.

Best vintages: 1945, 1959, 1971, 1975, 1990, 1994, 2007.

1975 • NOBEL PEACE PRIZE AWARDED TO SAKHAROV • KHMER ROUGE DICTATORSHIP IN CAMBODIA • DEATH OF FRANCO

Jo Heitz and his son David are the producers of this Napa Valley estate, close to the Mayacama Hills with the eucalyptus trees that perfume their wine. Jo Heitz started out modestly in 1961, on three hectares of grignolino, an Italian variety. Today, the estate covers 56 hectares, and the jewel in its crown is the pure Martha's Vineyard cabernet, named after Martha

one of the first California cult wines. I have never tasted it. For Robert Parker, it is a monumental wine. For James Laube, in his book *California Wines*, 'from 1966 to 1980, it was the star of the Napa Valley cabernets, with its characteristically sombre colour and its rich aromas of mentholated chocolate, blackberry and gooseberry'. Broadbent gives it five stars in 2000, with this remark: 'still sombre, rather intense, inimitable scent of eucalyptus; dry, a lot of extrait, excellent flavour and very long. Excellent wine'.

In 2008, a case of twelve bottles was auctioned for 18,000 dollars by Christie's in Los Angeles. I searched unsuccessfully for this bottle for several years in the collections of my American colleagues. My friend Éric Morlot, OIV Master (Office international du vin) finally found one for me from an Australian collector. This bottle travelled 40,000 kilometres before taking its place in my wine cellar.

> 'The wine, matured in tuns of American oak, then in casks of French wood, is black, silky and rich, of prodigious concentration and excellent ageing.'

May, a partner of the winery. From a gravelly and silty soil, it offers mentholated aromas of eucalyptus, fruit jam, chocolate, truffles. The wine, matured in tuns of American oak, then in casks of French wood, is black, silky and rich, of prodigious concentration and excellent ageing. The 1974 is

Martha's Vineyard, Napa Valley 1974

Appellation: Napa Valley, California, United States.

Vineyard area: 56 hectares.

Variety: cabernet sauvignon.

Average production: 50,000 bottles.

One of the twelve best wines of the 20th century according to the selection of Wine Spectator.

Best vintages: 1968, 1970, 1974.

MISE DU DO
MONOPOLE
1971
LEROY
AGENT GÉNÉRAL
AUXEY-MEURSAULT
COTE-D'OR
SOCIÉTÉ CIVILE DU DOMAINE DE LA ROMANEE-CONTI
PROPRIETAIRE A VOSNE-ROMANEE (COTE-D'OR)
PRODUCE OF FRANCE
LA TACHE
APPELLATION LA TACHE CONTROLEE
17.753 Bouteilles Récoltées
L'ASSOCIÉ-GÉRANT
N°
ANNÉE 1971
Mise en bouteille au domaine

'The ruby grenadine colour, bewitching, catches the eye. The flavours are rich and complex, evoking an alpine berry jam, with a unique refinement. The quality has been increasing these past few years.'

La Tâche is a grand cru produced only on the La Romanée-Conti estate, the most prestigious wine growing property in Burgundy. It belongs half to the Villaine family and half to the Leroy family. With Petrus and La Mouline, La Tâche is one of my three favourite wines, and I can say that when La Tâche is great, no wine in the world can equal it. I hold a precious memory of the dozens of bottles I have tasted. If I were to compare La Tâche to a woman, I would say that for its charm and its class it is the Lætitia Casta of wine! Only La Romanée-Conti surpasses La Tâche

in ageing, without equalling its plump quality and its silky flavours, its breathtaking concentration, its infinite persistence. When it is young, one often discovers in this wine aromas of violet, raspberry, black cherry, blackberry, blackcurrant, exotic spices, with a velvety texture, overflowing with supple melded tannins. The ruby grenadine colour, bewitching, catches the eye. The flavours are rich and complex, evoking an alpine berry jam, with a unique refinement. The quality has been increasing these past few years. The 1990 is breathtaking. Since then, the 1996, 1999, 2003 and 2005 are textbook wines. The old vintages are rather difficult to find – my oldest is 1944, two bottles restored by the chai master André Noblet. They were still very good, lightly *tuilé*, with flavours of faded roses, truffles, underbrush, and extremely mellow.

My favourite vintage is 1971, which I tasted with a petrus 1971 and a mouline 1976, to celebrate the new year in 2000. I have two bottles left. This is what Georges Lepré, the renowned sommelier at the *Ritz*, said about this 1971: 'A sublime scent, like satin in the mouth, one of the most sumptuous wines on the planet, to be saved for big occasions. Turkey with chestnut dressing and duck Auguste Escoffier should accompany it in a triumphant march.'

And also: 'The crimson colour, deep, the sublime scent of complexity and charm, hinting at resin, amber, faded roses, roasted coffee, mint, spice – and that satin texture in the mouth where all the scents of vanilla, pistachio, liquorice, come into harmony...'
My dream is to taste a wonderful bottle of 1999 or 2005 in 2031, at its apex. I will only be ninety years old!

La Tâche 1971

Appellation: La Tâche, grand cru, Burgundy, France.

Vineyard area: 6.06 hectares.

Variety: pinot noir.

Age of vines: 35 years.

Average production: 20,000 bottles.

Best vintages: 1990, 1996, 1999, 2003, 2005.

I became interested in Château-Lafleur, in Pomerol, around 1973. The first case I bought—and that I still have—is of the 1975 vintage, graded 100 by Parker with a fifty-year ageing potential. Since then, every year I have bought one or two cases of this divine nectar, to the point that I have assembled one of the world's best collections of Lafleur since the 1947 vintage (particularly in magnums, jeroboams or imperials in the best years).

I always maintained very good relations with the Robin sisters, Thérèse and Marie. Especially with Marie. I would often go to visit her. Shortly before her death in 2001, she gave me a small rosary, the only reminder she had kept of her sister. I carefully placed this present in my wine cellar close to the cases of her wine, and I am proud of this little relic of the last survivor of the most sumptuous and extraordinary wine in the world.

I have tasted a magnum 1947, and I have only the empty bottle, but I have kept all of the great vintages in magnums: 1961, 1971, 1982, 1989, 1990, 1998, 2000, 2005. Parker praises my 1961 magnum: 'One of the most extraordinary wines, opaque colour, dusky red bordering on black. Scent of black truffles, of very ripe sweet cherry;

Thérèse's rosary, given to me by her sister Marie Robin.

enormous corpulence and massive extraction, a terribly exuberant character with a thick and exotic finish bursting with tannins.'

Like Petrus, these magnums — a unique heritage — should no longer belong to me, but should be protected just like the works of art in the Louvre. The same goes for my four hundred bottles of Lafleur from 1947 to 2005. Unfortunately, since the price of this wine has soared, especially for the vintage 2005, the estate has refused to sell me a single bottle. I try to continue this collection, paying full price, when I can find some.

'These magnums should no longer belong to me, but should be protected just like the works of art in the Louvre.'

Magnum Château Lafleur 1961

Appellation: Pomerol, Bordeaux, France.

Vineyard area: 4.6 hectares.

Varieties: merlot 50 %, cabernet franc 50 %.

Average age of vines: more than 30 years.

Average production: 12,000 bottles.

Best vintages: 1945, 1947, 1950, 1961, 1966, 1971, 1975, 1982, 1985, 1989, 1990, 2000, 2005.

Mission-Haut-Brion is one of the greatest Bordeaux wines, occasionally surpassing its neighbour Haut-Brion in quality. It is a rich, potent wine, with a lot of tannins but an intense fruitiness. It can age fifty years. This 1961 magnum is in excellent shape and reigns in my wine cellar as one of the best bottles. Parker gives it 100/100. Broadbent gives it five stars, the maximum, with this pithy comment: 'Fabulous flavour. Masculine.' A virile wine.

One day in 1995, I was invited to Sologne by my friend Alex de Clouet, a gourmet with a passion for the good things in life and fine wines, especially bordeaux. It was he who taught me the nuances of the six wines of the La Romanée-Conti estate. At dinner, he brought out a bottle of La-Mission 1961. It was slightly low, but sublime, with a bouquet of spices, cigars, blackberry, blueberry. In the mouth, the wine was rich, smooth, sumptuous... I fell in love with this wine that I did not have in my cellar. So Alex, smiling, said to me: 'I have a perfect magnum in my wine cellar, a true collector's item. It will be yours if you outshine me at the hunt tomorrow. I don't know if I did better than him, but nevertheless he sold me that magnum a few months later...and at a bargain price.

La Mission-Haut-Brion used to be a religious community; the gothic chapel of the chateau attests to its origins. The wine has been renowned for some time: in the 18th century, it was already one of the most expensive Bordeaux wines. Le Féret of 1868 specifies that 'Americans in New York and New Orleans are great lovers of this wine'. Sold as national heritage during the Revolution, it knew various owners until its purchase in 1920 by the Woltner family, who developed a style that puts its strength in evidence. In 1983, the Château Haut-Brion bought the Woltner vineyards: La Mission, its neighbour La Tour and the white vineyard of Laville, all three crus classé. The La Tour Haut-Brion has now disappeared, and will reinforce the second wine, La Chapelle de La Mission-Haut-Brion. All of the neighbouring vineyards belong to the Clarence Dillon estate, named for the American Francophile who bought Haut-Brion in 1935. Today Prince Robert of Luxembourg, who succeeded his mother the Duchess of Mouchy, herself granddaughter of Clarence Dillon, administers the estate. The greatest I have tasted are the 1975 and the 2000.

> 'It is a rich, powerful wine, with a lot of tannin but an intense fruitiness. It can age fifty years.'

Magnum Château La Mission-Haut-Brion 1961

Appellation: Graves, and Pessac-Léognan since 1986, Bordeaux, France.

Vineyard area: 20 hectares.

Average age of vines: 45 years.

Varieties: cabernet sauvignon 50 %, merlot 40 %, cabernet franc 10 %.

Average production: 80,000 bottles.

Best vintages: 1961, 1975, 1989.

'A wine with a deliciously fruity bouquet of alpine berries, a wonderful balance and a plump texture, velvety melded tannins.'

Marcel Dassault taught me how to think, and I try to cultivate his qualities: curiosity, intelligence, tenacity, rigour, perfectionism, audacity, a sense of duty and, more difficult, humility. After my military service in 1963, I started to work at Dassault in Saint-Cloud. With an engineering diploma, I thought I would be hired as an executive, but I was told that before working on prototypes, I would have to start at the bottom, in the workshops.

So be it. I started as a rank P1 boilermaker. Then P2, P3, then study draughter, 4th degree technician, and finally manager for international sales of the Mirage, until 1989 when I left the company. I had known a heroic period, from the Mirage III in riveted duralumin to the Rafale made of composite materials. Marcel Dassault had purchased the Château Couperie, renamed Château Dassault, so that delegations visiting the factory might also discover chais in a world-renowned region. This Saint Émilion grand cru, for which the famous oenologist Michel Roland is a consultant, produces a wine with a deliciously fruity bouquet of alpine berries, a wonderful balance and a plump texture, velvety melded tannins giving it an exceptional charm.

After seeing articles in the press about my collection, particularly in *Le Monde* and *Paris-Match*, Laurent Dassault, grandson of Marcel Dassault, invited me to lunch at the estate in Saint-Émilion, and made me a gift of this bottle of 1961, vintage of the century, the last in his possession.

The aircraft manufacturer Marcel Dassault, great lover of wine, was the owner of the Château Couperie, renamed Château Dassault.

Château Dassault 1961

Appellation: Saint-Émilion grand cru, Bordeaux, France. Grand cru classé.

Vineyard area: 24 hectares.

Average of wines: 35 years.

Varieties: merlot 65 %, cabernet franc 30 %, cabernet sauvignon 5 %.

Best vintages: 1959, 1961, 1982, 1990, 2000, 2001, 2005.

The best bottle I have tasted: 1959, of which there is, alas, no more in the wine cellar of the estate.

'Rich, powerful, with often spectacular concentration, these wines can reach their apex at thirty years.'

I have known Angelo Gaja for some twenty years, and it is a pleasure to speak with him at every Vinexpo, where he is always considered the star of the great Piedmont producers. He represents the fifth generation of winemakers, and his wines are present on the most prestigious tables. His charisma, his marketing sense and the quality of his wines have built him an international reputation. 'Wine must be worked artistically and sculpted so that it always remains elegant', says this defender of the grand nebbiolo vintage, *fog wine*, tannic but elegant, that finds its best soil here. It is he who introduced French oak casks into Piedmont, and cabernet sauvignon for some of his wines.

My first purchases were the famous fragmented selections of Barbaresco Sori Tildin, Costa Russi, Sori San Lorenzo of the vintage 1988, and I was lucky enough to be able to purchase the prestigious vintage 1997, the production of which was limited to twelve thousand bottles.

Gaja's nectars offer to the nose aromas of black cherry, raspberry, liquorice, truffles, with vanilla notes and new oak. Rich, powerful, with often spectacular concentration, these wines can reach their apex at thirty years.

In my selection of one hundred extraordinary wines, I could not forget Signor Angelo Gaja, and I needed and old and representative vintage. However, in Italy, as in Burgundy, it is not as easy to find fifty-year-old bottles as it is in Bordeaux where bottling has been general since the 19th century. At the celebration of the one hundred fiftieth anniversary of the family *winery*, Angelo, with a big smile, gave me one of the oldest bottles of the family stock, the famous Barbaresco 1961, to which he attached a luxurious folder entitled '1858-2009'. Since 1994, I have had the privilege of tasting Angelo's wines with him, every two years at Vinexpo. His comments are meticulous and enriching. The best wines of his that I have tasted are Sori Tildin, Costa Russi and Sori San Lorenzo 1997. Those from 2001 aren't bad either!

Barbaresco, Angelo Gaja 1961

Appellation: Barbaresco, Piedmont, Italy.

Vineyard area: 100 hectares (Barbaresco and Barolo).

Varieties: nebbiolo 95 %, barbera 5 %.

Average age of vines: 25 years.

Yield: small.

Average production: 60,000 bottles of barbaresco.

Gaja's fragmented selections have been 'folded into' the Langhe appellation, wider, but the quality is the same.

Best vintages: 1961, 1971, 1989, 1990, 1997, 2001.

Piedmont wine producer Angelo Gaja.

Hermitage wines have always been ranked among the first in France, and have often been used to reinforce the great Bordeaux in difficult years; a tasting term was born of this phenomenon, describing a wine as 'hermitage'. In the 19th century, in *Topographie de tous les vignobles connus*, Jullien provides a short list of first-class red wines including seventeen *climats* of Burgundy, eleven *crus* of Bordeaux, and nine *mas* of Hermitage: the four from which come La Chapelle, then les Beaumes, les Murets, les Diognères, and two others that do not appear in the land registry.

I met Gérard Jaboulet several times in La Roche-de-Glun, a few kilometres from the Hermitage vineyard. *Dégustations* were always perfect in the company of this generous bon-vivant. In 1992, he said to me: 'I am going to put aside a few cases of 1990 for you. It's going to be a great one like the 1961.' I was thus able to obtain this 1990 in magnums. As for the 1961, it is listed among the twelve greatest wines in the world and its price has hit the ceiling: a case of six bottles has sold for 100,000 dollars. It is a very dense wine, still young: roasted, smoky aromas of spice, pear, flavours of plum, blackberry, crème de cassis, etc., immortally long. According to Parker, it is one of the most grandiose wines of the 20th century, graded 100/100 more than twenty times!

I had the opportunity to acquire this famous 1961, which is now included in my collection next to the 1947 acquired some twenty years ago. Today, given the exorbitant price of these great bottles, counterfeit bottles circulate. I have not had the chance to taste the 1961. But among the twenty or so vintages that I have tasted, I particularly appreciated the 1978 and the 1990.

> 'It is listed among the twelve greatest wines in the world and its price has hit the ceiling.'

Hermitage La Chapelle, Jaboulet 1961 & 1947

Appellation: Hermitage, Rhône, France.

Selection of 21 hectares on the estate, in the localities Les Bessarts, LeMéal, Les Rocoules, Les Greffieux.

Variety: syrah.

Age of vines: 50 years.

Yield: 35 hectolitres per hectare.

Average production: 80,000 bottles.

1961 : one of the twelve best wines of the 20th century for *Wine Spectator*.

Best vintages: 1929, 1937, 1947, 1961, 1978, 1989, 1990, 2003.

1961 • NUREYEV COMES TO THE WEST • FOUNDATION OF AMNESTY INTERNATIONAL • MASSACRE OF PRO-INDEPENDENCE ALGERIANS IN PARIS

1961 & 1947

77

This property, which belongs to the Baron de Rothschild family, is masterfully administered to produce a great wine every year, sometimes rivalling the famous Petrus. It used to be administered by an energetic woman with a tough character, Madame Ducasse, always present on the property every day, despite her ninety years, and the vineyard never stopped making great wines. The credit goes to her husband Louis, who restored its image by a draconian selection of varieties after a devastating frost in 1956. The renovated chais and buildings give it all the lustre of the prestigious Pomerol chateau it is.

Château l'Évangile is one of my favourite pomerols, along with Vieux Château Certan, La Conseillante, Lafleur and L'Église-Clinet. This land, between Petrus and Cheval Blanc, made up of gravel and clay, produces an immense wine de *longue garde*. Between 1970 and 1980, when the price of Bordeaux was at its lowest, I tasted the vintages 1947 and 1950 several times, and was always captivated by the quality and the complexity of this divine beverage.

'I have only one bottle of 1961 and it's one of the references to the heritage of my collection.'

I have only one bottle of 1961 and it is one of the references to the heritage of my collection. This is what Robert Parker writes about this wine: 'The 1961 gives off an enormous scent of coffee, sweet candied black fruit, creamy nuts and truffles. Its syrupy texture and its concentration as well as its richness and its viscosity are incredible. Like a port, this wine is full-bodied, massive, and recalls the grandiose 1947.' I am proud of having been able to acquire this bottle of 1961 some ten years ago from a wealthy English collector who was mad for port.

Château l'Évangile 1961

Appellation: Pomerol, Bordeaux, France.

Vineyard area: 14 hectares.

Varieties: merlot 78 %, cabernet franc 22 %.

Age of vines: 35 years.

Average production: 20,000 bottles.

Best vintages: 1947, 1961, 1975, 1982, 1985, 1990, 1998, 2000, 2005.

The great reputation of this vineyard dates from the 17th century. A century later, its wines were among the first to be bottled. Moreover, the oldest bottles of Bordeaux wines to be put on the market, Lafite 1784 and 1787, at the time when Thomas Jefferson, then ambassador of the young United States was at the court of Versailles, gave it international renown. In 1717 in London, Lafite was among the spoils of the English corsairs put up for auction. Louis XV appreciated it so much that it came to be called 'the king's wine'. A bottle from 1787 was auctioned for 160,000 dollars, the highest auction

The château Lafite-Rothschild.

price in the world, before being badly stocked and having the cork fall into the wine... In 1855, Lafite was ranked first among the premier crus, ahead of Latour and Margaux. The 1868 remained the most expensive wine *en primeur* for a century. One can still 'rather easily' find bottles dating from 1800 and 1900 of surprising quality, which attests to the remarkable longevity of this wine. It is Baron Eric de Rothschild-whose ancestor James purchased Lafite at auction in 1868 after a long period in the hands of the Ségur family - who re-established its reputation as of 1975. The vineyard is situated on thick gravel, and a small part on Saint-Estèphe is integrated into this Pauillac cru by special dispensation.

The vines are old, they are very short and their yield is small, especially since the least satisfying product is put into the second wine, Les Carruades. The 1985 bottle is adorned with a small Halley's Comet, and that of 1999 with a pretty solar eclipse. Since 1996, the bottles carry the Lafite cachet. The wines often have a mineral smell, aromas of blackcurrant, liquorice, blackberry, plum, caramel, vanilla, cedar. In the mouth, Lafite is sappy, generous, elegant, less massive than Latour, but soft

and powerful at the same time. Parker attributes to the 2000 a seventy-two second finish and a maturity in... 2050.

Concerning this famous bottle of 1959, considered the vintage of the century at Lafite, and with an extraordinary reputation, superior to the 1961, it comes from the personal

> 'In the mouth, Lafite is sappy, generous, elegant, less massive than Latour, but soft and powerful at the same time.'

wine cellar of Guy de Rothschild whom I had the pleasure of visiting in 2005. He was a good man, of rare generosity. It is in the company of Michel Bettane that I tasted – only once – this 1959. It developed a very complex bouquet of truffle, underbrush, black fruit, blackcurrant, spices. It is a wine that presents velvety tannins but with an uncommon concentration and strength. The wine is generous and can age at least another twenty years.

Château Lafite-Rothschild 1959

Appellation: Pauillac, premier cru classé, Bordeaux, France.

Vineyard area: 90 hectares.

Varieties: cabernet sauvignon 70 %, merlot 20 %, cabernet franc 5 %, petit verdot 5 %.

Average age of vines: 45 years.

Average production: 250,000 bottles.

Best vintages: 1825, 1848, 1870, 1899, 1929, 1959, 1982, 1986, 1996, 2000, 2005.

The reputation of this mythical Châteauneuf-du-Pape cru is due to the personality of Jacques Reynaud, who died in 1997 at the age of seventy-two. A legendary figure for me, like Henri Bonneau or Mademoiselle Robin of Lafleur in Pomerol. A counter-current to all the passing fancies of the winemaking world and especially of modern winemaking, Jacques Reynaud was a cultivated character, a lover of fine cuisine and of top-of-the-line shoes! He coaxed from his vines a wine of extraordinary quality. He was not talkative and liked to pass for a kind of hermit in his chateau hidden in a red and sandy countryside. And when someone found the chateau, Jacques Reynaud would eye the visitor from the threshold of his chai, with that clever and deceptively absent air, carefully avoiding inviting the visitor to come in. Today his nephew Emmanuel Reynaud elaborates the wine while perpetuating its quality; the vintages 2003, 2005 and 2007 have all the quality of the old vintages.

Contrary to other proprietors, drowning in an ocean of rounded pebbles, the Rayas vineyards are small clearings surrounded

'Rayas vines incarnate the culmination of the grenache noir.'

by woods planted in 1922 by Louis Reynaud, who had put his grapes on the northern sides in the soil of fine clay and limestone. These vines incarnate the culmination of the grenache noir. Rayas wine does not resemble other châteauneufs: it enjoys a 'cold' microclimate; it is very fine with aromas of cherry, blackcurrant, kirsch, liquorice, wild strawberry, blueberry, silky like a pomerol, flavourful, gourmand, in spite of its considerable concentration. Vintages like 1989 and 1990 are full-bodied and rich, strong, tannic and *de longue garde*. The older vintages are impossible to find. However, during a lunch at the *La Beaugravière* restaurant in Mondragon, the chef Guy Jullien gave me the tour of his wine cellar where he has one of the most beautiful collections of rayas, and I was able to acquire an impeccable bottle of 1959.

Château Rayas 1959

Appellation: Châteauneuf-du-Pape, Rhône, France.

Vineyard area: 8 hectares in all.

Varieties: grenache in red, claret in white.

Average age of vines: 35 years.

Average production: 12,000 bottles of red rayas.

Best vintages: 1959, 1961, 1978, 1989, 1990, 1995, 1998, 2003, 2005.

Lalou Bize-Leroy is a major figure in Burgundy. I discovered her philosophy in the '80s, when she was distributing the wines of the Romanée-Conti domain which she co-owns. The press often recounted with eulogistic enthusiasm her *dégustations* of Leroy wines. The Leroy house, having become a domain of biodynamic cultivation with very small yields, is often envied and criticized for its exorbitant prices: these are the most expensive wines in Burgundy. But they are magnificent wines: never filtered, with irrefutable longevity, deep colour, extraordinary opulence, rich and smooth, with flavours of black fruit, spices, plum, blueberry, juniper. The finest wines, like the exceedingly rare Musigny, have a silky structure and flavours of cherry, raspberry, violet, alpine berries. Seeing the staggering prices of the *cuvées confidentielles*, I made the mistake of not buying more Vosne-Romanée Aux Brûlées (300 to 600 bottles produced each year), Musigny (600 to 900 bottles), Richebourg (1000 to 2500 bottles). I looked, but was unable to find a bottle of Romanée-Saint-Vivant from right after the Second World War, which I thought would be a good reflection of the personality of Madame Leroy. However, at the home of an epicurean friend I did come across this beautiful bottle of Grands-Échezeaux 1959, a reminder of that sumptuous time when the Leroy house was already producing grand burgundies. In exchange, I resolved to take from my cellar a Petrus 1959, of which I fortunately have several more specimens.

> 'A wine never filtered, with irrefutable longevity, deep colour, extraordinary opulence, rich and smooth, with flavours of black fruit, spices, plum, blueberry, juniper...'

Grands Échezeaux, Leroy 1959

Appellation: grand cru Grands Échezeaux, Burgundy, France.

Vineyard area: 9.13 hectares, for some 15 proprietors.

Variety: pinot noir.

Average age of vines: 60 years.

Average production: 25,000 bottles.

Best vintages: 1990, 1993, 1995, 1999, 2002, 2003, 2005.

MOSEL · SAAR · RUWER

SONNENUHR

1959er
Wehlener Sonnenuhr
Trockenbeerenauslese
ORIGINAL-KELLERABFÜLLUNG
WACHSTUM JOH. JOS. PRÜM, WEHLEN/MOSEL

Among great German wines, the Johann Joseph Prüm estate is one of my favourites, along with those of Egon Müller, Herman Dönnhof and Robert Weil. If Manfred Prüm likes to say that 'a great wine is a wine that, while having concentration, gives the greatest of pleasures', his wines are nonetheless suitable for long ageing, despite their low alcohol content. The arid and schistose vineyard, situated around the city of Bernkastel, close to Moselle, is very steep: slopes up to 60 %, meaning that harvesting has to be done with a winch!

Joh. Jos. Prüm's Riesling, ages in traditional 1,000 litre-tuns and is considered the greatest in Germany. The rarest wines of the estate are the Trockenbeerenauslese (TBA), of which three hundred bottles are produced in good years. In 1990, the production was 100 litres. There is also Eiswein, ice wine, made from grapes harvested at the end of November, even early December, around six o'clock in the morning and of which one to four hundred half-bottles are produced. These two dessert wines are very sought-after, and usually sold at auction. Drunk young, they are a treat of which one never grows tired. With a consistency of fresh honey, they give off aromas of quince, passion fruit, mango. The TBA deserves all the superlatives: thick, dense, smooth, rich, syrupy, with an impressively smooth freshness and an infinitely long finish. I have only drunk this nectar five or six times, given its exorbitant price: 500 to 1,000 euros for a bottle of 370 millilitres. I was able to acquire this bottle of TBA 1959 at the estate, as a sample representative of that exceptional year. Here is a comment from specialists, Pierre Casamayor and Michel Dovaz: 'TBA 1959: a perfection dressed in a sheen of mahogany, with an empyreumatic, charred and botyrised Riesling smell, more candied than sweet, supported by a beautiful acidity reminiscent of little alpine berries.'

'With a consistency of fresh honey, they give off aromas of quince, passion fruit, mango. The TBA deserves all the superlatives: thick, dense, smooth, rich, syrupy, with an impressively smooth freshness and an infinitely long finish.'

Trockenbeerenauslese, Joh. Jos. Prüm 1959

Appellation: Bernkastel, Moselle-Sarre-Ruwer, Germany.

Vineyard area: 17 hectares.

Variety: riesling.

Age of vines: 50 years, not grafted.

Average production of the estate: 10,000 bottles.

Best vintages: 1949, 1959, 1971, 1976, 1983, 1994, 1997, 2001.

RISERVA 1955
BOTTIGLIA N° 268

BIONDI-SANTI

BRUNELLO

MARCA   PROPRIA

NTINA DELLA FATTORIA "IL GR

·MONTALCINO

When one speaks of the Biondi-Santi estate, one immediately thinks of the brunello di Montalcino, one of the most reputed varieties in Italy. It was selected around 1880 from sangiovese clones, the chianti variety, by Ferruccio Biondi-Santi, whose grandfather worked the vines on the soils of *galestro* – clayey shales, of the dry hills of Montalcino. His 1891 definitively established the wine's reputation. Today Franco Biondi-

'This variety, a cousin to the nielluccio, produces small grapes with thick skin that make a ruby wine whose flavour lasts forever in the mouth.'

Santi manages this vineyard with his son Jacopo. Their *Riserva* comes from the best vines that are more than twenty-five years old. It is aged four years in casks, like the brunellos before it. This variety, a cousin to the nielluccio, produces small grapes with thick skin that make a ruby wine whose flavour lasts forever in the mouth. These are wines worth waiting for: traditional, austere, with *tannins like they used to be*, and a nice acidity that permits the

Riserva – only 20 % of production – to age more than fifty years. And rare in Italy are proprietors who possess bottles of good-quality fifty-year-old wine!

For ten years I looked for the vintage 1955, considered one of the greatest Italian wines ever produced. I scoured the best wine cellars in Italy: Peck in Milan, Pinchiorri in Florence, etc. I found some, but with low levels or moulded labels. Then, in 2002, a friend of mine named Roberto Rossi inherited one hundred fifty bottles of Biondi-Santi brunello going back to 1945, including one of the famous vintage 1955. Signor Rossi would not drink a drop of alcohol, and as this bottle did not especially interest him, I was able to buy it for peanuts.

This 1955, considered one of the greatest wines produced in Tuscany in the 20th century, is one I have never had the privilege of tasting, and its rarity has prevented me from finding information about its flavour characteristics. The estate described this 1955 as an extraordinary vintage: 'intense flavour with notes of vanilla (…), grand structure, warm, very delicate and harmonious, persistent… sublime!'

Brunello di Montalcino, Biondi-Santi 1955

Appellation: Brunello di Montalcino, Tuscany, Italy.

Vineyard area: 12 hectares.

Age of vines: 30 years, and up to 80 years.

Variety: brunello (sangiovese grosso, variety of sangiovese).

One of the best wines of the 20th century for *Wine Spectator*.

Best vintages: 1945, 1955, 1964, 1982, 1995, 2001, 2004, 2006.

Château Musar was founded in 1930 by Gaston Hochar in the Bekaa Valley, at an altitude of 1,000 metres. His son Serge took over from him in 1959, and was named 'Man of the year' by the magazine *Decanter*. I have met him at every Vinexpo to taste his internationally renowned red wines. For the chosen few, however, he brought a few bottles of his white wine, declaring 'it's even more interesting than the red!'

In 1984, I was already interested in foreign wines, from South Africa, Australia, Chile and of course Lebanon, of which I had a few bottles of Musar 1981 and 1982. Certain people criticised me for this: 'with all the different wines we have in France, why bother with foreign wines?' But wine has been made in Lebanon for seven thousand years: traces can be found on the Phoenician frescoes, and it was traded out of the port of Tyre.

Serge continued to produce his wines throughout the sixteen years of war, as if everything were normal, even though lorries sometimes defied bombs to bring the

'**Musar is built to last: it resists oxidation like nothing else. It is only sold seven years after the harvest, and tasting it offers unusual emotions.**'

wine to the chai! Musar is built to last: it resists oxidation like nothing else. It is only sold seven years after the harvest, and tasting it offers unusual emotions: a smell of spices, sometimes balsamic, with notes of leather, very structured in the mouth, and very long. Serge Hochar's son, Gaston, continues to manage the prestigious family estate. He had spoken to me about the famous vintages 1959, 1964 and 1972 in red, and 1954 and 1964 in white. He was kind enough to send me by express mail this bottle of 1954 with a world-wide reputation, produced by his grandfather, who certainly deserved to be included in this book.

LABOR OMNIA VINCIT

Château Musar 1954

Appellation: Bekaa Valley, Lebanon.

Vineyard area: 180 hectares.

Varieties: cabernet sauvignon, cinsault, carignan, grenache, monastrell for red wines. Obeideh and merwah for white wines.

Average age of vines: 50 years.

Average production: 300,000 bottles.

Best vintages: 1954, 1959, 1964, 1969, 1972, 1977, 1995.

This bottle of Croatian white wine comes from a wine cellar in Kutjevo, built in 1232 by Cistercian monks, one of the oldest wine cellars known. The vineyard, at an altitude of between 250 and 300 metres, produces red and white wines, mainly from the varieties of riesling, chardonnay, pinot blanc and noir, sauvignon and merlot, and from this grasevina, also known as Italian riesling. For some time I have known of this cellar's international reputation, as well as its numerous gold medals in competitions in Zagreb or Brussels. The Turkovic family acquired this vineyard in 1882 and kept it until 1945. Then came the socialist period, and the old vintages were no longer to be found; however what is called a 'Wine Archive' was conserved, 70,000 bottles of which the oldest vintage is 1947. Kutjevo wines are imbued with mystery, like those of the Movia cellar in Moldavia or those of Massandra. The Kutjevo cellar was privatised in 2004; in that period I met Stephan Macchi in Croatia, a French 'luxury cook' who works on request for wealthy families. At my insistence, he succeeded in obtaining a beautiful bottle of Grasevina 1948 for me, a semi-dry white wine typical of that region, and only an archive wine, a survivor of the wars and disturbances of that Balkan region.

It is a late harvest wine, with 12.9 degrees of alcohol, 17 grams of residual sugar, and an acidity of 5.1 grams per litre. A wine de *longue garde* that always has an exceptional freshness, particularly due to its being kept in a medieval wine cellar. It is one of the rarities of my international collection.

'A wine de *longue garde* that always has an exceptional freshness, particularly due to its being kept in a medieval wine cellar. It is one of the rarities of my international collection.'

Grasevina 1948

Appellation: Continental Croatia, Croatia (former Yugoslavia).

Variety: grasevina, also called welschriesling or Italian Riesling.

Average age of vines: 60 years.

Production : confidential.

Best vintages: these (secret) wines have been tasted too rarely to be able to express an opinion.

Pre-war tasting cup from the Baltic region.

> 'The characteristic bouquet of nuts and candied fruits is unique, but with a breathtaking vivacity.'

Hungarian Tokaji, of which Voltaire wrote 'it invigorates every fibre of my brain and reanimates, at the deepest part of my soul, enchanting sparks of the spirit and good humour', fell into oblivion during the First World War.

We had to wait until 1985 for the Dionysus Society to bring back the great Hungarian tokajis, and I took advantage of the opportunity to buy the best before this wine was known. I was thus able to acquire five bottles of the rare eszencia Château de Sarospatak 1947 in 500-millilitre bottles, in a little wooden frame sealed with a Hungarian tricolour ribbon. Tokaji eszencia is obtained from grapes that have been dried out by *botrytis cinerea* (aszù), detached from the bunches and deposited into receptacles with perforated bottoms that allow the juice to fall, drop by drop by its own weight, without pressing. The nectar reached a sugar level of 600 to 800 grams per litre with miniscule alcohol content — one to two degrees. It is oily, with great spicy, empyreumatic complexity. Under the Ancien Régime, it was considered a nectar of immortality. Sought after by the Czars of Saint-Petersburg or the Emperor of Austria, the price hit astronomic highs. I have put away a bottle of this 'royal jelly' to drink in 2041 for my one-hundredth birthday.

I had the privilege of tasting a few millilitres of pure Tokaji eszencia, today exceedingly rare. However one can find Tokaji aszù 3 to 6 puttonyos, obtained by the mixture of aszù grapes having emitted their essence, ground with a quantity of wine or must (25 kilos of aszù for 136 litres of wine make 1 puttonyos).

The characteristic bouquet of nuts and candied fruits is unique, with a breathtaking vivacity.

The vineyard is in volcanic and sedimentary subsoil, on Mount Tokaj, an old five hundred-meter-high volcano. I have tasted 5 and 6 puttonyos some fifty times with various importers. 50 francs for 5 puttonyos and 800 francs for the eszencia 1947, my curiosity helped me find a deal in 1985...

Hungarian Tokaji Esszencia 1947

Appellation: Tokaji, Hungary.

Varieties: furmint and harslevelü.

Eszencia production: a few litres per year.

Best vintages: 1900, 1903, 1947, 1972, 1975, 1983.

Cheval Blanc, one of the two 'A' ranked Saint-Émilion grands crus, was the best Saint-Émilion wine until the return of the great Ausone wine in 2000. It is a very sappy wine, opulent, full-bodied, with extraordinary ageing capacity that must be decanted before drinking. Bernard Arnaud and Albert Frère purchased the estate in 1998, after having belonged to the Four-caud-Laussac family until 1832, after the dismemberment of the Château Figeac. In 1975, Jacques Hébrard, one of the co-proprietors and administrator of the estate, told me: 'If ever you see a bottle of Cheval 1947, don't let it pass you by! It still has fifty years in front of it.' I discovered very early on that the two best vintages were 1921 and 1947. So at wine sales, particularly in Drouot, I bought all the bottles, two or three per year at the time. At 1,500 francs per bottle, it was expensive, but few connoisseurs knew that this wine had a bright future, and would become as mythical as that famous Mouton 1945. I do not regret having bought seven bottles, including one that contributed to the renovation of the chateau, thus permitting me to taste it: it was still very good.

In his book *Bordeaux Wines*, Robert Parker writes: 'the 1947 is perfect, with a terribly smooth character, rich and complex, one of the great success stories of the century', and also, 'after tasting an impeccable magnum of Cheval-Blanc 1947 I realised how lucky I was to be in such a profession'. I had six bottles of this wine, often compared to a port, but I needed a magnum for my con-

knew the Fourcaud-Laussacs well: 'We usually bought a barrel every year. We chose it, but we were in severe competition with the Belgians who usually exported the best. Our barrel was bottled in magnums, one and a half bottles. My father drank only Cheval-Blanc, half a bottle at every meal. It is he who preserved it, he died at ninety. In 2008,

'I exchanged the magnum for eighteen bottles of Cheval-Blanc 1975 with an elderly gentleman who had had it in his wine cellar for fifty years and did not dare open it.'

servatory of rare wines. I searched for ten years. But perfect magnums, of high level and good origin, are rare. I finally found one in 1990, before the price went through the roof... and before counterfeits begin to circulate! I exchanged the magnum for eighteen bottles of Cheval-Blanc 1975 with an elderly gentleman who had had it in his wine cellar for fifty years and did not dare open it. He had bought twelve magnums directly from the chateau, at 500 francs apiece, (about 13 euros). His father

this magnum was worth 20,000 dollars in the United States. It's one of the rare ones of this world whose origin is certified and which is without doubt '*mis en bouteille au château*'.

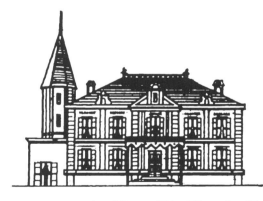

Magnum Château Cheval Blanc 1947

Appellation: Saint-Émilion grand cru, premier grand cru classé, Saint-Émilion, Bordeaux, France.

Vineyard area: 36 hectares.

Varieties: cabernet franc 65 %, merlot 34 %, malbec 1 %..

Age of vines: 40 years.

Average production: 100,000 bottles.

One of the twelve best wines of the 20th century for *Wine Spectator*.

Exceptional vintages: 1921, 1947, 1964, 1982, 2000.

CHEVAL-BLANC

The two Robin sisters, Thérèse and Marie, with their mother on the left.

In the auctions I attended, I noticed a man who spent considerable sums to purchase great wines. I said to myself that he could be a potential client for my Feytit-Clinet, whose vineyard rental system brought me three thousand bottles per year. Thus one day I decided to engage him in conversation and I boasted to him about the qualities of my wine. 'Bring me four cases to Nanterre. My name is Jerry Brace.' Eight days later, I delivered the cases to him. A wine fanatic, he had me taste a few, and before I left, he gave me a Cheval-Blanc 1941, the year of my birth. Afterwards, we got together in Drouot, sitting next to each other. One day in 1987, I wanted to purchase a magnum of Château-Lafleur 1947. Obviously very rare. The auction price is 8,000 francs. I bid 8,200 francs. And, surprise, Jerry Brace tells me: 'You want it, but so do I. And I have no price limit. So let me buy it, and I'll invite you to taste it. He took home the magnum for 9,000 francs.

Three months later, I was invited to his table and found myself before this famous magnum, along with other stunning bottles, like Mouton 1945, Latour 1947... Twenty-two years later, I still retain a precise memory of its flavour, and I tell myself that if I had bought it, I would never have tasted it. This is what Robert Parker writes about this wine that made tears of joy run down his cheeks: 'This wine leaves you speechless. Extraor-dinarily deep, it surpasses even Petrus and Cheval Blanc in this vintage. Graded 100, this 1947 presents a thick colour, lightly amber on the edge, reminiscent of the colour of port. Its richness and freshness are absolutely incredible and its finish, more than a minute long, covers the palate with several layers of concentrated fruit. This wine seems to be the very quintessence of this miniscule and marvellous vineyard.'

Although I have Lafleur 1947 in bottles, I have never been able to purchase an authentic magnum: it is exceedingly rare, worth 15,000 to 20,000 euros and there are numerous counterfeits. Nonetheless I can dream before the empty magnum I brought home. The *dégustation* of this 1947 remains memorable. Among the vintages I have tasted, I particularly appreciated 1961, 1975, 1982, 1990.

'Twenty two years later, I still treasure a precise memory of its flavour.'

Magnum Château Lafleur 1947

Appellation: Pomerol, Bordeaux, France.

Vineyard area: 4.6 hectares.

Varieties: merlot 50 %, cabernet franc 50 %.

Average age of vines: more than 30 years.

Average production: 12,000 bottles.

Best vintages: 1945, 1947, 1950, 1961, 1966, 1971, 1975, 1982, 1985, 1989, 1990, 2000, 2005.

Wine was not expensive in the 80s: I bought two bottles of Trotanoy 1945 for 250 francs apiece, the equivalent of 40 euros. Even Petrus 1982 I could buy for 250 francs! Trotanoy 1945 is a rare and extraordinary wine. This is what Parker writes about this exceptional bottle: 'Still impenetrable and

> 'Trotanoy is a 'sporty' nectar, dense and full-bodied, smooth, massive and rich.'

terribly tannic, this wine has a concentration and a richness of extracts so astounding that one can only hope that all of its components will melt together one day. If that were the case, this wine would have an ageing potential of a hundred years.' I have yet to find the opportunity to taste one of

these relics. I will wait until 2021, when I will be eighty years old, to open it with my son and grandchildren.

After Petrus, my two favourite Pomerol wines are Château Lafleur and Château Trotanoy. I have three hundred bottles of Trotanoy, all the great vintages, including the fabulous 1961 and the 1998. This estate has belonged to the Jean-Pierre Moueix Society since 1953. The wine is fine and silky, voluptuous. In the good red vintages, one perceives notes of gooseberry, black cherry, liquorice, blackberry, blackcurrant. In the older vintages, one finds mocha, coffee, truffle, caramel. The colour of the young wines is ruby, dusky red, dense, the tannins are abundant and melded. The older wines adopt a plum colour, leaving an amber ring in the glass. Trotanoy is a 'sporty' nectar, dense and full-bodied, smooth, massive and rich.

Since the famous 1971, I have tasted some twenty vintages including the 1982, long and bold, my favourite, reminding me of my grandmother's red and black berry marmalade.

Château Trotanoy 1945

Appellation: Pomerol, Bordeaux, France.

Vineyard area: 7 hectares.

Varieties: merlot 90 %, cabernet franc 10 %.

Age of vines: 35 years.

Average production: 20,000 bottles.

Best vintages: 1945, 1961, 1970, 1975, 1982, 1990, 1995, 1998, 2000, 2005.

The label of Château Trotanoy, year 1961.

The key to paradise, emblem of Petrus on the cases.

This is the most expensive wine of Pomerol, and even of all Bordeaux. Located in the centre of Pomerol on unique soil, a tiny piece of black clay, its soil gives small grapes with dark and concentrated juice. Petrus is probably the most mythical wine in the world, along with La Romanée-Conti. Thanks to Jean-Pierre Moueix (1913-2003), the legendary native of Corrèze, merchant and great art collector, Petrus became the most sought-after wine on the planet. This cult wine heightened the level of the entire appellation. Petrus has a deep colour. It offers a powerful scent of red and black fruit, blackberry, liquorice, caramel, chocolate, truffle... In the mouth, it is often enormously corpulent, with a dense texture, concentrated, a fabulous complexity; it is full-bodied, and even viscous. Certain vintages have a finish a minute long.

'In the mouth, it is often enormously corpulent, with a dense texture, concentrated, a fabulous complexity; it is full-bodied, and even viscous. Certain vintages have a finish a minute long.'

Magnum Petrus 1945 & 1947

Appellation: Pomerol, Bordeaux, France.

Proprietor: Jean-François Moueix, oenologist Olivier Berrouet.

Vineyard area: 11.5 hectares.

Varieties: merlot 95 %, cabernet franc 5 % (not always used).

Average age of vines: 40 years.

Average production: 30,000 bottles.

Best vintages: 1921, 1945, 1947, 1950, 1961, 1982, 1989, 1990, 1998, 2000, 2005.

I am lucky enough to own seventy-five different vintages since 1914, representing the greatest among them – except 1921 –, the exceptional vintages in magnums (1961, 1971, 1982, 1989, 1990, 1998, 2000, 2005) and seven imperials (1985, 1988, 1989, 1995, 2005, 2006, 2007). In 2008 in London, one could acquire a magnum of 1945 for the modest sum of 20,000 euros. From a very small harvest, it is still young and can age twenty years, 'Drinking it, one has the impression of tasting the essence of merlot', writes Robert Parker. It is less famous, but infinitely rarer than the 1947. These two magnums are the expression of the differences of the two vintages: 1947, exotic and opulent, with a demonstrative femininity; 1945, tannic and square, with an unfailing virility! The legendary vintage that is missing from my collection is the 1921, which I would live to find in a magnum. It was also the favourite vintage of Jean-Pierre Moueix, the artisan of the Petrus myth, and I would like to find that year in a magnum as well. Of the thirty or so vintages that I have tasted, my favourites are 1950, 1971, 1982, 1990. I am still waiting to taste the 1961.

Château Haut-Brion.

Haut-Brion is the best wine of the Graves de Bordeaux. Jean de Pontac founded this famous vineyard around 1500. It must have produced a salutary nectar, since Pontac died at the age of one hundred one, incredible longevity for that time. Later, Haut-Brion was among the favourite wines of Thomas Jefferson, ambassador of the United States in Paris, who ordered several cases of the 1784 vintage and of Yquem 1787.

In 1855, at the World's Fair in Paris, the courtiers of Bordeaux ranked it among the premier grands crus classés of Médoc, from which it is nonetheless separated by the city of Bordeaux. Today, Prince Robert of Luxembourg administers the estate.

Haut-Brion is distinguished for its elegance, its voluptuous texture, a greater suppleness than the other premier crus. Its high percentage of merlot gives it a flamboyant character and a great purity. In spite of that, it is a dense wine with great aromatic power. It often presents aromas of blackcurrant, morello cherry, liquorice, and the smoky and early scents that are the trademark of Graves soil.

The 1989 will go down in history as the greatest Haut-Brion ever produced. It deserves all the superlatives: impressive, sumptuous, phenomenal, breathtaking! It can age until 2050. It is one of my best tasting experiences of the past twenty years. I had the 'nose' to purchase a twelve-bottle case and one of six magnums for 300 francs per bottle.

I am also lucky enough to own two bottles of 1945, perfect and reconditioned by the chai master, Monsieur Portal; the new corks should last until 2050. At that time, back in 1990, I went every year to taste the reds

> 'Its high percentage of merlot gives it a flamboyant character and a great purity.'

and whites in his company; it is he who put me in contact with a great connoisseur, mad for Haut-Brion, who owned seventeen bottles of 1945, and three cases of 1961. I was able to choose the two most beautiful bottles, the highest level, which I traded for two bottles of Latour 1947.

Château Haut-Brion 1945

Appellation: Graves, and Pessac-Léognan since 1986, Bordeaux, France.

Vineyard area: 43 hectares.

Varieties: cabernet sauvignon 44 %, merlot 42 %, cabernet franc 14 %.

Average age of vines: 40 years.

Average production: 150,000 bottles.

Best vintages: 1859, 1875, 1900, 1929, 1945, 1959, 1961, 1982, 1989, 1990, 2000, 2005.

1945 • SURRENDER OF THE ARMY OF NAZI GERMANY • SUICIDE OF HITLER • HIROSHIMA AND NAGASAKI • ALLIED OCCUPATION OF GERMANY

'It is the greatest wine ever produced in this prestigious estate, and only 2,091 magnums were filled.'

Wine expert Michael Broadbent has tasted and graded more than seven thousand wines, and only the Mouton 1945 was awarded six stars. Robert Parker gave it 100/100. It is the greatest wine ever produced in this prestigious estate, and only 2,091 magnums were filled. This legendary wine is characterised by its extraordinary dark red colour, an complex smell: spices, eucalyptus, ginger, balsamic notes; in the mouth it is enormous, still viscous, rich and with an impressive persistence.

This vintage celebrates the year of victory. Its proprietor, Baron Philippe de Rothschild, called upon Philippe Jullian, a dandy chronicler of literary life, to design the label. Since then, many famous artists have illustrated the labels on bottles of this precious wine. Collectors covet bottles decorated by Jean Hugo (1946), Braque (1955), Dali (1958), Alechinsky (1966), Miro (1969), Picasso (1973), Soulages (1976), Delvaux (1985), Bacon (1990), Balthus (1993), Savignac (1999)... which explains why the smaller vintages, rarer, reach such high prices. But the most expensive is this 1945, of which many counterfeits are unfortunately in circulation, given its value: around 20,000 euros for a magnum. Philippe de Rothschild died in 1988; since then, his daughter Philippine has skilfully managed the estate and its superb Wine museum.

In 1985 in Drouot, I was fortunate enough to meet a collector who did not have the exceedingly rare vintage 1946. I had a bottle that I traded for this magnum 1945, at the time of equal value (since then, the price of the 1946 has dropped sharply, and the 1945 has shot up).

Magnum Château Mouton-Rothschild 1945

Appellation: Pauillac, second cru classé in 1855, premier cru since 1973, Bordeaux, France.

Vineyard area: 80 hectares.

Varieties: cabernet sauvignon 77 %, merlot 11 %, cabernet franc 10 %, petit verdot 2 %.

Average age of vines: 48 years.

Average production: 300,000 bottles.

Best vintages: 1945, 1959, 1961, 1982, 1986, 2000, 2005.

My favourite vintages: 1961, 1982, 1986.

1945 года
Украина, Крым, Ялта, ул. Мира, 6
Национальное производственно-аграрное объединение
МАССАНДРА
коллекционное вино
МУСКАТ
розовый десертный

It all happens in Ukraine. It is 2006 and I am in Yalta, on the seashore. The girls are pretty, the climate pure, with exotic scents, and the Crimean wines, all dessert wines, are jewels.

One evening, sitting by the bar of the *Orienda* hotel, I see a man of some forty years sipping a Louis XIII brandy from Rémy Martin. He orders a second one. The thirty-millilitre glass costs 300 euros!

Wow! I address him in Russian, he answers

'In the mouth, it is rich, powerful, with multiple flavours from another world. One can nevertheless distinguish notes of dulce de membrillo, date, papaya, caramel.'

in French. That is how I happened to meet Vadim Beliakov. He works in the luxury cosmetics industry in Moscow and has an apartment in Paris. We commiserate over wine. I tell him about my Feytit-Clinet, Vadim orders two hundred bottles and gets an idea: at home he has a post card telling the story of the

Yalta Conference, the meeting from 4th to 11th February 1945 where Churchill, Roosevelt and Stalin secretly decided the fate of the post-war world. Vadim advises me to find a bottle of Massandra 1945 for my collection. Then he said to me: 'I don't quite understand you but I like you, and you gave me a good price on your Pomerol. The 1945 will be a gift. We'll go together to buy it tomorrow.'

I thus brought back to my wine cellar this bottle from a historic vintage, and the post card of the Yalta Conference. Vadim became a great friend. Since then, I have tasted this dessert wine in Massandra, a gift from the director Mr. Boiko during the visit of the high dignitary of Crimea, to which I was invited. Its colour is mahogany, its smell exotic and complex. In the mouth, it is rich, powerful, with multiple flavours from another world. One can nevertheless distinguish notes of dulce de membrillo, date, papaya, caramel. Unforgettable flavours and a concentration that should preserve it another fifty years.

Massandra Muscat 1945

Appellation: : Crimea, Ukraine (then in the USSR).

Variety: muscat.

Vineyard area: 100 hectares.

Average age of vines: 60 years.

Average production: 100,000 bottles.

Best vintages: 1934, 1937, 1938, 1950, 1966, 1968, 1972, 1975, 1994, 1997, 2000.

Churchill, Roosevelt and Stalin at the Yalta Conference in 1945.

Three dusty bottles hidden among cobwebs in a twisting corner of Henri Bonneau's wine-tasting cellar... 'Get them! They're old, but there must be at least one good one among them!' The levels were perfect. We uncorked the first with multiple precautions. It gave off complex aromas of faded roses, truffles, smoked spices, underbrush. The colour

'The Réserve des Célestins is the best wine of this ancient estate. An extraordinary wine, powerful and massive, structured, tannic and concentrated.'

was lightly tuilé, bright, limpid, amazingly young. The wine was still bold, ample, beautifully long, with notes of candied prunes, roasted almonds, humus. It was a vintage 1942. We opened the second bottle, it was even better. Henri Bonneau brought the level back up with a little bit of the first one, and held it out to me: 'Here, Chasseuil, take this bottle for your museum of rare wines.' He was proud to know that this relic would be preciously guarded in the paradise of my collection. This reconditioned bottle, and the third, that he gave me as

well, are treasures. They were produced by his father Marcel.

I am lucky enough to have several cases of his greatest vintages. The Réserve des Célestins is the best wine of this ancient estate, established since 1667. An extraordinary wine, powerful and massive, structured, tannic and concentrated, the quintessence of Châteauneuf. With scents of roasted meat, pepper, truffles, spices, cedar, lavender, morello cherries, an extraordinary complexity with a peacock finale. The 1990 'Réserve Spéciale' is a monument that outdoes every Châteauneuf I have tasted to this day.

Tasting a bottle with Henri Bonneau, in his kitchen or his cramped wine cellar dotted with blackened barrels of another age, is a magical moment. I met this warm and simple man some ten years ago. We had a shared past: combat engineer during the Algerian War. That brought us together, and we understood each other immediately. He is a character of another time, a joker and a Gaulois with an inimitable southern accent and bonhomie. Fishing enthusiast, refined bon-vivant, he knows how to spread happiness.

Châteauneuf-du-Pape, Célestins, Henri Bonneau 1942

This escutcheon represents a tiara placed above the keys of Saint Peter. It is the symbol of the A.O.C. Châteauneuf-du-Pape appellation.

Appellation: Châteauneuf-du-Pape, Rhône, France.

Vineyard area: 6 hectares.

Old vines of 90 % Grenache, on the Crau, the best sector of Châteauneuf, a plateau of rounded pebbles.

Average age of vines: 40 years.

Average production: 9,000 bottles.

Exceptional years: 1978, 1989, 1990, 1998, 2001, 2005.

'Vega Sicilia is a monument of concentration and substance, with a fascinating complexity: dark ruby colour, bouquet of blackcurrant, spices, pepper, cigar, truffle, black fruit, vanilla...'

Since the beginning of the 20th century, this Grand d'Espagne has been the most sought-after. The vineyard was founded in 1864 by Don Eloy Lecanda Chaves, and took the name of Vega Sicilia in memory of the prior owners; nothing to do with Sicily. Although the estate spans 1,000 hectares, only 250 have vines. The red soil, composed of clay and limestone, is at an altitude of 600 metres: before cutting through the Porto Mountains, the Douro River dug the hills of this Castilian vineyard. The contribution of cabernet sauvignon gives it a structure that other Ribera del Duero wines lack, as plantations of foreign varieties can no longer be extended. The wine, which stays three years in the barrel, four years in the vat and three years in the bottle before being sold, has an excellent ageing capacity. Demand is such that one must register on a long waiting list to have any hope of one day buying it at the estate. The supply begins with the valbuena, from the most alluvial land, aged two years in casks and sold at five years, as its name indicates. Unico Reserva Especial is not a vintage, but rather an assembly of great vintages: the lot of 25, sold in 1990, includes 1970, 1985 and 1990. Unico is produced only in great years. Vega Sicilia is a monument of concentration and substance, with a fascinating complexity: dark ruby colour, bouquet of blackcurrant, spices, pepper, cigar, truffle, black fruit, vanilla... The older vintages evolve into  caramel, chocolate or liquorice. In the mouth, nice acidity, melded tannins, voluptuously soft and aromatic set in a powerful body. Vega Sicilia has an extreme elegance, pulpy , never vulgar.

My first purchase in the 80s was a case of twelve bottles of 1968, a great vintage, still astonishingly young and concentrated, and which can age until 2040. Luck smiled upon me during a lunch at the home of Laurent Dassault in Saint-Émilion: I met the oenologist of the estate, Pascal Chatonnet, who told me that he also consulted for Vega Sicilia.

I was thus able to visit the vineyards of Ribera del Duero, and the well-reputed *bodegas* Dominio de Pingus, Pesquera, Aalto; but it is not easy to get into Vega Sicilia, and I came home without the old bottle that I coveted for my collection. Pascal Chatonnet had mentioned the 1942, a very great vintage; a few months later, he invited me to the Château Haut-Chaigneau, his estate in Lalande-de-Pomerol. He wanted to give me the famous direct from the personal stock of Vega Sicilia that the chai master Xavier Ausas had prepared for me thanks to the benevolence of Don Pablo Alvarez Mesqueriz, proprietor. My greatest bottles tasted: 1968, immense, 1975 and 1994.

Vega Sicilia Unico 1942

Appellation: Ribera del Duero, Spain.

Varieties: tempranillo (adapted here under the name of tinto fino, 80 %), the rest cabernet sauvignon and other unidentified antique varieties.

Age of vines: approximately 60 years.

Production: 30,000 to 100,000 bottles per year.

Best vintages: 1942, 1962, 1966, 1968, 1970, 1975, 1985, 1989, 1990, 1994, 1998, 2004.

'Hello, Monsieur Chasseuil, Thierry Brouin calling. I just read four pages in *Paris-Match* about your wine cellar. Bravo!' Monsieur Brouin is in charge of the Burgundy estate of Clos-des-Lambrays, and it is always a pleasure to taste this great wine when I go to pick up my bottles each year. He adds: 'Did you know that we also have older vintages here in the Lambrays cellar? 1937, for example. The next time you come, now that you have

'I am convinced that in a few years the Clos-des-Lambrays will become a rare wine.'

the noble credentials of the most prestigious wine cellar in the world, we'll have you taste an old vintage.' What interested me was a bottle of 1937. The famous oenologist Michel Dovaz wrote that 'The pre-war Lambrays constitute a remarkable piece of the Burgundy legend.'

Passing through Morey-Saint-Denis to pick up my magnums of the great vintage 2005, I had prepared all of my arguments to convince Monsieur Brouin to sell me a bottle of that famous 1937. He received me with a big smile: 'Monsieur Chasseuil, we under-stand. Don't tire yourself out; we have prepared a bottle for your museum.' Like a dream...

In his book *Un siècle de millésimes*, Jean-François Bazin recounts: 'Lambrays 1937, the Pharos of Alexandria, without a wrinkle, full of fire, under the label designed by Hansi. We tasted a piece of history.' As for myself, I have not yet tasted it, but I have a bottle.

After the Joly and Rodier families, in 1938 the estate came into the hands of the Cosson family. Madame Cosson having refused to uproot the old vines, le Clos produced less and less wine. The vintages from 1960 to 1980 no longer equalled the quality of the Rodier years. In 1979, le Clos was purchased by the Saïer brothers from Alsace, who sold it to the Freund family of Coblence in 1996. Oenologist Thierry Brouin had carte blanche to resuscitate the wine. It started with the replanting of a part of the vineyard with the best pinot noir clones, then yields limited to 30 hectolitres, and the sorting of the grapes. I am convinced that in a few years the Clos-des-Lambrays will become a rare wine. Michael Broadbent writes of the vintage 1937: 'It is a very great vintage whose best wines have rarely been equalled' and gives four stars to the Clos-des-Lambrays.

Clos des Lambrays 1937

Appellation: Clos des Lambrays, grand cru since 1981, Burgundy, France

Vineyard area: 8.70 hectares.

Variety: pinot noir.

Age of vines: 40 years.

Average production: 30,000 to 40,000 bottles.

Best vintages: 1911, 1920, 1923, 1929, 1937, 1945, 1949, 1990, 2002, 2005.

For some thirty years, I have regularly gone to taste the wines of the Lamarche estate, particularly La Grande Rue. I love this name, this long, narrow plot in the middle of the grands crus of Vosne-Romanée: on the left La Tâche, on the right La Romanée, La Romanée-Conti and La Romanée-Saint-Vivant. The vines were criticised and envied for some time, but one must realise that François Lamarche inherited them in poor shape, and that he had to reconstitute the vineyard, build a new fermenting room, replace the equipment. Moreover, the wines improved in 1990, border on excellent in 1998, and the 2002, 2005, and 2006 are often first in blind tastings. François is now handing the vineyard over to his daughter Nicole and his niece Nathalie, two dynamic young women who inherited their ancestors' love for Burgundy, its land, and the pinot noir that has reigned there since the year 1395.

Nicole Lamarche, with her constant quest for perfection, now produces a Grande Rue of transparent ruby colour, with a subtle bouquet of alpine berries, a balance, a velvety finesse, but also a potency that allows

'A Grande Rue of transparent ruby colour, with a subtle bouquet of alpine berries, a beautiful balance, a velvety finesse, but also a potency that allows for long ageing, with that oeil-de-perdrix colour typical of this variety.'

for long ageing, with that oeil-de-perdrix colour typical of this variety.

I noticed this bottle of 1934 in 1990, in the personal wine-tasting cellar of François Lamarche, during the exchange of a few Échézeaux for my pomerol. There were three, which I eyed every time I came. But in 2005, there was only one left... that François Lamarche gave me not very long ago: 'What you do for wine heritage is good. This is the last one. We will recondition it for you with a good cork.' 1934 is a great vintage in Burgundy.

La Grande Rue 1934

Appellation: Vosne-Romanée premier cru, then grand cru La Grande Rue since 1992, Bourgogne, France.

Vineyard area: 1.65 hectare.

Variety: pinot noir.

Average age of vines: 40 years.

Average production: 6,500 bottles.

Best vintages: 1934, 1949, 1959, 1969, 1978, 1990, 1993, 1999, 2002, 2005.

I had the honour of shaking Yuri Gagarin's hand at the Paris Air Show, in 1963 I believe, and to get his autograph. I wanted to honour him by having a bottle in my collection from 1934, the year of his birth. This was possible thanks to Helena Turicheva, the interpreter during my stay at the Magarach Wine Institute, on my sec-

'I wanted to honour Yuri Gagarin by having a bottle in my collection from 1934, the year of his birth.'

ond visit in 1999. That is when I discovered the prestigious cellar of old wines that holds a million bottles. And in this cellar, pure heaven, a tunnel where thirty thousand bottles sleep under six hundred references. Since then, I have added to my collection a bottle of 1968, the year of Gagarin's death. The Massandra wine cellar reproduces the great dessert wines of the world, in that other world of wines in Crimea. Quality production is developed on very favourable lands, where the Greeks produced the wines of Antiquity. It is a conservatory of the grape varieties of the entire world, and it produces

equivalents of all great dessert wines. The different white, rosé or black muscats are the muscats of Livadia, Massandra, Gurzuf, Kastel, Red Stone, Southcoast, Kutchuk-Lambat, Alurka, Taurida. This is how Olivier Poussier describes the muscat Gurzuf 1937: 'On the nose, this complex wine unveils aromas of herbal tea, incense. Its aromatic palate is highlighted by wax and yellow fruit paste. Flavours of rancio and dried fruits like an old Mandarine Napoléon liqueur.'

Post card given to me by Gagarin, with his autograph.

Massandra Muscat 1934

Appellation: Crimea, Ukraine (then in the USSR).

Vineyard area: 100 hectares.

Variety: muscat.

Age of vines: 60 years.

Average production: 100,000 bottles.

Best vintages: 1930, 1934, 1937, 1938, 1950, 1966, 1972, 1975, 1994, 2000.

One day in 2004, I get a call from Helena Turicheva: 'Michel, he is going to sell some bottles from the Massandra cellar at Sotheby's in London, doubtless at a good price, because Massandra needs money: they have to buy corks at Amorim for the reconditioning of old bottles.'

Massandra had already sold bottles at auction in 1990. It was its first opening towards the West. That 2004 sale saw an 1894 cabernet sauvignon sell for 4,300 euros. The record belongs to a sherry from 1775, sold for 50,000 dollars in 2001! As for me, I bought a few old bottles of the aleatico, bastardo, saperavi, red muscat, etc. varieties, and I was lucky enough to acquire a bottle of cagore 1933. This bottle is rare, since it is the first year for this kind of wine produced in Crimea. Here is the history of this wine: it used to be made in Cahors with grape must heated to 60°C, and was used as liturgical wine by the Orthodox Church. Peter the Great, who suffered from an ulcer, treated it with Cahors wine, and had created a vineyard of the same type in Azerbaijan, cultivated by winemakers from Cahors. The cagore of Crimea is made from the saperavi variety of Ayu-Dag where grapes have been grown for more than two thousand years. Saperavi makes a very full-bodied and very tannic red wine, with good acidity, which makes it resemble the Cahors malbec. I tasted this cagore 1933 at Massandra. It has 16° of alcohol, with 180 grams of sugar per litre. Amber-red in colour, it has aromas of Corinthian grapes, tea, smoke. It is harmonious in the mouth, with a very nice balance, delicate and silky like rose petals, sweet, with notes

'This bottle is rare, since it is the first year for this kind of wine produced in Crimea.'

of alpine berries, ripe wild strawberries. The finish is young for its age. It can still age for decades. I brought back for my collection all the great vintages of 'Chagors' produced: 1933, 1936, 1939, 1944, 1947, 1951, 1957, 1971.

I thus constituted a collection of the three hundred best references of all of the different kinds of wines of Massandra.

Small lacquered jewel box from Yalta

Massandra Cagore 1933

Appellation: Crimea, Ukraine (then in the USSR).

Variety: saperavi.

Age of vines: 70 years.

Best vintages: 1933, 1934, 1937, 1938, 1950, 1966, 1972, 1975, 1994, 2000, 2001.

> **'Chambertin is particularly robust, even brawny, interminably long in the mouth, and of course with excellent ageing capacity.'**

In my wine cellar I had the bottles of the principal grands crus of Burgundy, but I was missing a pre-war Chambertin, the famous Chambertin, Napoleon's favourite wine. These are evidently rare wines, from a time when few winemakers bottled their wine themselves. As for grandfather Armand Rousseau, he did so since the early 20s. When I was invited to the Château du Clos de Vougeot for the fifty-year jubilee of the Méo-Camuzet estate, I was lucky enough to meet an illustrious connoisseur, curious about the great dessert wines of Crimea. That is how he traded this bottle of Chambertin 1933 for a White muscat 1910 from Massandra that was in my collection.

After Armand Rousseau, his son Charles reaffirmed the notoriety of his prestigious crus: Clos-des-Ruchottes, Clos-Saint-Jacques, Clos-de-Bèze, and Grand-Chambertin. This elite winemaker is one of the last great figures having known the pre-war vineyard, along with Henri Jayer, Pierre Ramonet... They produced wines respecting the fragile pinot, often conserving that characteristic 'oeil-de-perdrix' colour rather than making bottles of black wine, as fashion dictated. He passed the torch to his son Éric a few years ago. The generation gap can spawn divergent views, but in the end the experience of the father and the modernism of the son work together so that these past few years the various vineyards of the Rousseau estate offer wines that have their place among the greatest wines of Burgundy, with an exceptionally full aroma, subtle and soft. Éric's wines are sumptuous, velvety, with perfect richness and balance, with flavours of red and black fruit. Chambertin is particularly robust, even brawny, interminably long in the mouth, and of course with excellent ageing capacity.

I congratulate this winemaker who incarnates everything there is to love: modest, simple, peaceful. I am glad to have started to buy this wine from his father in 1985. And by twelve-bottle cases! It was the golden age! Today there is always a crowd at the gate, and it is a privilege to obtain merely a few bottles.

Chambertin, Armand Rousseau 1933

Appellation: grand cru Chambertin, Burgundy, France

Vineyard area: 14 hectares, including 2.15 hectares in Chambertin.

Variety: pinot noir.

Average age of vines: 40 to 45 years throughout the estate.

Average production: 8,800 bottles.

Best vintages, for the nine grands crus and premier crus of the estate: 1933, 1937, 1945, 1949, 1959, 1978, 1990, 1996, 1999, 2002, 2003, 2005, 2006.

1933 • MERMOZ AND THE AÉROPOSTALE BETWEEN SENEGAL AND BRAZIL • ANGEL FALLS IN VENEZUELA IS THE HIGHEST WATERFALL IN THE WORLD

123

1933

'The price I paid for a Nacional 1931: six Petrus 1975, six 1982 and twelve 1990!'

It was during a wine tasting that I met Cristiano Van Zeller, then manager of the mythical Quinta do Noval, an estate founded around 1715 that reigns above all port wines with its Nacional vintage. At that meeting I bought from Van Zeller a case of Nacional 1963, an excellent year. He explained to me that 1931 was the port vintage of the century. An article in *Le Point* in 1987 confirmed this, evaluating it at 38,000 francs, next to 3,500 for Mouton-Rothschild 1945. Michael Broadbent writes in *Vintage Wine* that this wine is 'considered the Everest of *vintage Port*!' In another leading work, Vintage Port by specialist James Suckling, the 1931 is described as 'the most intensely concentrated, black as ink, one of the greatest wines ever produced'. In 1931, these five thousand feet of ungrafted vines, every vintage of which – and there are but few – is an event, produced the most mythical wine of the 20th century. My bottle has an original capsule and a perfect level. I am not aware of the existence of another bottle.

I found the trail that led to my Nacional 1931 at Vinexpo in 1993, when I was searching for a Penfold's-Grange 1955. I learned that an Englishman had one and I was able to meet him. The price I paid for the trade: six Petrus 1975, six 1982 and twelve 1990!

This property now belongs to the AXA Millésimes group, managed by Mr. Christian Seely, whose skills have raised the latest vintages to the level of the greatest ones. My favourite vintages are 1963, 1966, 1970 and 1997.

Quinta do Noval, Nacional 1931

Appellation: Porto, Portugal.

Vineyard area: 2.5 hectares.

Varieties: turriga nacional, sausao, turriga franca, tinto cao.

Age of vines: pre-phylloxera.

Average production: 2,000 bottles per year produced when possible.

Best vintages: 1931, 1963, 1966, 1975, 1994, 1997, 2000, 2003.

1929

CHÂTEAU LATOUR

GRAND VIN

1er GRAND CRU POMEROL

Mme Edmond Loubat
Propriétaire

MISE EN BOUTEILLES
AU CHÂTEAU

MÉDAILLE D'OR

IMP. B. ARNAUD - LYON - PARIS

My Château Feytit-Clinet is located across from the Château Latour à Pomerol. I was well acquainted with Madame Lily Lacoste, who became the proprietor in 1961 after the death of her aunt, the famous Madame Loubat, who had built the notoriety of Château Petrus and purchased Latour in 1917. I had the privilege of dining several times in her beautiful dining room, where she told me the story of Petrus and what made it famous. Madame Lacoste passed away in 2006, at dawn on her hundredth year. She was still completely lucid, playful and alert, and she still played the piano. What a rich and instructive experience for me to have been close to this *grande dame*! I had known her since 1975, a great year for Petrus. Back then she sold me a Petrus 1961 that was missing from my collection – probably the greatest of her century along with 1921 – for 1,000 francs. She also gave me a bottle of Latour à Pomerol 1961, insisting: 'It's the best of all 1961 bordeaux!'

She was right. Robert Parker later gave it 100/100, ranking it among the two best Bordeaux of the century, with these comments: 'Irresistible for its aromatic richness and its depth, slight resemblance to port, sensational bouquet of blackcurrant, liquorice; smooth, incredibly concentrated, phenomenally rich.'

I received my bottle of 1929 from the hands of Madame Lacoste as well. Her price is a secret between us. It was in the

'It's the best of all 1961 bordeaux!'

period of small yields, the grapes were not destemmed, and the macerations were interminable. Wines like that will never be made again. This 1929 was described by Jean-Claude Berrouet, oenologist for Petrus and Latour à Pomerol, as a 'magic living wine', full of vivacity, almost thick enough to chew, intensely aromatic. My favourite is the 1982 in a magnum.

Château Latour à Pomerol 1929 & 1961

Appellation: Pomerol, Bordeaux, France.

Vineyard area: 8 hectares.

Varieties: merlot 90 %, cabernet franc 10 %.

Average age of vines: 40 years.

Average production: 35,000 bottles.

Best vintages: 1929, 1947, 1961, 1982.

'It is a monocépage, a monocru, still vintage, produced sporadically according to the quality of the harvest: some forty vintages in the last ninety years.'

Salon champagne is the *Le Pin* of champagne, my favourite bubbly diamond, along with two other *confidentiels*, Egly-Ouriet and Selosse. These three champagnes belong to a particular category, compared to the prestigious estates like Bollinger, Roederer, Krug, which each produce several hundred thousand bottles. Its beginning dates back to 1911, when Aimé Salon, a rich fur merchant, gourmet and member of the famous 'Club des Cent', planted two small plots of chardonnay in Mesnil-sur-Oger for his personal use and for his friends. In 1914, he founded his estate, and as of 1920 Salon became the official champagne of *Maxim's*. This Blanc de blancs with its fine bubbles is suited for long ageing thanks to its pronounced acidity, due to the fact that the wines do not undergo malolactic fermentation. It ages eight to ten years on the shelf and is only offered for sale after about twelve years. In the right quantity, it is a dry champagne, impressively long. It is also a monocépage, a monocru, still vintage, produced sporadically according to the quality of the harvest: some forty vintages in the last ninety years. After the death of Aimé Salon in 1943, his family continued his work until its sale in 1963 to Besserat de Bellefon. Salon has belonged to the Laurent-Perrier group since 1988, but the estate is managed independently.

I have been interested in this confidential champagne for twenty-five years, and I have a good stock of magnums, starting with the famous 1990. If you must drink a vintage Krug at least once in your life, you mustn't fail to taste several bottles of Salon, particularly the 1995 or the 1996, sublime, with a great vinosité and fine bubbles, it is a rare champagne, and I like to commune with it, lips and nose in the glass, with the bubbles jumping up to my aroused nostrils! 1928 is a mythical vintage in champagne and, for Salon it is the first universally recognised great vintage and still perfect today.

Salon Blanc de Blancs 1928

Appellation: Champagne, France.

Vineyard area: 1 hectare personally owned, plus purchases from the Cooperative du Mesnil.

Variety: chardonnay.

Age of vines: 50 years.

Average production: 50,000 bottles, only in the best years.

Best vintages: 1921, 1928, 1934, 1947, 1959, 1961, 1979, 1982, 1990, 1996.

'It has a very rich and complex style, an exceptional aromatic intensity, often of roasted hazelnuts, brioche, fresh almonds, vineyard peach.'

B ollinger is a family estate founded in 1829 by Jacques Joseph Bollinger. Since then, his descendants have acquired more vines, always of excellent quality, enlarging their vineyard to 163 hectares, a vineyard that guarantees their supply and 90 % of which is ranked as grands crus and premiers crus. Jerôme Philipon now administers the estate, and the cultivation has remained entirely traditional. Their vines supply approximately 60 % of the estate's grape needs. The rarest

product of the estate is a blanc de noirs, a white champagne from pinot noir grapes, in addition to ungrafted French vines, 45 ares in Ay cultivated *en foule* (without alignment and in very high density) as in the 19th century, and producing some one thousand five hundred bottles per harvest. This great wine bears the French tricolour flag and the mark of Vieilles Vignes Françaises. The first vintage was produced in 1969. This champagne is the rarest and most expensive of the Bollinger line. It has a very rich and complex style, an exceptional aromatic intensity, often of roasted hazelnuts, brioche, fresh almonds, vineyard peach. The winemaking process is an accumulation of small details that make for the production of the best wine. Bollinger wines are matured in oak barrels of 205 and 220 litres maintained by the estate's *tonnelier*. They age on their dregs – longer than at other estates – and by separate vintages, thereby permitting a precise assembly. Malolactic fermentation (second fermentation that reduces acidity) is not systematic it depends upon the year. The *vins de reserve* age in corked magnums. Another particularity – costly – that contributes to the quality: the wines are not filtered, and are often the most potent of champagnes. The Bollinger style is signalled by the pinot noir: corpulent wines with excellent ageing capacity. The R.D. vintages (*récemment dégorgé* – recently circulated) have aged a very long time on their dregs and take on a very *vineux* character. Bollinger ages well. The older champagnes have been fashionable for the past few years. That was not the case in the 80s, and I was one of the few people to be interested in the older vintages, very inexpensive at auction. I was thus able to acquire a magnum and two bottles of 1928 in Drouot for 800 francs. The magnum, drunk with foie gras, was still bubbly, with a golden colour, a good consistency, long in the mouth... In remembrance, I chose for this book a bottle of 1928, 'one of the most legendary champagnes,' according to Swedish expert Richard Juhlin who has graded four thousand champagnes, and who notes that the champagne served in 1929 at the Nobel Peace Prize ceremony in Stockholm was a Bollinger.

Bollinger Champagne 1928

Appellation: Champagne, France.

Vineyard area: 160 hectares.

Varieties: pinot noir, pinot meunier, chardonnay.

Average production: 180,000 vintage bottles, including 30,000 R.D. and 1,500 Vieilles vignes françaises.

Best vintages: 1928, 1953, 1959, 1961, 1969, 1975, 1979, 1985, 1990, 1995, 1996, 2002.

My preference goes to the vintages 1959, 1975, 1990, 1995, 2002.

One morning in September 2009, I get a phone call from an elderly gentleman. What does he want so early in the morning? 'My name is Monsieur Viellemarette, I live in Rambouillet, and I saw the television special about your wine cellar. Bravo! My father would drink only La Romanée-Conti, La Romanée, and Chambertin, Napoleon's favourite wine. He was a doctor, and we would drink it every Sunday, and my personal favourite was La Romanée. I have a present for you: a bottle of La Romanée 1926, the year of my birth. I have no children, and I would be proud to have it lie in your admirable collection. Pass by and pick it up the next time you come to Paris, we would be happy to have you to lunch.' And that is how I received this bottle.

La Romanée is a miniscule terrain: 0.85 hectares, facing east close to La Romanée-Conti and Richebourg. Exclusive property of the Counts Liger-Belair since 1826, it produces an ageing wine that expresses all the subtlety and the complexity of the Burgundy pinot noir. Formerly distributed by the Bouchard Père et fils Establishments, it was magnificently resuscitated, as of the vintage 2000, by Count Louis-Michel Liger-Bélair.

A red wine, flamboyant, loaded with red and black fruit, violet, spices, with a flavourful roundness, a clean and potent body... and so long that for me it is the 'pearl' of the Côte de Nuits, as a great connoisseur and personal friend Didier Romieux has so often repeated to me. Happy are those who can taste, at least once in their life, this nectar from the smallest of the great climates of Vosne-Romanée, which is also the smallest appellation controlee of France. 1926 signals the hundredth anniversary of this family monopoly.

'The 'pearl' of the Côte de Nuits. Happy are those who can taste, at least once in their life, this nectar from the smallest of the great climates of Vosne-Romanée.'

La Romanée 1926

Appellation: grand cru La Romanée, Bourgogne, France.

Vineyard area: 0.85 hectare.

Variety: pinot noir.

Average age of vines: 55 years.

Average production: 3,500 bottles.

Best vintages: 2002, 2003, 2005, 2006.

'...very particular, extremely concentrated, very rich, oily, with breathtaking aromatic potency.'

Since 1975, I had been looking for a great wine of the Soviet Union. I knew from a friend that there were excellent wines in Crimea, where grape vines cover 33,000 hectares. In 1997, I learned that Professor Djenieev, director of the Magarach Institute in Yalta and representative of the O.I.V. (International Organisation of Vine and Wine) in Crimea, was coming to Paris. Since I knew that he was at the Élysée Palace where he was to be received by the president, I tried my luck and was able to reach him by telephone. I immediately proposed to show him Pomerol, Petrus... The same day I was at the train station in Poitiers to pick him up, along with his son Yuri! We went to Pomerol, where I showed them several chateaux and had them taste my

Professor Djenieev's watch,
given to me by his wife in 2003.

pomerol, and then we returned to my home, where I showed them my wine cellar and my collection. We obviously spoke of vines and grape varieties, while drinking a Mouline of Guigal, a Chambertin of Rousseau and L'Évangile, and they spent the night at my home.

As they were leaving, Professor Djenieev handed me a bottle: 'Here you are, Monsieur Chasseuil! I admire your work on wine. Here is a bottle of 1924, the year of Lenin's death, from the Magarach Institute. It was meant to be a gift for President Chirac. It is better that it stay with you, and you will have a reminder of Crimea. And I invite you to spend ten days in Yalta in September.'

I did in fact go to Yalta, and gave him six bottles of French grands crus. During my stay, he gave me the tour of the Institute, with its collection of three thousand grape varieties from around the world. I tasted some fifty dessert wines and this very particular Magarach muscat, extremely concentrated, very rich, oily, with breathtaking aromatic potency. Yquem to the fifth power. The vintage 1937, which I also tasted, seemed as young as a 1975.

This 1924 might well still have fifty years ahead of it. And even though no bottle leaves the Institute anymore, I left with three other bottles: from 1931 and 1941 (our respective birth years) and 1945. Bonds of friendship united us, and when he died of a heart attack in 2003, his wife sent me his gold watch in memory. It lies in my museum next to the bottle from 1931.

Magaratch Muscat 1924

Appellation: Crimea, Ukraine (then in the USSR).

Variety: muscat.

Vineyard area: 1 hectare.

Average age of vines: 80 years.

Average production: 2,000 bottles.

Best vintages: 1924, 1934, 1937, 1938, 1947, 1966, 1968, 1975.

DE LIQUEUR NATUREL
DU
MAS AMIEL
MA
PROPRIÉTAIRE DU MAS AMIEL

'It has an immense richness in the mouth, smooth and infinitely long, with liquorice, blackberry, blueberry, candied prunes, and of course the chocolate with which it is often associated.'

In 1816, Raymond Étienne Amiel won this estate, located in the Maury vineyards, in a card game. The Dupuy family ran it afterwards. I had the luck of meeting Monsieur Charles Dupuy in the 90s. At the time I had some Feytit-Clinet 1982 available, and I was able to trade a case for a few bottles of his family stock, including this precious 1924, his last bottle, and a 1941, the year of my birth.

On the poor soil of the Maury hills, the sweltering sun that shines nine months of the year and the tramontane winds produce very dry and overripe grapes, with a very concentrated and sweet juice. After the mutage of alcohol, which stops the fermentation, the wine rests for about eight months in the cellar, then for a year in demijohns in the sun to acquire its rancio. It is then treated for at least four years, and sometimes up to fifteen, in oak tuns. The best vintages exhibit tuilé and copper tones; the scent is very rich with aromas of caramel, and spices. It has an immense richness in the mouth, smooth and infinitely long, with liquorice, blackberry, blueberry, candied prunes, and of course the chocolate with which it is often associated. The complexity of the oldest vintages is reminiscent of vintage ports. It is nearly impossible to find old Maurys. They are sought after and particularly appreciated at the end of a meal, like an old port. I have rarely had the opportunity to taste them, but I have indelible memories of the pre-war vintages.

Maury Mas Amiel 1924

Appellation: Maury, Roussillon, France.

Vineyard area: 155 hectares (Maury and Côtes du Roussillon).

Variety: grenache 90 %.

Average age of vines: 60 years.

Corkscrew from the 1920s: the brush was used to dust off the bottles.

1924

137

> 'With a deep red colour, this wine has incredible ageing potential.'

This wine estate is special for the exceptional location of its vines on the south-western hill of Saint-Émilion, as well as for its wine cellars dug into the limestone, continuously in construction according to the meticulous directives of the proprietor Alain Vauthier. The name Ausone is in reference to the Latin poet (310-395) who is reputed to have owned a villa here. The Dubois-Challon and Vauthier families have been established here since around 1790, and the Vauthier family became the proprietors in 1990. Under the leadership of Alain Vauthier the quality of the vine increased spectacularly, especially in the vintages 2000, 2001, 2003 and 2005. Almost as expensive as Petrus, almost as rare as Le Pin, Ausone once again became the tenor it used to be around 1900, regaining its unique character. It is most often a rich and intense wine, with melded tannins, complex and extraordinarily precise, a pure *vin de côte*. It expresses itself through elegance, purity, finesse, texture. In particular one finds notes of cherry, raspberry, blackberry, blackcurrant, spices, liquorice. With a deep red colour, this wine has incredible ageing potential. Michael Broadbent gives five stars to the Ausone 1874 tasted in 1995 ('perfect weight, balance and floor'). His description of the 1921 could be from no one else: 'the aroma made one think of seaweed and the sweat of a young athlete'! Robert Parker cites 2100 as the apex of the vintages 2003 and 2005. Monsieur Vauthier is practically alone in having never agreed to sell me a bottle directly, never mind a jeroboam or an imperial, kindly proposing that I see a wine merchant. As a result I had to pay three or four times the price at the estate! I spent a fortune to acquire the best vintages, and was unable to buy large bottles, since merchants reserve them for export. Paradoxically, he did me a favour in 1990: I had entrusted him with five bottles of old vintages (1921, 1937) for reconditioning, and when I went to pick them up I was surprised to find six. 'I added one from 1983 to complete the case. You'll find it's a good vintage.'

Château Ausone
1921 & 1959

Appellation: Saint-Émilion grand cru, premier grand cru classé, Saint-Émilion, Bordeaux, France.

Vineyard area: 7 hectares.

Varieties: 55 % cabernet franc, 45 % merlot.

Age of vines: 55 years.

Average production: 18,000 bottles.

Best vintages: 1900, 1929, 1945, 1955, 1982, 1990, 1995, 1998, 2000, 2001, 2003, 2005.

My first meeting with Jean-Jacques Sabon was strange at the very least. I had sprained my ankle hopping through the hundred-year-old Châteauneuf vines, more precisely in the rounded and multicoloured pebbles that look like pebble beaches. The waitress at the hotel where I was staying advised me to go see a well-known healer in the region. His name was Jean-Jacques Sabon! And there we were spending the evening talking about our passion for wine and visiting his wine cellar. In a dark corner, I notice some old bottles, 1921 and 1959. There are not many old vintages in Châteauneuf; there was no tradition of keeping them. I begged Jean-Jacques to sell them to me, but received a very kind, but firm, refusal.

In early 2009, I was the subject of several television broadcasts and magazine articles. A short time later, Jean-Jacques phoned me: 'I had no idea your passion went so far. Come to Châteauneuf for the Saint-Marc, I've chosen two lovely bottles for you, which deserve to be in your extraordinary collection.' These two excellent vintages, 1921 and 1959, thus joined my precious bottles.

The Sabon family has been established in Châteauneuf-du-Pape since the 17th century. Séraphin Sabon was the artisan of the Châteauneuf-du-Pape appellation, next to the famous Baron Leroy. When I met Jean-Jacques, he was bringing out the first vintage – 1996 – of the Secret des Sabon, the estate's prestigious vintage, produced from one hundred ten-year-old vines. He produces only one thousand two hundred bottles on average. Afterwards I bought all of the vintages. 2001 and 2007 are particularly good. It is a majestic wine, dense and full-bodied, very concentrated. Its texture is extraordinarily smooth. It has scents of spices, blackberry, black cherry, raspberry, truffle, even chocolate. The tannins are melded and silky, the alcohol quite present (sometimes more than 16°). His exceedingly rare vintage can age fifty years. The line continues with the Cuvée Prestige, a great keeping wine, the Cuvée Réservée, a virile wine, and finally Les Olivets, matured in tuns for fifteen months.

'It is a majestic wine, dense and full-bodied, very concentrated. Its texture is extraordinarily smooth.'

Châteauneuf-du-Pape, Domaine Roger Sabon 1921 & 1959

Appellation: Châteauneuf- du-Pape, Rhône, France.

Vineyard area: 45 hectares.

Varieties: grenache 65 %, cinsault, monastrell and syrah for the red wines.

Average production: 70,000 bottles.

Best vintages: 1959, 1961, 1978, 1990, 1998, 2001, 2005, 2007.

> 'In my view, 1921 is the vintage of the century, ahead of the 1929 that I have tasted twice, and the 1937.'

Romanée-Conti
1921 & 1945

Appellation: Romanée-Conti Monopoly, grand cru, Burgundy, France.

Vineyard area: 1 hectare, 80 ares and 50 centiares.

Variety: pinot noir.

Average age of vines: 50 years.

Yield: 25 to 30 hectolitres per hectare.

Average production: 6,000 bottles.

Best vintages: 1915, 1921, 1929, 1937, 1945, 1961, 1990, 1996, 1999, 2002, 2005.

My two favourite vintages out of the twenty I have tasted: 1929 and 1990.

One day in 1985, I go to a sale of Romanée-Conti in Neuilly accompanied by wine expert Alex de Clouet. Nice catalogue, full house, I sit in the back. Next to me, I recognise Henri Salvador. He buys a case of Pommard, then a case of Clos-Vougeot.

Then the auctioneer announces a bottle of Romanée-Conti 1921 – exceptional! The only one I have seen in my life – and two from 1945. The starting price for the three bottles is 6,000 francs! Henri Salvador bids 9,500 francs. I bid 10,000.

The gavel falls. They are mine: the amazing 1921 that I estimated at 20,000 francs by itself, and the two 1945. In my view, 1921 is the vintage of the century, ahead of the 1929 that I have tasted twice, and the 1937: '1921 is a myth and a legend', writes Serena Sutcliffe.

'Spices, exotic scents, essence of perfumes, faded roses – tea, smoke, cedar, coffee – a sublime bottle, absolutely unforgettable', says Michel Bettane.

'The greatest wine, the most balanced, the most sublime', observes Michel Dovaz with his legendary succinctness.

La Romanée-Conti is the most prestigious vineyard in Burgundy, established in the 17th century. The Prince of Conti purchased it in 1760 and gave it his name. Today it is the property of the de Villaine, Roch and Leroy families.

The 1945 is an amazing wine. It is also a symbol: the wine of victory. Even more, the last harvest of a great vintage of agonising French vines: decades were spent desperately treating Romanée-Conti for phylloxera attacks, but the fight was hopeless, the grapes were ancient, they had been reproduced from themselves for centuries in all directions. After the last frost of 1945, the harvest was miniscule – six hundred eight bottles –, but very concentrated thanks to early blooming and a hot, dry summer. Afterwards, there was no choice but to pull the vines out. 'One must realise that we are not pulling a vine, but *the* vine, the last of its kind', wrote Jean-François Bazin. So this 1945 is indeed a mythical wine. This is a tasting commentary from 1990, by Geoffrey Troy:

'Dark colour, marvellous scent of oriental spices in which plums and exotic berries mix. In the mouth, a sheet of fruit and immensely long – perhaps one of the greatest burgundies ever made.' A bottle was sold at Christie's in Geneva in 2007 for 48,140 dollars. I have perhaps one of the last authentic bottles: most of those circulating among collectors are counterfeit. 1947s are seen in England, even though the land was lying fallow that year! A collector served a Conti 1948 at a wine-tasting dinner, even though there is no 1948: the first vintage after replanting is 1952. And the three magnums of 1945 that he owns are fakes. Indeed, after the reconditioning of my Romanée-Conti 1944, André Noblet, the chai master, told me: 'With only six hundred eight bottles of 1945, it was out of the question to make magnums.'

As for my bottle of 1945, it is authentic. 25 years ago, wine was not expensive enough for counterfeits to be made, and it will never be sold. Next to the Romanée-Conti, I of course have the other wines of the estate. La Tâche is nearly its equal, 'the most irresistible wine of the estate' according to Robert Parker.

> 'It is the year of my father's birth. It is the oldest bottle of Petrus in my collection; I paid a fortune for it.'

This bottle from 1914 has a history. I absolutely wanted to have it since it is the year of my father's birth. I paid a fortune for it, and it is the oldest bottle of Petrus in my collection. Its label is different from the label that adorns Petrus today, on which Saint Peter displays the keys to Paradise. The vineyard then belonged to the Arnaud family. On the label, one can read:

World's Fair 1878 and 1889
Gold Medal
Petrus Arnaud premier grand cru
Pomerol

With the medals shown here and there on the label.

Given the difficulty of finding the original label, my 1914 was reconditioned with a modern label.

In the showcase of my 'museum-cellar', this bottle represents my family history: the First World War, my grandfather Joseph injured at Verdun. Then my father, born in 1914, who was a postman, and hairdresser in the evening after his rounds on his bicycle: forty-five kilometres each day in this hilly countryside, on gravelly roads, when he did not have to carry his bicycle across the fields! And his cape! Blue felt, it weighed at least twenty kilos when it rained, and I still recall how he had to ring it out and let it dry in front of the fireplace before leaving again in the afternoon. I have kept the leather satchel in which he sometimes transported a million francs in that period, today 1,500 euros, to pay money orders at the various farms.

It is only when our parents pass away that we realise all they have done for us! Some people write books about their parents; for my part, I am still looking for a Yquem 1886, or an exceedingly rare Petrus of that same year, the year of my grandfather Joseph's birth. From the year of my own birth, 1941, there is nothing exceptional, except Cheval Blanc, even if it cannot equal the illustrious 1947.

Three unremarkable vintages live in my wine cellar, they correspond to dates that are important for me: 1941 saw a beautiful summer but harvests late in autumn; few bottles are available. 1914 is rare, a late harvest, there is little wine, but a good year. 1886 suffered from frost, then mildew; then as well, the harvest was very late.

Petrus 1914

My grandfather's watch

Appellation: Pomerol, Bordeaux, France.

Vineyard area: 11.5 hectares.

Varieties: merlot 95 %, cabernet franc 5 % (not always used).

Average age of vines: 40 years.

Average production: 30,000 bottles.

Best vintages: 1921, 1945, 1947, 1950, 1961, 1982, 1989, 1990, 1998, 2000, 2005.

1904
Grands Crus du Bas-Armagnac
Bas Armagnac
Vieux
Garanti pur Vin de
Blanche
du Domaine
Grand Cru Classé du
G. Joseph LABE
Propriétaire
CAZAUBON (GERS)

When speaking of rare bottles, one mustn't forget the great armagnacs. The name of this brandy supposedly comes from the Germanic *Herremann*, the name of a companion of Clovis, Latinised to *Arminius*, then *Arminiac* and finally *Armagnac*. His wine-producing region of Gascony owes much to the Emperor Probus who, in 267 C.E., authorised the replanting of the vines uprooted on the order of the Emperor Domit-

'The oldest vintage available for sale.'

ian one and a half centuries before, evidently to protect Roman vineyards. Armagnac brandy (the oldest in France) was already known in the 13th century and described by Franciscan cardinal Vital Dufour, trained at the Faculty of Medicine in Montpellier (the oldest in France), as beneficial for health: it 'dissolves kidney stones, cures burns, eliminates phlegmons, treats strep throat' etc., among forty virtues detailed in a book, including the advantages of moderate usage for pregnant

women! These days Armagnac is at least recognised as being good for the arteries and the heart!

The 15,000 hectares of vines are divided into three territories: in the west, Bas-Armagnac produces rich and smooth brandies; in the centre, Ténarèze produces very full-bodied brandies that age well; in the east, Haut-Armagnac, with much less vine density, brings vivacity to eaux-de-vie, and is drunk younger.

Contrary to cognac, distilled in two firings with the elimination of the first and last fractions of the distillate, Armagnac is distilled in a continuous stream, which provides more aromatic richness and a better ageing capacity. This ageing is done in oak tanks of 400 to 420 litres.

Although it is difficult to find vintage cognacs (this was prohibited by the profession for a long time), this practice is common in Armagnac where one can find all the vintages, for example since 1893 in Castarède. My favourite armagnac is the Laberdolive estate. This dynasty was born in 1856 at the Escoubes estate in Cazaubon, in the Gers region. Since 1893, the Jaurrey estate, planted with folle-blanche franche de pied that the sandy soil has protected from phylloxera, is the most well-known. The other domains, Pillon with colombard and bacco, and Labrune with ugni blanc, complemented the 40-hectare Laberdolive estate. The hundred-year-old pot still is wood-heated. The brandies age in casks from trees on the property and are not reduced.

Pierre Laberdolive was kind enough to sell me several bottles of his famous 1904, the oldest vintage available for sale, sparingly of course. This 'Grand Bas-Armagnac' distilled by Joseph Laberdolive, nicknamed 'the Pope of Armagnac', aged in a 100-hectolitres wooden cask until 1967, before being stocked in demijohns. It has reached maturity.

Laberdolive Armagnac 1904

Appellation: Armagnac, South-West, France.

Vineyard area: 40 hectares.

Varieties: folle blanche, colombard, bacco 22A (hybrid of folle-blanche and noah), ugni blanc.

Age of vines: 40 years.

Best vintages: 1893, 1904, 1911, 1923, 1929, 1942.

Thirty years ago, wine sales were just beginning. Wine was usually sold by lots after furniture was auctioned off, and speculation was non-existent. It is the great vintage 1982 that started it all. And of course no one knew that it was the Tokaji of Hungary. For good reason: after the Soviet invasion of 1956, all the bottles had been pillaged or broken, and the production of Tokaji aszù or eszencia forbidden in order to favour ordinary wine destined for the Russian market.

In 1980, a bottle was put up for auction after a sale of paintings: Tokaji 1901.

No one wants it, so I take a chance: '100 francs'. The gavel drops! Had I said 50 francs, it would have been the same thing. Behind me I hear someone say to his neighbour: 'That guy's mad!' I blush with shame and I feel strange, because I know I just acquired a mythical wine of a very rare year. Like a dusty Van Gogh that would pass unnoticed! Back home, I examine the traditional little 500-millilitre bottle, I clean off the capsule and discover the royal coat of arms of the Prince of Hungary, which also figures on the label. It is indeed my Van Gogh, a historic bottle, worthy of the Louvre!

This bottle is 6 puttonyos, the maximum quality, just ahead of the eszencia, which registers 800 grams of sugar per litre. Moreover, it belonged to the Hungarian royal family: the Archduke Otto of Hapsburg-Lorraine, son of the last king of Hungary, Emperor of Austria Charles I, and Empress Zita. Tokaj is the name of a modest city close to the Ukrainian and Slovakian border, mentioned in the Hungarian national anthem. For a very long time, the eponymous wine enjoyed an immense reputation. Czars would dispatch a regiment of Cossacks to accompany this precious nectar to Moscow. *Soma vedique* (elixir of immortality in Sanskrit), able to prolong life, a feast wine, a cure for pains, that matures very slowly in the labyrinthine cellars of Tokaj, covered with a charcoal-grey cloth.

'This bottle contains 6 puttonyos, the maximum quality, just ahead of the eszencia which registers 800 grams of sugar per litre.'

I also have a case of the vintage 1972, about which I would say: 'The scent is dense, but soft. In the mouth, the aromas have a rare complexity – caramel, fig, prune, tobacco, coffee... The acidity seems to surf on the sugar.' A nectar to be enjoyed in the company of a beautiful woman... blonde like the wine!

Tokaji 6 puttonyos, Otto of Habsbourg 1901

Appellation: Tokaj, Hungary.

Vineyard area: 6,000 hectares, for 15,000 proprietors.

Varieties: mostly furmint, with harslevelu and muscat ottonel.

At the time, I was still selling my Feytit-Clinet door to door. One day, I deliver a case to the *Deux Magots* in Paris. This well-known bar is hosting an exhibition of drawings of the principal chateaux of Médoc. I stop in front of the Château Margaux: well executed, perfect attention to detail. It is signed Marc Dekeister.

An elderly gentleman contemplating the work says to me:

'That artist is brilliant! Look at the front of the chateau.'

'The wine isn't bad either,' I retort.

'You're preaching to the choir. I have more than two hundred bottles of Margaux in my wine cellar. 1928, 1929, 1934, 1947, 1953, 1961, 1982. Only the great ones.'

I am interested in the 1953, a very good vintage, but also the year Corinne Mentzélopoulos, the proprietor of Château Margaux, was born!

'Will you sell me one for my collection?'

'Deliver me a case of your pomerol, and in exchange you can choose one.'

A month later, I am in his wine cellar in the Marais, deep, twenty stone stairs, and I discover cases of lined up along oak beams. In a corner, an embossed case of 1928 magnums. 'My grandfather was an art dealer. He bought the equivalent of a barrel per year. You know, back then, it wasn't expensive. I was born in 1928, but in the case there is also 1900 and 1904.' I must be dreaming: 1900! The perfect wine, I must have it! In 1999, Robert Parker writes: 'Château Margaux 1900 seems immortal. It is one of the most renowned nectars of the century, fabulously rich and incredibly smooth; this wine, with aromas that could fill a room, has great opulence.' He grades it 100/100, adding that it can age another twenty to thirty years. The

old gentleman says to me:

'I dare not open this 1900 magnum. I am alone. I have drunk two magnums, this one is my last. But I'd be happy to trade it for a twelve-bottle case of 1982 or 1990. I drink a bottle per day. At my age, it keeps me young: I'm still on my feet, I'm not blind, and I'm not deaf.'

1982 graded 98/100, or 1990 graded 100/100! I only have one case of 1990 left, but it's a deal. This 1900 is a relic, as well as a magnum, with the original capsule, and it is authentic, one of the last survivors. Because there have been many counterfeits, particularly fraudulent reconditionings. As for the most expensive bottle in

'This 1900 is a relic, as well as a magnum, with the original capsule, and it is authentic, one of the last survivors...'

the world, I believe it is a Margaux 1787 'given away' for 500,000 dollars and broken in a restaurant, with insurance paying 225,000!

Château Margaux 1900, the third factor in a beautiful trinity of magnums, along with Mouton 1945 and Cheval Blanc 1947.

Magnum Château Margaux 1900

Appellation: Margaux, premier cru classé, Bordeaux, France.

Vineyard area: 80 hectares.

Varieties: cabernet sauvignon 75 %, merlot 20 %, cabernet franc and petit verdot.

Average age of vines: 35 years.

Average production: 200,000 bottles.

One of the twelve best wines of the 20th century for *Wine Spectator*.

Best vintages: 1900, 1928, 1953, 1982, 1986, 1990, 1996, 2000, 2005. The greatest succession of extraordinary vintages since 1982, thanks to Corinne Mentzélopoulos, proprietor.

I acquired this crystal carafe in 1985 at an auction in Drouot, an auction at which several old cognacs were sold: Croizet 1870, Paulet 1811, Bisquit-Dubouchet 1858, etc. I am not aware of another specimen, at least not full. Indeed, this hand-blown Baccarat carafe is an exact replica of the first carafe of the 19th century (1873), while the more recent models are industrially produced. Rounded and slightly misshapen, with a twisted neck, irregular and skewed fleur de lys discs, there is no doubt that, as the catalogue

'It is a hand-blown bottle more than one hundred years old.'

claims – 'Grand Fine Champagne in Baccarat flask, early 20th century' –, it is indeed a hand-blown bottle more than one hundred years old! There is a simple way to identify these old Louis XIII bottles: there are twenty-three teeth on the perimeter of the carafe, whereas more recent models only have twenty. Furthermore, more recent corks are in the shape of a fleur de lys, while the older ones are hollow, in the shape of an indented ball. Finally, the bottom of old carafes does not have the engraved inscription 'Rémy Martin Cognac France'.

This carafe was accompanied by a miniature bottle of more recent manufacture with a label attached by a thin tricolour ribbon: 'This Grand Champagne cognac was served at the royal banquet held for Their Majesties King George VI and Queen Elizabeth at the Château de Versailles on 21 July 1938'.

According to experienced collectors, this miniature bottle could be as valuable as the bigger one! The Rémy Martin company is one of the most prestigious, along with Frapin, and has one of the most exceptional stocks of old cognacs. I particularly appreciated the cognac sold for the one hundred twenty-fifth anniversary (1850-1974), of which I purchased three bottles at the Drouot auction. My collection includes several hundred bottles of the best cognacs since 1790, including a few that are already put aside for a family *degustation* in 2030.

Rémy Martin Cognac Louis XIII
1900 (approximate)

Appellation: Cognac, Charentes, France.

The varieties used for cognac are folle-blanche (10 %) and ugni blanc (90 %), but nothing can equal cognacs of pure pre-phylloxeric folle-blanche from the 19th century.

Best vintages for cognac: 1893, 1929, 1937, 1939, 1946, 1947, 1948, 1957, 1964.

'After more than a century, these two dessert wines are still wonderful to taste. Coutet is a premier cru classé of Barsac from 1855; Arche is a second cru of Sauternes.'

Glass grapes showing the colour of the fruit at the moment of harvest.

After more than a century, these two dessert wines are still wonderful to taste. Coutet is a premier cru classé of Barsac from 1855; Arche is a second cru of Sauternes. With age, these wines acquire a golden colour, then mahogany, and finally chocolate brown, which takes nothing away from their extraordinary complexity, offering dulce de membrillo, passion fruit, dried apricot, ginger bread, resin, beeswax...

At the end of the 80s, Daniel Hallée, manager of the *Wine-Bar*, great lover of fine and very old wines, told me that he knew a 'fanatic' of dessert wines, a Japanese gentle-man. I was able to meet him in a restaurant on rue Pierre-Charron sometime later. He was one of the directors of Suntory whiskies. In particular, he collected great sauternes, except for Yquem. In his wine cellar, he has complete cases of suduiraut, guiraud, climens, 19th-century coutet, in perfect condition with impeccable levels; as well as an incredible collection of whiskies and cognacs! Since I also had quite a few old liquors, I was able to exchange these two bottles and a suduiraut 1899 for three 1942 Laberdolive armagnacs, a prestigious estate and his favourite. Meticulous, this Japanese gentleman even had the labels of these old bottles restored so as to present them on his table. I have drunk other bottles of this age, especially Arche 1893, Yquem 1904 and 1906, which usually left me with rare and unequalled taste sensations.

Château Coutet 1900
Château d'Arche 1893

Château Coutet

Appellation: Barsac (Sauternes), premier cru classé, Bordeaux, France.

Vineyard area: 28 hectares.

Varieties: sémillon, a little sauvignon and muscatel.

Average age of vines: 55 years.

Best vintages: 1929, 1934, 1949, 1971, 1988, 1989, 1997, 2001.

Château d'Arche

Appellation: Sauternes, second cru classé.

Vineyard area: 40 hectares.

Varieties: sémillon, a little sauvignon.

Average age of vines: 40 years.

Best vintages: 1893, 1906, 1921, 1947, 1959, 1967.

This château from the 17th and 18th centuries, surrounded by gardens designed by Le Nôtre, produces a wine of great aromatic complexity thanks to its soil of clay, limestone and silica. It is located in the municipality of Preignac and since 1992 has belonged to a subsidiary of an insurance company, AXA Millésimes, who purchased it jointly with the Fontquernie family. This wine is unique in its kind, combining finesse and richness, bold, smooth, and with an acidity that allows for long ageing. In 1989, this richness made possible the production of a small quantity of 'Crème de Tête' worthy of the greatest wines of yesteryear. In several *dégustations*, I myself have verified that this vintage is superior to Château-Yquem of this same year.

Suduiraut has also established itself ahead of the other great wines of the appellation in 1899, 1921 and 1928, three legendary vintages. I have tasted all of the great vintages, like the fabulous 1947, 1959 and 1967.

'This wine is unique in its kind, combining finesse and richness, bold, smooth, and with an acidity that allows for long ageing.'

Very complex wines with flavours of honey, apricot, pineapple, almond, caramel, candied quince, but the one that left me with the greatest memory is the 'Crème de Tête' 1982, compared to the other wines of Barsac and Sauternes, only moderately successful that year!

I was able to purchase two bottles of this famous vintage 1899, and had the corks replaced at the château in 1995, to keep this legendary vintage even longer. I also have an impeccable bottle of 1900: the level one centimetre from the cork...to the point that it seems as if this dessert wine even preserves corks!

Château Suduiraut 1899

Appellation: Sauternes, premier cru.

Vineyard area: 86 hectares.

Varieties: sémillon, a little sauvignon.

Average age of vines: 35 years.

Best years: 1899, 1921, 1928, 1947, 1959, 1967, 1982, 1988, 1989, 1990, 1997, 2001, 2005, 2007.

A crystal and silver Puiforcat ewer dating from 1860, used to decant sauternes.

The notoriety of Château Latour is very old: during the Hundred Years' War, a battle between Bretons and English took place there. In the 17th century the vineyard was renowned and in the 18th century, it became one of the most expensive Bordeaux wines. Thomas Jefferson, during his journey in France in 1787, ranks it as a premier cru along with Mar-

'Latour is my favourite Medoc wine.'

gaux, Lafite and Haut-Brion. The ranking of courtiers in 1855 keeps it at the first place, under the administration of the descendants of the Ségur family. After being in English hands from 1963 to 1993, it now belongs to a businessman from Brittany named François Pinault. Michel Dovaz published a review of the vintages of Château-Latour since... 1735! The 1899 has always had an illustrious reputation; in 1976 it 'stupefied everyone by its charm and its

relative freshness,' recounts Michael Broadbent. Since Latour is distinguished for its longevity and its quality, even in small years. Compact, with potent tannins, concentrated, full-bodied, rich and massive, it is a wine that waits twenty years before releasing its notes of blackcurrant, truffle, blackberry, prune. I tasted the fifteen best vintages of the century at a perfect *degustation*. Even the small vintages from the early 20th century are impressive, with scents of underbrush, ceps, or truffles. Indeed, Latour is my favourite Medoc wine. My best memories are the 1900 and the 1949; 1961 is one of the legends of its century.

This 1899 was rescued from a forgotten case that spent fifty years in an English wine cellar. Its owner was kind enough to trade it for a few bottles of Yquem, of which he is a great lover.

Château Latour 1899

Appellation: Pauillac, premier cru classé, Bordeaux, France.

Vineyard area: 78 hectares.

Varieties: cabernet sauvignon 79 %, merlot 18.5 %, cabernet franc 1.5 %, petit verdot 1 %.

Average age of vines: 50 years.

Average production: 180,000 bottles.

Best vintages: 1870, 1899, 1900, 1928, 1949, 1961, 1982, 1990, 1996, 2000, 2003, 2005.

In the Massandra wine cellars in Crimea, the oldest bottle dates from 1775. There is also 1837. As for the cellars, they were built in 1894: seven parallel 150-metre tunnels. The wines from that period were produced by the oenologist prince Golitzin. My exchanges of great Bordeaux wines with Massandra over ten years allowed me to develop a good relationship with the director, Nikolai Boiko. One day when I was visiting the wine cellar, I noticed bottles with a glass escutcheon on the neck. On each

Czar Nicholas II and the imperial family.

'This Lacrima Christi from 1897 is one of the sixty remaining bottles.'

one was engraved '*Livadia, His Majesty Estate*'; these are bottles from the personal wine cellar of Czar Nicholas II at his summer residence, the Livadia Palace. There remain only sixty with the czar's escutcheon. The oldest bottles in Massandra are considered national treasures, and cannot be sold without the authorisation of President Viktor Yushchenko.

This Lacrima Christi from 1897, the year the building of the Massandra wine cellar was completed, is one of the sixty remaining bottles. It has now made its way to my tunnel-shaped cellar, built with my own hands in 2000. Of course, this Lacrima Christi comes from Massandra. Lacrima Christi del Vesuvio is a wine from the slopes of Vesuvius, coming from a tear that fell from the cheek of Christ as he contemplated the debauchery of the demons established in Naples, or so legend has it. While the 1866 *Jullien* ranked it as a great red dessert wine, these days it is rather white and dry and without much character. As for the Lacrima Christi, it was apparently a *vin de goutte* from Malaga, Spain. Today, it dresses some Malaga vineyards. Italy and Spain both claim to be at the origin of the name, but the Russians could care less. They make port, malaga, marsala; they make all the great dessert wines on the planet, all at home. They have five thousand grape varieties from around the world, one hundred feet of each variety. They have eight farms of 5,000 hectares each.

Massandra is another world that no one knows, another world that makes the same things as we do. In my wine cellar I have all the great wines of the world; in Massandra, they make them. But only three vintages of Prince Golitzin's Lacrima Christi are known. The vine is still young, deep, vanilla-flavoured, fabulously complex: dried apricot, candied fig, caramel. This dessert wine is often superior to those we know in sauternes, jurançon or coteaux-du-layon.

Massandra, Lacrima Christi 1897

Appellation: Crimea, Ukraine (then in Russia).

Variety: lacrima christi, Italy.

Age of vines: vineyard lost.

9.5 degrees of alcohol, 280 grams of residual sugar.

CHATEAU - CHALON

BOURDY Père et Fils

Propriétaires

ARLAY (Jura)

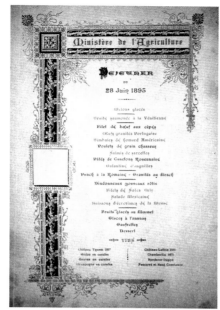

Menu of the annual meeting
of the Chamber of Agriculture in 1895.

Olivier Poussier, elected greatest sommelier of the world in 2000, attracted my attention to the Château-Chalon of the Jean Bourdy estate, producers for twenty-five generations since 1475. And especially to their 1895, immense and interminable... I already had a good range of 20th-century vintages, including the famous 1921 and 1947, but nothing from before 1900.

I made a request of Monsieur Jean-François Bourdy, but 'we have nothing left, Monsieur Chasseuil. The last 1865 was just sold for 3,940 euros'. Naturally, I was not about to give up. I insisted, and finally obtained a bottle of 1895 from the family stock, a bottle from before the phylloxera. I was thrilled! This bottle can age another hundred years: indeed, Château-Chalon, like sherry, is an indestructible wine. A bottle of 1774 was opened, from the wine cellar of Doctor Miller in Arbois, which 'yet tasted quite fine'.

This very particular wine ages in barrels for six years with no interference, and develops on the surface the famous yeast veil *saccharomyces oviformis*. This wine defies time. It is potent and dominating in the mouth, peculiar, with notes of hazelnut, walnut, honey, resin. Drunk at a temperature of 16° to 18°C, a bottle can remain open for several weeks, even several months, without a deterioration of its taste.

The bottles are the famous *clavelins*, with a 620-millilitre capacity: this represents what remains, after evaporation, of a litre of young wine, from barrelling until bottling. They are stamped with the inscription 'Château-Chalon', and often sealed with wax.

'This wine defies time. It is potent and dominating in the mouth, peculiar, with notes of hazelnut, walnut, honey, resin.'

Henri Bouvret, who was an illustrious taster of Château-Chalon, described the 1893 as follows: 'Smooth ensemble delivering a quintessence of nuts', and advised me to taste it with an omelette of partridge eggs accompanied by fresh morel mushrooms! It is an unknown wine that marks the palate for life with its unique and surprising taste, as well as being interminably long.

The area of appellation covers a mere 50 hectares of well-exposed blue-grey limestone shales sheltered by cliffs that allow for good ripening of the grapes. The yield is very strictly limited to 20 hectolitres per hectare.

Château-Chalon, Bourdy 1895

Appellation: Château-Chalon, Jura, France.

Vineyard area: Only 50 ares of the 50 hectares of the appellation.

Variety: savagnin.

Age of vines: 60 years.

Best vintages: 1865, 1895, 1921, 1929, 1942, 1947, 1959, 1967, 1971, 1976, 1983, 1990.

1895 • LUMIÈRE BROTHERS' CINEMATOGRAPH • X RAYS DISCOVERED BY RÖNTGEN • MARCONI'S WIRELESS TELEGRAPH

JURA

Vin de Paille

1893

BOUVRET 308 d POLIGNY

My friend André Bouvret would provide me with wines from the Jura, especially old Château-Chalon 1921, 1947, 1959, etc. First of all for my collection, but also to introduce this very particular wine to my friends. It is an acquired taste, and one must be initiated before fully appreciating this wine — particularly with comté, a dish of morel mushrooms, or a poularde de Bresse with mushrooms. André Bouvret was the greatest specialist of Jura wines I have ever known.

One day, I meet him in Paris, and with a big smile he offers me two bottles of straw wine 1893. Impossible to find, of course! Their history is incredible: before the First World War, a winemaker had hidden below the floor of an outbuilding a dozen demijohns of straw wine, to protect them from the German invaders. They were buried in sand, only the waxed necks showing. Next to them, a slate with 'The Krauts won't get

> 'Straw wine does not owe its name to its colour, but rather to the drying of the grapes on beds of straw, for several weeks and even several months, before being pressed.'

them' written in chalk. And covering it all, the worn oak parquet of the *fourniou*, the oven.

Only seventy years later did the heirs discover them upon removing the floor. At that time, they were not very expensive. I bought a few bottles for 800 francs (120 euros) each. Like Château Chalon, straw wines can easily age one hundred years.

Straw wine does not owe its name to its colour — even though the colour can sometimes resemble that of straw —, but rather to the drying of the grapes on beds of straw, for several weeks and even several months, before being pressed. By that time the grapes are nearly dry — *passerillés* in the vernacular —, and there is not much juice, but it is extremely concentrated.

Tasting this wine, with a colour of polished gold, is an unforgettable experience for me: an aromatic festival of date, dulce de membrillo, candied apricot, with a touch of nut. It is potent, smooth, and infinitely long. When the famous Marcel Guigal came to visit my wine cellar in 2008, I had him taste it. He told me that it was the best thing he had ever drunk in his life! As for me, I can say that it is a unique wine that bears little resemblance to straw wines today, and its more than seventy years in demijohns left it a freshness and aromas superior to the greatest vintages of Château-Yquem (1921, 1937, 1967). It is a textbook bottle and can age for decades.

Straw wine of the Jura, Bouvret 1893

Appellation: Jura, France.

Variety: savagnin.

Vineyard area: 50 hectares.

Age of vines: 60 years.

Production: confidential.

Best vintages: 1865, 1893, 1921, 1929, 1947, 1959, 1983, 1990.

Brass tap used in the early 20th century to draw wine from barrels.

'1893 is considered one of the greatest years in Armagnac.'

S ix bottles, purchased at an auction that I shall not soon forget. The same auction as the 1938 MaCallan whiskies. These six bottles, lot 174, purchased for 1,200 euros plus fees, in a mouldy cardboard box, blackened, with illegible labels. Later I was to learn that the contents of this sale came from the stock of *Harry's American Bar*, on the rue Danton in Paris, which had been having problems since the attacks of 11 September: Americans no longer dared to fly, and thus no longer came to drink the 1938 whisky at 3,000 francs for a 30-millilitre glass...

In my laboratory, the room where I examine my purchases, I appraise the bottles one by one: glass, label, capsule, colour of the liquid and other little secrets. I concluded that these six bottles are authentic. Then I begin the inquiry of the Armagnac producers' trade union and do not stop until I reach the widow of Count François de Lamaëstre, proprietor of the Château de Gimat in Vic-Fezensac, in the Gers region. She informs me that this liquor has been exhausted for fifteen years, just like the prestigious Réserves 1989, 1948, 1830. At that time, the 1893 sold for 13,000 francs, packaged in a '*cloche basquaise*', with a label emblazoned with a black waxen seal (the mark of the count's ring). The countess sends me a portrait of her husband, and I can put a face to the name of this man who adored his 19th century armagnacs. Now I have a story, a piece of heritage to share when I have people taste it in my conservatory.

This 1893 comes from pre-phylloxeric vines, irreplaceable, and the quality of which, just like the quality of the wines they produce, is no longer as prestigious since the introduction of American rootstock. Furthermore, 1893 is considered one of the greatest years in Armagnac.

Wax seal with the coat of arms of the Marquis de Lamaëstre engraved on his signet ring.

Lamaëstre Armagnac 1893

Appellation: Armagnac, South-West, France

1893 • EDVARD MUNCH'S *THE SCREAM* • DEATH OF TCHAIKOVSKY • GREAT NORTHERN PACIFIC RAILROAD BETWEEN SAINT PAUL AND SEATTLE

1893

167

In 2007, I was the guest of honour at the annual *degustation* of Massandra wines, an event that assembles some fifty oenologists and scientists from the Magarach Institute and the Magarach winery. Each one is in charge of a wine that he must analyse and comment on: colour, aromas, flavour, future. The wines are uncorked and tasted beforehand. Among the six mil-

'The first Massandra port, of monastrell grapes, is the greatest.'

lion litres of wine produced every year in Massandra, there are some six hundred dessert wines. The rotation of *dégustations* is organised such that after twelve years all of the wines have been verified. And it has been this way since 1897, when the construction of the seven-tunnel wine cellar was completed. When they are 'faded', they are removed from the collection. The oldest vintages that are still interesting lie in the 'Paradise': sherry 1775, madeira 1837, Crimean muscat 1865, Massandra pinot gris 1888, Livaria port 1891, Ayu-Dag cahors 1933... many Crimean wines are made fol-

lowing the example of European wines. During this *degustation*, I had the great honour of being introduced to Professor Nikolai Pavlenko, PhD, head of the chemistry department of the Magarach Institute for vine research. It is he who advised me to choose this bottle of Massandra red port 1891, from the wine cellar of the Romanov emperors: the first Massandra port, of monastrell grapes, is the greatest. Port is also made there from cabernet and morastel.

The Ay-Danil production centre, on the Black Sea coast, produces the most prestigious red 'ports', just like Livadia, former summer residence of the czars. In 2001, an expert from Sotheby's described the 1891 thus: 'amber, ruby reflections, velvety, chocolate, black cherry, Splendid wine. Will age a long time yet.'

Massandra Red Port 1891

Appellation: Crimea, Ukraine (then in Russia).

Variety: monastrell.

Age of vines: 80 years.

Production: secret.

Best vintages: Aï-Danil 1893, 1899, 1902, 1903, 1945, Livadia 1891, 1892, 1894, 1918, 1936, 1944, 1965.

1886

Украина, Крым, Ялта, ул. Мира, 6
Национальное производственно-аграрное объединение

МАССАНДРА

коллекционное вино

Мед с алтайских

лугов

Князя Голицына

This bottle of Massandra lets me evoke World War II. Like its fellow bottles from the wine cellar of Prince Golitzin, it was stored in the cellar in 1897. But facing the German advance in autumn of 1941, the 'evacuation number 297' was decided: a million bottles placed in wooden crates, labelled and numbered, and evacuated by rail in the Caucasus in Central Asia.

The grape variety is not known, we only know that it contains a small amount of honey. In a heavy bottle of the champagne type, it is opaque in colour, black-amber and greenish. It offers an intense smell of honey, complex, incredibly concentrated and multidimensional aromas of smoke, spices, exotic pepper, old cigars, balsamic. In the mouth, the palate is covered with an intense sweetness of sugar, dried dulce de membrillo, fig, candied prune. It has an incredibly long finish, more than two minutes.

It is an amazing wine that has retained good acidity and good freshness in the finish. Young for its age, it can age several more decades. There are only a half-dozen bottles left of this lost wine, invented by Golitzin (1845-1915), that prince who was the artisan of the Massandra collection, along with Alexander Yegorov (1874-1969). Nikolai Boiko, manager of the wine cellar, continues to preserve this national treasure and to oversee the production of more than fifty different dessert wines. The vintages 1987 and 2003 are exceptional.

I have been to Massandra practically every year since 1997. I found this rare bottle, and with infinite patience and fanatic diplomacy, I was finally able to convince the manager Mr. Boiko to sell me a bottle for a secret low price in 2005.

> 'It is an amazing wine that has retained good acidity and good freshness in the finish.'

Portrait of Prince Golitzin, oenologist to the czar Nicholas II.

Massandra, The Honey of Altea Pastures 1886

Appellation: Crimea, Ukraine (then in Russia).

Variety: unknown.

Age of vines: vineyard lost.

Best vintage: 1886.

This is a legendary wine since it was lost after the 1890 phylloxera epidemic. Robert de Goulaine praised it in his book *Livre des vins rares ou disparus*. Gilles du Pontavice, informed expert, told me: 'Drinking a constancia from the 19th century has been my dream for twenty years.' Luckily, I have owned this wine since 1987 and have tasted it several times. One day, my friend the sketcher of chateaus Marc Dekeister told me that thirty kilometres from my home there is a chateau whose vaulted wine cellar was overflowing with empty old bottles. Perhaps a few were still full...

'A legendary wine since it was lost after the 1890 phylloxera epidemic.'

Armed with a bottle of Feytit-Clinet, I introduce myself to Count Pierre de La Coste, heir of this chateau, unoccupied for ages, who gives me permission to visit his wine cellar: nothing thrilling. However, the count lets me know that there is a closet in the first-level basement that contains some unsorted bottles. Many are empty or nearly empty, old Samos muscats, some rum, some cognac, etc. However, in a corner, three bottles, small, black, with dirty and mouldy labels. I examine them and am able to read: 'Constancia, J.P. Cloete, Cape Town'. Constantia! What are they doing here? 'A member of my family was the French ambassador to South Africa in the late 19th century, and he lived in this chateau', the count tells me. And we make a deal.

The story of this legendary wine begins in 1685 with Simon Van der Stel, governor of the Cape, and to whom the East India Company had given land. Van der Stel chose the best grape varieties to produce a sweet wine, in both red and white. Upon his death, the vineyard was sold and divided. Then Hendrick Cloete, having come from the neighbouring Stellenbosch vineyards, improved the vineyard with the pontac and white muscatel varieties, to make the famous wine that consoled Napoleon on Saint Helena, and about which Hugh Johnson writes: 'in the early 19th century, European courts already preferred this wine over Yquem, Tokaji or Madeira'.

After the destruction of the vines by phylloxera in 1890, the proprietor, ruined, committed suicide and the vineyard was abandoned for eighty years. It was replanted by Mr. Lowell Jooste. In 2008, I learn that he is to come to Bordeaux; it is my opportunity to meet him, and to taste and recondition these three bottles. We arrange to meet at his hotel. I tell Mr. Jooste that I worked in South Africa from 1967 to 1970 and that I have often regretted not having taken advantage of my time in that country to look for bottles of constantia. He tells me that with the Boer War in 1900, the vineyard abandoned for three generations, there was no chance of finding any, and that I would do best to search through wine cellars in England. We open the three bottles, along with two others that I had found in England in 1990, and we piously taste them. The colours vary from mahogany brown to prune black. A complex scent, sweet flavours, candied fruits, dulce de membrillo, apricot, caramel. Infinitely long, a rare discovery of unknown flavours. After reconditioning, I now have four perfect bottles (the fifth having been used to top off the levels of the other four) that should last fifty more years. It goes without saying that they are exceedingly rare.

Since 1980, the vines have been replanted, and the Klein Constantia and Groot Constantia estates produce this wine. Unfortunately it bears little resemblance to the pre-phylloxeric wine, but then again the same is true for the great French wines.

Klein Constantia 1885

Appellation: Constantia, South Africa.

Varieties: muscat and others.

Age of vines: 30 years.

Production: 30,000 bottles

Area: 6 hectares

Best vintages: 1987, 1989, 1992, 1995, 1997, 2001, 2002, 2004.

To discover old vintages still existing on family estates (which produce the best cognacs), one must search in tiny villages: 'Chez Landais', 'Chez Gauthier', 'Chez Moreau'... But people in Charentes are discreet, tight-lipped, wary, and keep their old cognacs like family secrets. That day, it is beautiful out, and I set off across the vineyards to breathe in the air of this particular climate, touch the earth, caress a vine... The country roads are narrow, winding, steep: I am in Grande Champagne, land of the premier crus. In the distance, I make out a tiny hamlet lined with cypress trees. It looks just like a post card. It is Lignères-Sonneville. I stop to admire this amazing countryside.
There is a small house close by. A dog wel-

'This is Grande Champagne, the heart of Cognac!'

comes me, turning in circles, and then a man comes out. Raymond Dudognon. After five minutes of conversation, he invites me in for a *degustation*. We sniff and taste one, two then three nectars. I tell him that I am looking for something exceptional. He leads me to the back of the chai, under the cobwebs, where a small cask is sleeping. 'This is Grande Champagne, the heart of Cognac!' he exclaims, proudly nodding his head. 'Very old, inherited from my forebears, supposedly descendants of Henry IV.' He himself is seventy-five. With his grandfather's blown-glass pipette, shaped like an elongated olive, he serves me. Exotic scents waft through the chai; I am amazed right from the first drop, what more can I say! I leave from this first visit in 1985 with two bottles of Réserve des Ancêtres - only fifty years! Then, through the years, he agrees to sell me sixty-year-old cognac, then seventy-year-old, and a sincere friendship is born. Then one day, as he leaves his storehouse under the moonlight, he gives me a

bottle of his paradise 1874. It is true that he was amazed when he visited my wine cellar, and I sense he is proud that such a bottle will lie next to a Napoleon 1805 or a Paulet 1811.

Raymond Dudognon passed away in 2002, and his daughter Claudine, who took up the torch, gave me the blown-glass pipette of her ancestors, along with a 'Médaille d'or' bottle, of which the famous connoisseur Michel Bettane writes: 'This famous Médaille d'or is one of the most prestigious aromatic symphonies I know, and the nec plus ultra of the appellation, something akin to a Latour 1961 or a Mouton-Rothschild 1949.' That is an understatement! For my part, it is always an immense pleasure after a good meal to sip a few millilitres of the Réserve (Héritage), a one-of-a-kind Grande Champagne cognac, of extraordinary purity, distilled the old-fashioned way, with coal briquettes, and that once again was awarded 19.5/20 in an international *degustation*.

Dudognon Cognac 1874

Appellation: Cognac, Charentes, France.

Vineyard area: 11 hectares.

Varieties: montils, soares (colombard) and ugni blanc, 1 hectare of folle-blanche.

Age of vines: 40 years.

Liquors in the storehouse: 10,000 litres of old cognacs, up to 100 years.

The range of old cognacs: Très vieux, Réserve des ancêtres, Héritage, Médaille d'or.

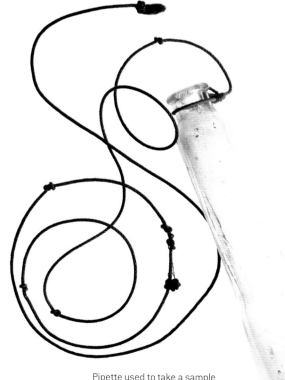

Pipette used to take a sample of cognac from the barrel.

Mary Domergue, my benefactress, who left me Feytit-Clinet

I discovered Château Feytit-Clinet in 1979. I was participating in the New York Marathon, and to celebrate my 2000th place, I invited some runners from Massachusetts to drink some Château-Dassault that I had brought. They had bought pomerol from a certain Madame Domergue from Lynn, Massachusetts. The wine was strong and good. I made the connection to this lady's brother-in-law, René Domergue – brother of Jean-Gabriel Domergue, famous Parisian painter –, a good man, ninety years old and living in Paris. He collected the canvasses of the masters, which filled his apartment and even his wine cellar. His only family was his sister-in-law Mary Domergue who lived – or rather survived – in the Château Feytit-Clinet. He was very proud of his wine and I drank it several times in his home. One day, he asked me to hang some paintings on his walls: Bonnard, Renoir, Domergue... 'to change things around'. One Saturday morning in 1983, I still remember, while taking paintings out of the cellar, I discovered a case of bottles with a shape from another age, stamped 'Feytit-Clinet Grand cru classé'. A miracle, they were from 1870 and 1893. René Domergue told me:

'They come from my brother Jean-Gabriel; he drank nothing but good and old wine, with young ladies with long necks. Since you have helped me to change my paintings, I'll give you one bottle from each case. You'll get more later.'

And thus these two bottles of Feytit-Clinet 1870 and 1893 became part of my collection, together with 1945, 1947 and 1961. Later on, I became the owner of one half of Feytit-Clinet, and my son bought the other half in 1997. In 1993, with my family, I drank a sublime bottle of 1893: its dusky ruby colour, its aromas of coffee, caramel, truffle, ceps, its richness and its exceptional flavour left me an indelible memory. Feytit-Clinet is a wonderful terrain, admirably

> 'Its dusky ruby colour, its aromas of coffee, caramel, truffle, ceps, its richness and its exceptional flavour left me an indelible memory.'

well located on the famous Pomerol Plateau between Trotanoy and Latour. It thus comes as no surprise that this wine won a gold medal in Paris in 1894. After being neglected for a long time until 2000, I am immensely proud that my oenologist son Jérémy, gave it back all its splendour, as attested by the fact that the specialised press ranks it among the five best Pomerol wines, beside L'Évangile, La Conseillante, and in 2007 Robert Parker graded it superior to the untouchable Château-Lafleur.

Château Feytit-Clinet 1870 & 1893

Appellation: Pomerol, Bordeaux, France.

Vineyard area: 7 hectares.

Varieties: merlot 90 % and cabernet 10 %.

Age of vines: 35 years.

Average production: 15,000 to 20,000 bottles.

Best vintages: 1893, 1900, 1929, 1945, 1961, 1982, 2005, 2006, 2008.

Dessert grenaches are no longer made the way they used to be, those Grenaches from low-yield, hundred-year-old vines, harvested late in the region of Châteauneuf-du-Pape. Bottles from the 19th century are impossible to find. My grandfather was a stonemason, and his wife ran the village bar-tabac in La Chapelle-Bâton, where I was born. They naturally served old liquors and digestifs. Many years later, I discovered a few old bottles in a cupboard, including two bottles of grenache 1868. For once, I could not resist the temptation to taste one. The colour was a slightly tuilé dusky red, the aromas like those of an old tawny port, intense, complex. Sweet flavours, infinitely long, prunes, coffee, liquorice, candied fig, cocoa, a symphony of exotic flavours. I will drink the other with my family, or perhaps I will keep it as a testimony of the wines that used to be made, modestly, with no pretentiousness, for country cafés, but with very old, pre-phylloxeric vines with limited yield, and careful harvests.

There were three cafés in La Chapelle-Bâton. After the war, I remember people playing cards in the evening; my grandmother would bring out a basket of apples and walnuts, and people would drink and laugh. At midnight, my grandfather would say: 'You'll surely have a little glass of pineau before you leave!' I tell this little story to show that we should still be able to enjoy ourselves while 'drinking in moderation' (as journalists write without anyone forcing them to do so), and also rediscovering the ancient art of drinking these old varieties of vin cuit, the muscats of Lunet, the banyuls, ports... and the art of living, good manners, beautiful things like those liquor cabinets of yesteryear, ornate and covered in mother-of-pearl, ivory or ebony, and that can still be seen in some salons, but tragically empty...

> '**Sweet flavours, infinitely long, prunes, coffee, liquorice, candied fig, cocoa, a symphony of exotic flavours.**'

Grenache 1868

Origin: Probably Languedoc or the southern Rhône Valley, France.

Variety: grenache, natural sweet wine.

My grandfather Joseph-Louis Chasseuil.

179

1868 • BEGINNING OF THE MEIJI ERA IN JAPAN • DOSTOYEVSKY'S *THE IDIOT* • CRO-MAGNON • DEATH OF ROSSINI

Opium pipes and nails from the ship *Marie-Thérèse*.

A former colleague from Dassault, Nicolas de Potapoff, introduced me to Monsieur Chastan, 'gold hunter' in a claim in the South China Sea, more precisely in the Gaspar Strait, between the Indonesian islands of Banga and Belitung, where at least twenty-five wrecks of European ships have been identified. A veritable nautical cemetery on the Silk and Spice Road! With his Pentagon company and local partners Monsieur Chastan discovered the wreck of the *Marie-Thérèse*, a three-masted ship that left Bordeaux for Saigon, and ran aground in shallows before sinking to a depth of 20 metres on 29 February 1872. Among its cargo was a quantity of bottles of champagne, madeira, malaga, Bordeaux (3,100 full and 2,000 empty), opium pipes, plates and silverware... five safes, two compasses and a thermometer. The Gruaud-Larose was identified thanks to inscriptions on the cases, and the oenology faculty of Bordeaux performed the examination. During this examination, Professor René Pijassou wrote: 'An exceptional bouquet with aromas of orange, old leather, spices, tobacco and dead leaves still distinguishable. The colour is slightly changed, somewhat brownish pink, but very dense and deep. In the mouth, the attack is clear, with a pronounced taste of wine, albeit rather fleeting and tenuous lacking somewhat in scope and persistence. A high salt content is nevertheless evident...'

All of this cargo was sold at auction at the Cité mondiale du Vin de Bordeaux in the 80s. But Monsieur Chastan had kept the best, including one bottle that still had its original tin capsule, oxidised, but amazingly watertight: the level of the wine was incredibly good. For this reason, it had not been reconditioned at the chateau, contrary to the other two hundred bottles. This is the bottle I obtained from him, and for which I exchanged a case of my pomerol, Feytit-Clinet 2000. I also have six perfect bottles, reconditioned at the chateau. In 1995, I drank the seventh, along with other late 19th century Médoc wines. It was still good after one hundred thirty years, in spite of all its adventures, from its shipwreck in the China Sea to its repatriation to its recorking.

I very much like this Saint-Julien, an appellation that produces very fine and full-bodied wines, such as the renowned Léoville-Lascases. I have a very good memory of the Gruaud-Larose 1982, 1986 and 1990.

'I very much like this Saint–Julien, an appellation that produces very fine and full–bodied wines.'

Château Gruaud-Larose 1865

Appellation: Saint-Julien, second cru classé, Bordeaux, France.

Vineyard area: 80 hectares.

Varieties: cabernet sauvignon 55 %, merlot 30 %, cabernet franc 15 %, plus petit verdot and malbec.

Average age of vines: 40 years.

Average production: 250,000 bottles.

Best vintages: 1928, 1945, 1953, 1961, 1982, 1986, 2005.

An enigma to resolve: a bottle bearing the name 'Zucco' with, on the capsule, three women's legs in the shape of a helix, and white wine. I was able to taste it with my friend Jean Solis, since I had four bottles: a discreet scent, dry in the mouth, a taste of nuts, with a long finale, reminiscent of sherry mixed with yellow wine, a dry but potent wine, excellent, like nothing I had ever tasted. Later I had to trace this wine back to its source. The tin capsule and the image it represents pointed me towards Sicily. As for 'Zucco' it is an estate that belonged to Henri d'Orléans, Duke of Aumale, ancestor of the Count of Paris, fifth son of King Louis-Philippe and husband of his first cousin, Princess of the Two Sicilies. A rich man, he was the largest real estate owner in France. His life was split between military activities and periods of exile imposed by the Republic, and crowned by the gift of his Chantille chateau to the Institut de France. On his large estate west of Palermo, which he purchased in 1853 from the Princes of Partane – 6,000 hectares in 1897 – he grew wheat, olives, lemons and pistachios and produced extremely varied vines, including the famous zucco, quite renowned. A dry wine, strong, rare, the wines of which were guarded day and night, or so it would appear, In 1866, it sold in Paris for 3.35 francs per bottle, the price of a good bordeaux. The duke died in Zucco in 1897, and the vineyard disappeared. I know nothing more about him or his wine, but this wine certainly deserves to be included in the hundred extraordinary bottles in the wine cellar. The grape variety of this wine seems to be insolia, still grown in western Sicily. The masseria (estate) of the Duke of Aumale was located in the small city of Terrasini. It has become a museum in honour of the duke. Visitors can see a bottle of zucco 1875 offered by my friend Carlo Dossi. My three bottles are the oldest known and still drinkable.

> 'A discreet scent, dry in the mouth, a taste of nuts, with a long finale, reminiscent of sherry mixed with yellow wine, a dry but potent wine, excellent.'

Vino di Zucco, duca d'Aumale 1865

Appellation: Sicily, Italy.
Varieties: insolia.
Age of vines: vineyard lost.

This historic bottle brings back incredible memories. In 1976 I went to Moscow to meet up with a charming Tamara I met during an earlier voyage. In our group, I met a Frenchman named François Doublet, who had come to marry Larissa, a 'TV bombshell'. Since I spoke English, he asked me to be his interpreter for a certain number of formalities. Back in Paris, he invited me to his home in Saint-Cloud.

'You should also marry your little Tamara. We could go to Moscow together. I'm a nurse

'This bottle comes from the wine cellar of the czar in Saint Petersburg.'

at the Garches hospital... By the way, I want to thank you. Here's this bottle of cognac for your collection. I have more: you know, Larissa has friends in high places, this bottle comes from the wine cellar of the czar in Saint Petersburg...', he said as he gave me this Hine 1863. Then he opened a drawer full of plundered icons of golden wood, very colourful. Next to them, I see an enormous kitchen knife! That knife scared me. Sometime later, I was summoned to Paris by the D.S.T., the French domestic intelligence agency, where I was received by a man named Para: 'Monsieur Chasseuil, would you like to work at the French embassy in Moscow? You could be reunited with Tamara.'

I was dumbfounded. How did he know? 'Don't think too much, Chasseuil. We know everything about you... and you would have a good salary there.' I could thus have ended up in an entirely different life, and Tamara was indeed gorgeous! I decided to talk to Commandant Suche from the security service at Dassault, a former gendarme (at the time I was working in the prototype office and was a military reserve officer).

His advice was to stop short: it reeked of espionage. I followed his sound advice, and I am happy I did! A few months later I was surprised to read in the newspaper headlines that François Doublet had been shot in the head. That double agent, not at all a nurse but manager of the *Restaurant des Tournelles*, was a formidable spy. The press swarmed around me: 'You shared a room in Moscow, what did you know?' Larissa spent some time in prison in Fleury-Mérogis, then her case was dismissed.

But let us return to this bottle of Hine 1863. It bears a second label reading: 'Shipped to Saint-Petersburg – 28 April 1909 – Fine Champagne Réserve Nicholas II'.

It has quite a history, and for me personally, deep sentimental value. I saw Tamara again by chance in 2006 in a luxury boutique in Moscow. Thirty years later...

Hine Cognac 1863

Appellation: Cognac, Charentes, France.

As a have said before, my parents both worked in my native village of La Chapelle-Bâton. A born collector, I started at the age of twelve with postage stamps. Then I searched for old documents related to stamp-collecting. Before coming down with 'colletionitis' of rare wines, I was fascinated by those old documents, those parchments from 1550 to 1850 that bore, sometimes printed, sometimes hand-written, the name of the departure city of a letter that was its own envelope, often sealed with a little ribbon of coloured silk.

In 1990, I had to sacrifice some of these

'This bottle from the time of the last King of France is one-of-a-kind.'

precious envelopes, called 'postal marks', in order to obtain this royal bottle. Indeed, while I was hunting through philatelist shops on the rue Drouot, and at the same time through the neighbouring auction house, I made the acquaintance of an antiquarian dealing in old stamps, who was also interested in 16th and 17th century parchment letters. His father, an antique

dealer as well, had a hand-blown wine bottle bearing an insignia with a mirror image of the monogram LPO, for Louis-Philippe d'Orléans, under the royal crown. I had to have this bottle at any price; it must join my Austerlitz 1805 and Tuileries cognacs. He had bought it after an auction in 1987, at the Chevau-Légers auction house in Versailles. My passion for collecting old wines progressively overtook my earlier passion for philately. The exchange was breathless and painful: six of my rarest envelopes, or rather six of those little folded papers tied together with silk. I still remember the oldest one, dated 1570, written with a goose feather on a piece of sheepskin parchment. But there are others of these envelopes of another age, transported from one village to another on horseback, many generations before my father would get on his bicycle... whereas this bottle from the time of the last King of France is one-of-a-kind. A wine bottle in original condition with a waxed cork on a background of woollen tow from the personal wine cellar of King Louis-Philippe d'Orléans, who supposedly gave it to his grandmother according to a family tradition.

Louis-Philippe d'Orléans 1850

Appellation: Burgundy bottle of wine.

Insignia attesting to the royal origin of this bottle.

You might wonder what vinegar is doing among the hundred mythical bottles of my wine cellar. The level of excellence reached by a hundred fifty-year-old balsamic vinegar – let us not forget that it too comes from the vine –, equals that of an old syrupy malaga or a pedro ximénez. I could drink a teaspoon of it every day because 'the mouth, the oral cavity, the most important physical attribute given to man by God' becomes coated with voluptuous aromas of an indefinable and unforgettable complexity! Rossini said that it cured his scurvy. Tenor Luciano Pavarotti was an unconditional lover of this vinegar, and they say that a few drops on parmesan or strawberries is a supreme sensual pleasure! Once again, it is thanks to my friend Carlos Dossi, that Milanese bon-vivant living in Paris, the lord of prosciutto, the king of Sassicaia, that I learned the art of tasting traditional Modena balsamic vinegar.

Traditional Modena balsamic vinegar is made from heated grape must, then matured by slow fermentation and progressive concentration by long, slow-paced age-ing process of transferring it to increasingly smaller barrels of different wood essences: 80-litre oak barrel, 60-litre cherry wood barrel, 50-litre ash wood barrel, 40-litre chestnut barrel, 30-litre blackberry-wood barrel, 20-litre acacia barrel, and finally a 10-litre juniper barrel. This series of trans-

> **'The level of excellence reached by a hundred fifty-year-old balsamic vinegar equals that of an old syrupy malaga or a pedro ximénez.'**

fers is called 'bourrage'. The balm obtained by this process after a legal minimum aging time of twelve years – thirty years for the best vinegars –, is put into jugs, then sold in traditionally-shaped 1000-millilitre bottles for prices varying from 150 to 1,500 euros. This 'royal jelly' is more expensive than the best caviars, and rivals saffron at the zenith of great gastronomic products. The best producers are Leonardi and Pedroni.

Demand never stops growing and for the first time an auction was organised. The highest price came from a Chinese restaurateur: 1,800 euros for a fifty-year-old 100-millilitre bottle.

I was lucky enough to obtain this wonderful hundred fifty-year-old bottle thanks to my friend Philippe Cohen, proprietor of the Château Vieux Taillefer, and Laurent Cazottes, artisan distiller. They introduced me to Rosanna and Pascal Irtelli, representatives of the Dinaro company, importer of exceptional Leonardi balsamic vinegars. Passion did the rest; I purchased this bottle for a friendly low price. Hundred or hundred fifty-year-old vinegars are usually not sold on the market, but rather passed from father to son as wedding gifts. My bottle is already a relic; I would need a second one to resolve myself to open it and taste it.

Leonardi Balsamic, Vinegar 1850

Variety: essentially trebbiano and lambrusco of Modena, but also a few other varieties. Brilliant dark brown colour. Syrupy density. Complex, penetrating, bewitching aroma. Sweet and sour, velvety, multidimensional flavour.

Three appellations: Modena balsamic vinegar, common, a combination of wine vinegar and concentrated grape must, acidic but aromatic; traditional balsamic vinegar from Modena, as well as from Reggio Emilia, made only from concentrated grape must aged for a minimum of twelve years. I am referring here to *traditional balsamic*, which has been protected for ages by an appellation contrôlée and is ranked as a condiment. The other, which cannot be called *traditional*, remains a vinegar.

BⁿE G. BONANN

1850

Siracusa

cchio

Sunday 26 June 1988 at the Galerie des Chevau-Légers in Versailles, the contents of the prestigious wine cellar of the restaurant *Le Coq Hardy* in Bougival are auctioned off. Many legendary bottles: Mouton 1859, Yquem 1847, Lafite 1865, Sherry 1847... But the one I want is the exceedingly rare Syracuse 1850! I talk to Didier Segon, an expert I know well: 'It's too rich for you, and it's too rare. I tasted it with the auctioneer and it's Yquem times ten. Insane!'

Another connoisseur adds: 'Yquem 1847 is worth 50,000 francs; Syracuse is even rarer. If you want it you're going to have to break open your piggy bank!'

I arrive early. There are not many people in the room: most people prefer to spend this beautiful sunny Sunday outside; also, the catalogue was not distributed because of a postal strike. This is my chance. Plus, no one knows Syracuse. The twenty or so 19th

'Syracuse was the rarest and most prestigious wine, far ahead of the famous Constancia or the Commanderia of Cyprus. The vineyard was lost in the 19th century.'

century Yquems on the block should eclipse this bottle, lot 433.

The auctioneer starts at 1,000 francs. I let the price go up, without too much confidence. At 3,000 francs, everything stops. A few long seconds pass, still nothing. It can't be! No one is reacting. I am in the first row, I mechanically announce '3,200' and the gavel falls. It's mine!

'One or both?'

'At that price,' I say, 'both!'

Perhaps this syracuse is not worth very much after all. And then, as is often the case, I am broke, and these two bottles cost me 6,400 francs plus fees. A month's salary out the window, crazy! I am sorry, but at the same time I am ecstatic. My guardian angel tells me that I was lucky.

In the back of the catalogue I found the following commentary: 'Great Syracuse wine considered the height of dessert wines in the 19th century, along with the legendary Shiraz wines or the no less famous Constancia. Syracuse wines are muscat wines, very popular at Court, and have become extremely rare today. Perfect bottle in original condition, tasted in 1987. Fabulous.' Signed by the auctioneer.

Syracuse was the rarest and most prestigious wine, far ahead of the famous Constancia or the Commanderia of Cyprus. The vineyard was lost in the 19th century.

I have kept these two bottles in a privileged corner of my wine cellar for more than twenty years. They are relics worthy of the Louvre Museum.

Syracuse 1850

Appellation: Syracuse, Sicily, Italy.

Variety: muscat.

Oily dessert wine, mahogany colour, a historic Sicilian wine.

Antique wine glass.

On 24 January 1985 in Paris, under the ivory gavel of Master Guy Loud-mer, assisted by Messieurs Maratier Sr. and Jr., valuers, a wine auction took place. Four lots of three bottles of Château-Bel-Air Marquis d'Aligre from the mid-19th century were to be sold. The history of these bottles is reported in an article in the *Monde illustré* of 25 September 1858: 'Two first-rate restaurateurs offer to veritable connoisseurs who accept to pay the price, a Bordeaux wine of which little was produced, and this little was for a long time monopolised by one man, the Marquis d'Aligre. It was called 'forbidden Margaux'. Indeed, these olive-coloured bottles bear on opposite sides of the shoulder two medallions in relief, one:
MARGAUX BEL-AIR MARQUIS D'ALIGRE
And on the other side, in a festoon:
DEFENDU D'EN LAISSER
(LEAVING BEHIND FORBIDDEN)
This 'défendu', a legendary abbreviation and plein cru Margaux that the Marquis d'Aligre, proprietor of the Château de Bel-Air, could not suffer seeing sold in the market. All went into his wine cellars for his personal use or that of his aristocratic friends. Upon the death of the marquis, artist Frédéric Gaillardet (*Tour de Nesles*) and the Count d'Ignonville bought what was left of the famous bottles, later to be sold to two restaurants that only had thirty-three bottles left.'
It is true that the Marquis d'Aligre, descendant of a tanner from Chartres, was a Peer

of France and owned more than 20,000 hectares of property. He could thus afford not to sell his wine, and even to present samples at the 1855 World's Fair, which explains why it was not included in the ranking of Médoc crus. In 2000, I tasted two bot-

'The wine, of a light tuilée colour, was amazingly vineux after one hundred fifty years.'

tles, still well preserved. They had a considerable amount of sediment, but the wine, of a light tuilée colour, was amazingly vineux after one hundred fifty years.
At this 1985 auction were twelve of these bottles, in perfect condition and recently

reconditioned at the chateau. No one was interested, and I was able to buy four lots for 7,200 francs. Examining them in my wine cellar, I noticed that one of them bore the seal:
« MARGAUX BEL-AIR MARQUIS DE POM-MEREU ».
It is the name of the Marquis d'Aligre's son-in-law, who inherited the chateau. Only one full bottle bearing this seal is known, and it is mine!
I also discovered a third sort of bottle in 1990, thanks to my meeting with the epic Max Calasou, whose wine cellar contained thirteen thousand bottles. He told me of a bottle bearing a seal with the words 'INTER-DIT D'EN VENDRE (SALE FORBIDDEN)', and of which he had only a broken half. A few of these bottles, still full, were discovered by chance in the cellar of the Château de Roque-taillade. They bore this famous inscription as well as a hand-written label: 'Vin de Louise - Soussans - 1848' (Soussans, today in the Margaux appellation, is the municipality in which the Château Bel-Air is located).
This fortified castle, built in 1310 by a son-in-law of Pope Clement V, has never been sold, and a friend of the family was able to obtain two impeccable bottles for me from the Viscount Jean-Pierre de Baritault du Carpia, the proprietor, in exchange for a case of Château-Figeac 1990, his favourite wine.

Château Bel-Air Marquis d'Aligre Marquis de Pommereu 1850

Vin de Louise 1848

Appellation: Margaux, Bordeaux, France.

Vineyard area: 17 hectares.

Varieties: cabernet sauvignon, cabernet franc, merlot, petit verdot and malbec.

Age of vines: 35 years.

Yield: low.

'In France, Lunel muscat is a liqueur wine of Languedoc produced with small grapes of the muscat variety, originating in Greece.'

This bottle was a gift from Sergei Foster, representative of Massandra in London. I met him at the annual *degustation* of wines from this cellar. I gave him a tour of the vineyards of Burgundy and Bordeaux. Naturally, he wanted to see my collection, and we became friends.

After touring my wine cellar, he opened the trunk of his car and took out a black chest stamped with the gold coat of arms of Massandra.

'Monsieur Chasseuil, I have the pleasure of offering you this bottle of Lunel muscat from 1848. I wanted to drink it, or to trade it for a few bottles of Petrus; but now I want nothing. I am proud to know that it will lie in your unique collection.'

He attached the tasting commentary of the Sotheby's expert: 'Alcohol 20.5°. Residual sugar 230 grams per litre. Red amber colour, a touch of green. Very potent aromas, crème brûlée, pleasant, full and thick. Sensitive alcohol. Notes of burnt caramel and coffee cover the palate in a symphony of flavours. Sweetness and perfect harmony. Very long finish with a strong aftertaste of candied fruits, refreshing. Marvellous wine. Excellent fruity acidity in the finale.'

It appears that there are only three bottles left in the paradise of Massandra. The one I own bears a seal with the words 'Duff Gordon and Co'. It is the name of a trading house in Cadiz, founded in 1772 by the Scotchman James Duff, British consul in Cadiz, joined by his nephew William Gordon, who was to become Sir William Duff-Gordon as his uncle's heir. His great house, which exported wine to numerous countries and had an agent in Russia, was incorporated into the Osborne family and firm, then dissolved in 1890. The name subsists as a brand of port of the Osborne group. The name Duff-Gordon was distinguished by Sir Cosmo D-G., grandson of William, and his wife Lucy, fashion designer, who were passengers on lifeboat number 1 of the *Titanic*, with only twelve passengers on board. The life vest of Lady Lucy's secretary, signed by the twelve passengers, was sold for 60,000 pounds in London in 2006. In France, Lunel muscat is a liqueur wine of Languedoc produced with small grapes of the muscat variety, originating in Greece. It can thus be assumed that this bottle passed from France to Cadiz, London or Hamburg, before landing in Prince Golitzin's wine cellar.

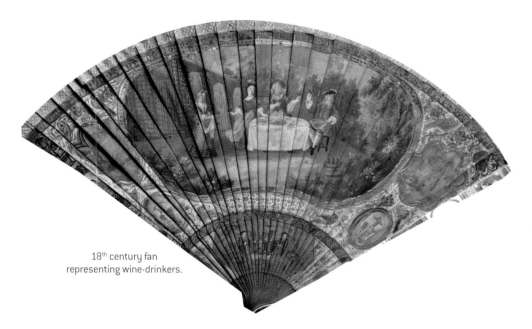

18th century fan representing wine-drinkers.

Muscat de Lunel 1848

Appellation: Lunel vineyard, Languedoc, France.

Crimea, Ukraine (then in Russia).

Variety: muscat.

Founded in 1822, the Nicolas wine cellar was the most prestigious in the world from 1920 to 1985, 'standing in' for the Massandra cellars during this period. It has always been innovative, especially in advertising and posters, launching the first cartoon advertisements in 1921. Its annual catalogues presented an incredible selection of old vintages, sometimes delivered 'ready to drink' after decanting! Through the years, I have purchased all the Nicolas catalogues since the year 1928, and seeing the exceptional 19th century vintages for sale in the period between the two World Wars always makes me dream.

'When I bought this 1848 port, no one was willing to pay 100 francs for it.'

Examining the 1929 catalogue, I read of the first page, printed red on gold paper: 'For the first time, the Nicolas establishments publish the nomenclature of the prestigious bottles of their private 'Grande Réserve', priceless one-of-a-kind collection of the most beautiful jewels of the soil of France.' Of France, but also of other countries. I thus discovered that I had one more relic in my collection: an 1848 bottle of port that I had thought was a generic port, somewhat the worse for age. In fact it was an exceptional port, described thus in the catalogue: 'King's Port – Imperial 1848 – Pure marvel of smoothness, finesse and elegance – 100 francs.'

The Latour, Margaux 1900 on the following page were 200 francs. Since these two premier Médoc grand crus are currently worth 10,000 euros, it is easy to estimate the value of the 1848 port. And to think that when I bought it, no one was willing to pay 100 francs (the nominal price in 1929, the equivalent of 1147 euros today!). Why? Because it was too old, because the label was not shiny, because in France in the 80s no one was interested in port. But I was interested, and that is how I was able to build up a reserve of the most renowned ports in their best years, like Noval Nacional 1963 (a case), Ramos Pinto 1937, Croft 1945, Taylor 1948, etc. Three hundred bottles that I love more every day.

King's Port 1848

Appellation: Porto, Portugal.

Best vintages of port: 1912, 1927, 1931, 1945, 1948, 1963, 1977, 1985, 1994, 1997, 2000, 2007.

Graphic of the Nicolas brand in the 30s.

'With its high percentage of merlot, as well as cabernet, it is a unique Médoc wine that resembles the best pomerols.'

I know Château-Palmer through its extraordinary 1961, of which I was able to acquire an original case of six perfect bottles.

I have both pleasant and unpleasant memories of an auction in the 80s. Good memories because I bought this rare 1847. A bad memory because I was broke again and had to be creative to find a way to pay the bill. Especially since I had also bought Palmer 1961, Lafite 1878 and 1891, Mouton 1868, Poyferré 1870, Montrose 1893. The equivalent of two months of salary! Fifteen years earlier at Dassault, before 'moving up' to the prototype department, I was a boilermaker. I hadn't lost the knack of working with my hands, so for two week-

ends I worked refurbishing damaged cars. I also repainted cast iron radiators and did other odd jobs. But you get nothing for nothing, and I have no regrets!

Palmer, named for General Charles Palmer who purchased it in 1814, was ranked third cru in 1855. At the time it belonged to the famous Pereire bankers and had been ravaged by oidium. It probably does not deserve that rank, but today I personally rank it as second cru, just behind Château-Margaux. With its high percentage of merlot, as well as cabernet, it is a unique Médoc wine that resembles the best pomerols. Dark ruby in colour, it is very full-bodied, rich, round, dense with abundant melded and supple tannins. It offers the nose fireworks of blackcurrant, violet, black cherry, plum, liquorice. The older vintages of the 19th century take on notes of ceps, truffle, cedar, hummus. The legendary 1961, immortal, incomparable, is sought-after by gourmets, just like the 1966 and the 1983, though less sumptuous. I have tasted some twenty different vintages, but I have not had the privilege of tasting the 1961. I enjoyed the 1928, fabulous, with notes of mocha, ginger... then the 1966 and the 1983, as well as the 2005, of which Robert Parker says that it will still be mature beyond 2050.

Château Palmer
1847 & 1870

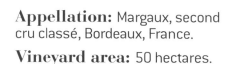

Appellation: Margaux, second cru classé, Bordeaux, France.

Vineyard area: 50 hectares.

Varieties: merlot 45 %, cabernet sauvignon 45 %, petit verdot 5 %.

Age of vines: 40 years.

Average production: 120,000 bottles.

Best vintages: 1961, 1966, 1982, 1983, 1989, 2000, 2005.

Pewter ewer with a golden spout from the 19th century.

I had heard so much about the famous François Audouze, a wine enthusiast who organises sumptuous meals accompanied by old wines, that I decided to phone him, curious to visit his wine cellar. He received me very kindly to talk about wine, as he had heard about my collection. In his successive cellars of simple breeze-block, tens of thousands of bottles were jumbled, of all vintages, great and small, and a few prestigious bottles: a case of Romanée-Conti 1979, some Yquems from the beginning of the 20th century, and especially, to my great surprise, two impressive magnums of Romanée-Conti 1945. I only have that mythical wine in bottles, and that is enough. Indeed, André Noblet, the famous steward of the estate, assured me that no magnums were made in 1945, only six hundred eight bottles.

I admit I was rather disappointed. Until I noticed, standing in a corner, a few small, dirty pear-shaped bottles. Some were waxed, others were not, some empty bottles still gave off a bouquet of old sherry or old yellow wine, some with no label, others carrying a succinct label: *Cyprus*. We discussed the bottles, and I deduced that it was the rare wine known as *Commanderia*. I did not have any, and I wanted two bottles. But François Audouze would not yield, even when I offered him in exchange old Massandra wines, or a straw wine of Jura from 1893, still incredibly good for its age. The negotiations stopped there.

A few months later, he came to visit my wine cellar and was surprised by the diversity of rare foreign wines. He took from his pocket a small bottle of Commanderia of Cyprus of about 350 millilitres, with the original wax. In exchange, I gave him a big bottle of 1893 straw wine. I had been looking for this wine for thirty years!

Commanderia is the oldest branded wine in the world: in 1191, Richard Lion Heart gave the island to the Knights of the Temple, and they in turn developed the vineyard and its reputation. It is the ancestor of Madeira and Marsala, according to Alexis Lichine. It was served at the 'Kings' banquet' in 1352. Under Turkish domination, it resisted. Even phylloxera was unable to conquer it. This chapped wine, made from sun-dried grapes, is matured in solera. It is easy to find in Cyprus, but recent vintages do not equal the older ones. As for the 1845, François Audouze describes it as 'total refinement', with notes of black pepper, liquorice, sometimes candied orange. A commentary on the *degustation* of a bottle from the same lot: 'Exceptional scent of fresh nuts, candied fig, a wisp of volatility, which gives it even more style. In the mouth, a festival of wax, blood oranges, orangettes and caramel... a potency from another world!'

Commanderia of Cyprus 1845

Appellation: Island of Cyprus.

Varieties: mixture of red mavron and white xynisteri blanc.

Porcelain glass from 1850,
given to me by Antonio Sanchez.

'The Pedro Ximénez
variety gives one of the
thickest dessert wines in
the world, since the must
can reach 400 to 500
grams per litre.'

In 2006, I was officially invited by the city of Jerez de la Frontera to the Wine Show, and international display dedicated to dessert wines, accompanied by sweet delicacies from around the world. That year, the countries invited were Romania, Lebanon and Turkey, and more than a thousand wines were presented. There I met Antonio Sorgato, director of the Bodega Toro Albala, who showed me the estate of Montilla-Moriles and introduced me to the proprietor, the original oenologist Antonio Sanchez, who collects everything, from poisons to gunpowders, exhibiting them in a museum. The web site of the estate says 'Is it a wine cellar with a museum, or a museum in a wine cellar?' Antonio Sanchez is a genius who produces incomparable Pedro Ximénez.
I had the privilege of visiting his museum and his stock of old wines, of which the oldest is from 1844, the founding year. I of course spoke to him about my collection, and he gave me a small glass tube, 50 millilitres, containing the oldest wine of his estate, from the pre-phylloxeric la Noria vine (only 1 % of the estate), and a unique bottle of 1844 taken from a 180-litre barrel in the paradise of the estate.

The Pedro Ximénez variety produces one of the thickest dessert wines in the world, since the must can reach 400 to 500 grams per litre. At least 3 kilos of grapes are needed to make 1 litre of wine. After the harvest, the grapes are placed on sheets, in the burning sun in August, balanced by the fresh Atlantic breezes. The wine is matured in casks of American oak until bottling. It is very dense in the mouth, with phenomenal persistence. It can keep for centuries. The Bodega Toro Albala is located in Aguilar de la Frontera and, since 1922, on the site of an electrical factory the tunnels of which are used as an ageing cellar. The estate produces 30 % of its wines and purchases the rest. The wines have the appellation Montilla-Moriles, an appellation that was separated from Jerez in 1993. The white Pedro Ximénez variety is dominant, and by far, the only one at Toro Albala to use oloroso, contrary to Jerez. It is strong and dry. If it carries the mark P.X., that means alcohol was added. Old-style winemaking processes use earthenware jars in which the wine is refined in clay. *Flor*, a mysterious mould, insures the slow ageing of the wines. Señor Sanchez, a rare man, sensitive, with many qualities, let me taste some twenty of his best vintages, including the 1900, 1910, 1939 and 1945. The 1939 left me with a memory of complex, multidimensional aromas, with soft and bewitching flavours (caramel, crème brûlée, mocha, balsamic), infinitely long...

Pedro Ximénez, Toro Albala 1844

Appellation: Montilla-Moriles, Andalusia, Spain.

Variety: pedro ximénez.

Vineyard area: 75 hectares.

Age of vines: 40 years.

Average production: 150,000 bottles.

Best vintages: 1844, 1910, 1939, 1945, 1961, 1967, 1971, 1975.

Here is another bottle of Massandra. There will be none older. Since 1997, I have returned every year to the Black Sea coast to revisit the wine cellar of Czar Nicholas II and its paradise that encloses thirty thousand bottles. I got along well with the director, Mr. Nicolai Boiko, and at each of my visits I have brought a few great bottles from the French vineyards. In October 2008, I introduced him to Olivier Poussier, the best sommelier in the world, who had come with a team from the television programme Envoyé Spécial to prepare a show about rare wines.

'Here is another bottle of Massandra. There will be none older.'

The rarest wines among the six hundred references in the paradise of Massandra are the sixty-one last bottles carrying the seal of Czar Nicholas II. I had already taken out seventeen bottles, and at each trip I eyed the Madeira 1837, only five bottles, the oldest vintage after the untouchable 1775 sherry. None of these bottles may be sold without the authorisation of President Yushchenko. The week of the reportage is approaching. Foster Sergei, a friend of mine who represents Massandra in London, is there as well. I told him that I dreamt of having that Madeira 1837 in my wine cellar. So he whispers something to Boiko: after all, French television is there, it's a great moment. And the last day, a miracle! After a *degustation* of thirty vintages of excellent quality, Monsieur Boiko asks the cameraman to come closer. We are in front of the cast iron grille, the holy of holies of the paradise of paradise; he opens the small grille, dons white woollen gloves, clasps a bottle of Massandra 1837: 'I phoned President Yushchenko, we know that Monsieur Chasseuil has one of the most prestigious collections in the world. We could not let him return to France without his favourite bottle, this Madeira from 1837, the year of Pushkin's death. And this way, you will have a nice memory on French television.'

Massandra Madeira 1837

Appellation: Crimea, Ukraine (then in Russia).

Age of vines: 80 years on average.

The different madeiras produced in Crimea are Ai Danil, Massandra, Kuchuk-Uzen, Alushta, Koktebel and Crimean.

Best vintages produced according to Massandra oenologist Alexandre Yegorov (1874-1969), are: 1900, 1903, 1905, 1915, 1923, 1934, 1937, 1945, 1947, 1950, 1952.

205

1837 • INAUGURATION OF THE FIRST RAILROAD TRACK BETWEEN PARIS AND SAINT-GERMAIN-EN-LAYE • BEGINNING OF THE REIGN OF QUEEN VICTORIA

IMPERIAL   RESERVE

BROWN MADEIRA

Grand Madère

1835

> '**Vines in narrow terraces cover the volcanic hills around the perimeter of the island, cultivated in small mixed farming operations.**'

The island of Madeira, located off the coast of Morocco, has belonged to Portugal since the 15th century. A subtropical climate, too humid for grapes, summers too hot... nothing seems to have predisposed Madeira to make a great wine. But human thought and action made this exploit possible; vines in narrow terraces cover the volcanic hills around the perimeter of the island, cultivated in small mixed farming operations: it is indeed astounding to see bananas growing next to grape vines! The science of winemaking did the rest.

Madeira wine is ranked into four qualities, each one tied to a noble variety: sercial (generally dry), verdhelo (semi-dry), bual (colourful, sweet) and malvoisie (malmsey, the sweetest). People often forget to mention that at least 60 % of the wine comes from the tinta negra mole variety, a cross of pinot noir and grenache, recently promoted to the rank of noble variety. The wine used to be loaded onto boats stopping on their way to Asia. Eau-de-vie was added so that the wine would survive the voyage, and it turned out to be better when it returned. Later, *estufas*, ovens in which wine with added alcohol is heated for six months at a temperature between 40 and 46°C. It is then funnelled into casks left in the sun, sometimes for more than twenty years for the best wines. It is important to mention that excellent Madeiras are made without being heated. Madeira contains between 17 and 22° of alcohol depending on the style, from dry to sweet. Its colour varies from golden yellow to chocolate brown. The dry wines have flavours of nuts, orange, vanilla, almond, balanced by a good acidity. The sweet and semi-sweet wines are rich and smooth, intense and complex, with notes of dried fruits, honey, even caramel, balsamic aromas like vanilla.

One of the best producers is the Barbeito firm, founded only in 1946, but which has acquired and preserved vintages as old as the 1875. Unfortunately, these bottles from the 19th century will soon have disappeared. Around 1985, when I was already interested in all of the derivatives of wine – madeira, marsala, malaga, port, constancia, cotnari, essenczia...–, I was able to acquire, for 650 francs per bottle, a case of twelve bottles of Madeira 1835 from the Nicolas wine cellar in Charenton, the most prestigious wine cellar of all time, along with those of Massandra in Ukraine.

I recently realised the true value of these bottles by looking at a Nicolas catalogue from 1929: this old Madeira was 'given away' for 300 francs, the same price as Latour 1870 and Lafite 1865. For me, Madeira is the brandy-wine with the longest ageing potential. The best vintages I have tasted are a barbeito-bual 1863 and a malvoisie 1916, with Claude Gilois of Vins du Monde, as well as a sercial 1944 from Henriques.

Nicolas Imperial Madeira 1835

Appellation: Island of Madeira.

Variety: tinta negra.

Best years: 1835, 1863, 1870, 1875, 1912, 1916, 1954, 1966, 1968.

'The excellent pedigree of this wine becomes evident with age, with nuances of honey, hazelnut, almond, vanilla, coffee, liquorice, candied fig, caramel, cocoa...'

Marsala is an English creation dating back to 1773, when John Woodhouse, English connoisseur, added eau-de-vie to the dry wine he sent to England. Its reputation was soon made, and Admiral Nelson strongly promoted the *Marsah Allah* wine, literally *Port of God*. It was with English help that Giuseppe Garibaldi seized Marsala in April 1860, the first step in the conquest of Italy, and which would end with its reunification under the crown of the Dukes of Savoy.

Old bottles are very rare, but the excellent pedigree of this wine becomes evident with age, with nuances of honey, hazelnut, almond, vanilla, coffee, liquorice, candied fig, caramel, cocoa... Every time I see a bottle, I rush to purchase it. How many are left? In my opinion, no more than one hundred bottles; soon there will be none, and then 'the world' will notice the disappearance of this bacchic heritage. Thanks to Marco de Bartoli, whom I have never met but with whom I have spoken by telephone, I was able to purchase several bottles from 1830 to 1945 for my collection. He has nothing older, and he is unanimously considered the best producer in Sicily, as well as the most innovative. The only vintage I have tasted, 1945, was breathtaking. I also have a few bottles produced by Florio, and very well reputed. There are five types of Marsala, from dry to semi-dry to sweet. The *fine* is the simplest and must age one year. The *superiore* ages at least two years; it is more complex. The *superiore riserva* ages at least four years and adopts aromas of dried fruits. The *vergine* ages at least five years in oak casks, little alcohol is added and it retains a dry character. The same goes for the *stravecchio*, which must age ten years and register 18° of alcohol. For the last two, very ripe grapes are necessary. There are several varieties that heighten the palate of sensations: grillo, inzollia, catarrato for white; nero d'Avola, perricone, nerello mascalese for red. It is an *aperitif*, but also an excellent companion for desserts and sheep's-milk cheeses.

Bartoli Marsala 1830 & 1860

Appellation: Marsala, Sicily, Italy.

Varieties for red Marsala: nero d'Avola, perricone, nerello mascalese.

Varieties for white Marsala: grillo, inzollia, catarrato.

Most renowned years: 1830, 1860, 1900, 1935, 1945, 1955, 1968.

Best producers: De Bortoli, Florio, Pelegrino.

'The Rugiens 1811 was surprising for its age, a bouquet of vanilla, tea, meadow mushroom, no faults, good acidity, good alcohol level, sweet.'

Daniel Hallée, a bon-vivant who lives on the rue Saint-Lazare in Paris, introduced me to Félix Clerget, owner of extensive terrains in Burgundy: Clos Vougeot, Volnay-Caillerets, Pommard-Rugiens, etc. It was in the 80s, and at the time Félix would sell me his grands crus for 4 francs per bottle... We would taste the barrel, and then we would uncork the bottles: Vougeot 1929, Rugiens 1937, etc. I would leave with the trunk of my car full, and he would always give me an old bottle as a bonus.

One day, when I asked him what his oldest bottle was, he brought me to the second level of his basement and showed me an 1811 wrapped in a charcoal-grey cloth called 'the mushroom'.

'This is the last one. We drank the other one with Grandfather twenty years ago, and did we ever laugh: we tasted it blind, and he really was blind! Everybody was mad for the beverage with scents of faded roses. In reality, the wine had a good amount of volatile acidity and did not show its age. Volatile acidity preserves the wine, and Rugiens stays fresh.'

'What do you plan to do with that 1811?'

'Since I don't have any children, it could be here for some time. It's not the contents that are so interesting, it's the fact that it's an 1811. You are a collector. Do you want it?'

We were sitting on the edge of the well in the courtyard, the weather was fine, Félix was in good shape, we had had quite a bit to drink, and that 1811 was bothering me. It was my lucky day.

'I'm curious to taste it.'

'Let's go. We'll change the cork, and you'll taste a drop while I draw you on the label, and we'll top it up with some very good wine to rejuvenate it a bit.'

The 1811 was surprising for its age, a bouquet of vanilla, tea, meadow mushroom, no faults, good acidity, good alcohol level, sweet. 'This feels good,' said Felix, 'nothing like the other one!'

I brought an undreamed-of treasure to my sanctuary. It is true that at the time no one was interested in these old vintages. Since then, Félix has passed away and every year, in his honour, I drink an exceptional bottle of his Volnay-Caillerets 1976 or 1978. The 1976 was assessed very highly by Andreas Larsson, the best sommelier in the world, who came to visit my wine cellar on 5 December 2009, my birthday.

Clos de Vougeot, Félix Clerget 1811

Appellation: Clos de Vougeot, Burgundy, France.

Variety: pinot noir.

Best vintages: 1929, 1959, 1978, 1999.

Stone statuette of Saint Vincent, patron saint of winemakers.

All the wines of the year 1811, white or red, are reputed, even liquors that have been kept for a long time, and particularly great brandies. It is the year of the comet called 'Napoleon's Comet', and not Halley's Comet that we read about everywhere. Its tail was 176 million kilometres long and the whole world could admire it. This sherry comes from the prestigious cellar of the Nicolas brothers in Charenton, which is in itself an assurance of quality. It was advertised for 250 francs in the first Nicolas luxury catalogue published in 1929. Next to it, the well-known grands crus such as Margaux 1870 for 350 francs, Latour 1874 for 300 francs (today it is worth at least 5,000 euros). These bottles ranked as 'Prestigious' in the catalogue were only sold to certain clients, those who agreed to have Nicolas himself deliver them an hour before *degustation* so as to decant them with all their artistry and verify their quality. Marvellous customer service! I bought this one at auction in 1995 in Angers for 800 francs, without a precise idea of the value of old sherries. I was the only one to buy them, along with madeiras and malagas. What luck! The auctioneer smiled, and most of the connoisseurs exclaimed 'Who is this mad eccentric who is paying so much for bottles that must be completely deteriorated?'

Since then, sherry has acquired great historic renown, the 19th century vintages have become very rare, but it is still misunderstood. There are several types of sherry: white *fino* and *manzanilla*, delicate and very dry, deserve to be drunk with grilled Mediterranean prawns; *amontillado* and *oloroso*, rich and complex, with amber colours, always dry, have notes of caramel and nuts, and they are impressive for their complexity and their potency, and they can stand up to exotic dishes; then come the soft, sweet wines, with colours varying from mahogany to ebony, with notes of candied prunes, Corinthian grapes, dates, coffee, cocoa, infinitely long and persistent... eternal and unforgettable wines.

I am referring to vintage sherries, aged in the same cask, but there are also *soleras*, Less renowned: they are dated from the oldest wine; the wine to be bottled is extracted, replaced with younger wine, and so on, and the old wine raises the younger wine. I have tasted quite a few vintage sherries at the wine fair held every year in Jerez de La Frontera, and I have indelible memories of them.

'This sherry comes from the prestigious cellar of the Nicolas brothers in Charenton, which is in itself an assurance of quality.'

Nicolas, Sherry
1811

Appellation: Sherry or Jerez, Andalusia, Spain.

I have been collecting Yquems for forty years. I have around five hundred bottles of one hundred ten different vintages. One day in 1990, I meet a man called Merlaud, a great lover of Yquem. He tells me that he has a bottle of 1811, the best year of the 19th century, graded 100/100 by Parker, the year of the comet. Wow! I have been looking for this wine for ten years. I go to see him at his home outside Méri-

'It is the rarest of dessert wines, the Rolls Royce of sauternes, beloved by Thomas Jefferson and the Russian czar...'

gnac. I examine the bottle meticulously, because there are many counterfeits: it is authentic, the level is perfect, it was reconditioned at the estate, I need not worry for another hundred years! But he wants 100,000 francs (about 15,000 euros)! After long negotiations, he trades it for five bottles of Yquem 1921, the best of the 20th century (I only have two left). At that time, each one was worth 3,000 francs, in 2008 that is 5,000 euros. And I finally have this famous 1811. It is the rarest of dessert wines, the Rolls Royce of sauternes,

beloved by Thomas Jefferson and the Russian czar...

The Lur-Saluces family became proprietor of Château d'Yquem in 1785 by an alliance with the Sauvages of Yquem, before selling the majority of the shares to LVMH in 1997, after an epic battle.

The harvest is performed by picking, grape by grape, fruit extremely botrytised by noble rot. The yield does not exceed ten hectolitres per hectare. And there was no Yquem in bad years such as 1930, 1951, 1952, 1964, 1972, 1974 and 1992.

Yquem is unique to its kind. Tasting it, depending on the year, one perceives aromas of pineapple, passion fruit, mango, honey, candied orange, apricot, peach, coconut, crème brûlée and, for the old vintages, caramel, date, hazelnut, Corinthian grape, candied prune, dried fig, etc. This wine can preserve even more flavours after two hundred fifty years. The first known vintage is 1753. I have personally tasted some thirty vintages, and my favourites are 1937 and 1967.

Château d'Yquem 1811

Appellation: Sauternes, premier cru supérieur, Bordeaux, France. Ranked only premier cru supérieur of Gironde wines in 1855.

Vineyard area: 100 hectares.

Varieties: sémillon 80 %, sauvignon 20 %.

Average age of vines: 30 years, but some very old plots.

Average production: 100,000 bottles.

Best vintages: 1811, 1847, 1864, 1870, 1900, 1921, 1937, 1945, 1947, 1967, 1975, 1990, 2001, 2005, 2007, 2009.

Porcelain label used on the neck of the carafe.

Back when I was working at Dassault, the works committee would organise ski weekends. One Saturday in 1964, in a nightclub in the Samoëns ski resort, I met an American woman, daughter of a general working on an American military base in France. She was studying at the Marymount School in Bougival. We were drinking whisky when she told me that her family lived in Elvis Presley's old house and that 'my father often drinks 1805 sherry from the Battle of Trafalgar!' I knew next to nothing about sherry at the time. Later, I saw her again at Marymount. She liked speaking French, so we talked about my collection and I told her that sherry would go well with the old rums I brought back from Martinique after my time in the Army.

And one fine day, this pretty blonde brings me a bottle of 1805 sherry embossed with the symbol of Nicolas, wrapped in a plastic American flag, which I have kept. I did not realise the value of this gift from a very rich young American. We had become friends, but lost touch. I guard this bottle religiously, as it has many stories.

Of course it belonged to the Nicolas brothers, wine merchants *extraordinaire*, and it commemorates the victory of Admiral Nelson over the Napoleonic fleet on 21 October 1805. It is one of the oldest vintages preserved in good condition. But it is also a bottle given to me by a young woman I would like to have known better...

Like marsala or madeira, Andalusian sherry is not well known in France. There are several types: dry, semi-dry or sweet. There are many producers, but the most prestigious is incontestably Emilio Lustau. It is not easy to find sherry more than thirty years old, called Vors (*Very Old Rare Sherry*, since it is the English who developed the commerce of sherry). As for 18th century

'Like marsala or madeira, Andalusian sherry is not well known in France.'

sherries, they are very rare. Paradoxically, the oldest currently available are in the cellars of Massandra in Crimea, where Olivier Poussier, greatest sommelier in the world, and who accompanied me there in 2008, tasted and eulogised it. It is then that I learned to taste old sherries: a great vintage leaves you an indelible memory of its particular flavours and its *longueur* in the mouth, just like an old Château-Chalon.

Jerez de la Frontera 1805

Appellation: Sherry or Jerez, Andalusia, Spain.

In 1985, a friend of mine told me that the famous restaurant *Le Coq Hardy* in Bougival, where he occasionally dined, has exceptional brandies, including the Grande Fine Champagne Réserve d'Austerlitz 1805, from the emperor's stock, with the escutcheon 'N' for Napoleon.

In 1988, I receive a catalogue of a wine auction in Versailles, Galerie des Chevau-Légers, and I see that lots 478 and 479 are two bottles of this famous 1805. On Sunday 26 June 1988, I attend the auction. Quite an auction: Mouton-Rothschild 1859 sells for 10,200 francs, Lafite-Rothschild 1865 for 8,500 francs, Yquem 1847 for 63,000 francs, Yquem 1870 for 10,600 francs... Five hundred lots of rare wines, to the point that no one seems interested in the few lots of spirits. If the price is low, I have a chance. 'Lot 478, starting price 1,000 francs!' At that price, even though I am broke, it is a bargain (and these bottles are historic: Napoleon, Austerlitz...) The price goes up: 1,200, 1,500, 1,800, no one else? I go up to 1,900. Bang! The gavel falls, it's mine! One or two bottles? Both! I have already bought Petrus 1951 for 2,950

francs and 1953 for 2,800, Yquem 1904 for 4,000. Alas, I will have to liquidate part of my stamp collection at the Carré Marigny to pay the bill...

But this bottle is a page out of history. It follows the Trafalgar bottle, and commemorates that 2 December 1805 when, in southern Moravia, Napoleon I strategically defeated the Emperor of Austria and the Czar of Russia, leading them to believe that his army was weak and defenceless. Meanwhile in Cognac, the liquor in these two bottles began its slow ageing. Napoleon brandy has even become a registered name, designating a liquor in which the youngest brandy is at least six years old. But this vintage is mythical and exceedingly rare. I placed these two bottles in a showcase, next to two authentic letters written by Napoleon, one from 1811, the other from 1808 addressed to his son the King of Rome.

> 'Napoleon brandy has even become a registered name, designating a liquor in which the youngest brandy is at least six years old.'

Cognac Napoléon, Grande Fine Champagne Réserve d'Austerlitz 1805

Appellation:
Cognac, Charentes, France.

Letter signed by Napoleon.

219

> 'The aromatic palate of an old Malaga is unequalled: syrupy, bold, smooth, it leaves it a unique and undying memory.'

Six centuries before the birth of Christ, grape vines were already cultivated around Malaga and in the hills of the back country, for the fruit as well as for wine: raisins were a valued product. The sweet wine was exported throughout the world, until phylloxera ravaged the vines. The Civil War battles destroyed the vineyard, reduced over a century from 100,000 to 1,000 hectares. The renewal of the vines dates from the 60s. One of the most renowned estates is Lopez Hermanos, founded in 1885 by Salvador Lopez; that family continues to practice the traditional winemaking method: the grapes are dried in the sun on sheets of grass for up to twenty days. The pressed wine is matured in *soleras* like sherry, older wine raising the younger wine.

Traditional malaga has the colour of mahogany, brown tuilé or old gold. The aromas are coffee, dried fruits, candied prunes, chocolate, liquorice, caramel... In the mouth, it is a long and majestic wine, silky, of extravagant complexity. The aromatic palate of an old Malaga is unequalled: syrupy, bold, smooth, it leaves a unique and undying memory. However, malagas from before 1900 are no longer to be found. The two bottles in my collection are much older. They come from the excavation of the *Marie-Thérèse*, a ship that ran aground on 29 February in the Strait of Gaspar, between the islands of Sumatra and Borneo. This three-masted vessel left the Port de la Lune in Bordeaux on 2 November 1871, loaded with wines, liquors and faiences. It was only discovered in 1992. Next to these bottles of malaga, (37 full and 143 empty), there were also some old Gruaud-Larose. I was lucky enough to meet Monsieur Jean-Marc Chastan, director of the Pentagon company, which had purchased the exploration concession in the China Sea. After a good deal of negotiation, I was able to persuade him to trade these two bottles of malaga for a few cases of good pomerol. A bottle from 1918 tasted in 2005 in the Massandra wine cellar etched unknown flavours into my palate, unequalled, infinitely long, suggesting that this bottle will last at least another fifty years. Old malagas are impossible to find, but it is possible to taste twenty-year-old bottles at the estate of Lopez Hermano. A bottle from 1914 from Massandra was tasted at my home on 5 December 2009 in the company of the world's greatest sommelier Andreas Larsson, who was surprised and amazed by the extraordinary quality of this wine.

Malaga from the *Marie-Thérèse* 1800

Varieties: pedro ximénez, muscatel (Alexandria muscat).

Label dating from the 19th century.

VENDANGES DE LA REVOLUTION
1789

I dated this cognac 1789, but the label carries the year 1790: indeed the 'counting' of a cognac begins a year after the harvest.

In 1994, in the Nanterre auction house, I am sitting next to a lady of provincial appearance. I buy a few lots of old wines, and then it's time for a lot of three bottles of cognac: Lozay 1790, Varez 1859, Landes 1876. That is why I am here. At the very least I need the bottle of 1790, thus from a 1789 harvest, a pure folle-blanche. The auction begins, the price rises, and then stops, the lady sighs, nodding her head, taps her hand on her knee. I wait in silence, then bid with a resolute air, and the gavel falls, it's mine, I have my three bottles! But the lady yells: 'This is shameful! They're giving it away!' Unfortunately for her, she had not indicated a reserve price. I give her a contrite look; she informs me that the sale of these bottles was intended to repair the roof of her chateau near Saint-Jean-d'Angély, the Chateau de Dampierre-sur-Boutonne. Then she tells me that these three bottles used to belong to Doctor Texier, former owner of the chateau, and that they have been preciously passed on from one generation to the next... to end up being sold for peanuts. I went to see her to learn more about this story. In the municipal archives, I found a small lexicon published by Doctor Texier, with his photograph. One of his colleagues had the kindness to give me a copy. It was through marriage that Doctor Jean Texier had come to own this chateau, with the box beams of its open gallery covered with mysterious alchemy symbols. On one gallery is written 'If you come to share our blonde light, greetings. But if you want to share it for a long time, come with only your heart. Bring nothing from the world, and do not repeat what people say'. He was the founder of the Trésors du Saintonge tourist path (Dampierre has been open to the public since 1924) along with Archambaud de Grailly, descendant of a great family, of which Jean de Grailly is the most illustrious member: supreme military commander of Aquitaine for the King of England, in 1348 he was one of the first twenty-five members of the prestigious Order of the Garter, and the husband of Rose d'Albret. This fascinating chateau has not had luck with roofs: sold as national heritage to a planter in 1795, it was paid for with... brandy, and lead taken out of the roof; it was later sacked and burned by the Germans in 1944, and victim of another fire in 2002. Nonetheless it is still open to the public, with exhibitions of alchemy and the legends. As for this famous bottle of 1789, adroitly hidden in the Château de Dampierre, and which the Germans failed to find, the cork was replaced in the presence of experts, whose certificate includes the following comments: '44°, extraordinary, superb rancio, rare complexity, sumptuous bottle with rich aromas of folle-blanche of Grande Champagne'.

'44°, extraordinary, superb rancio, rare complexity, sumptuous bottle with rich aromas of folle-blanche of Grande Champagne.'

Cognac 1789

Appellation: Cognac, Charentes, France.

Doctor Texier, former owner of the Chateau Dampierre-sur-Boutonne where this bottle of 1789 cognac was found.

Spirits

It is 2006. I go to Paris to attend an auction at Drouot. It is the best auction I have seen for cognac, armagnac, whisky. Once more my bank account is empty, but I absolutely need a bottle that is missing from my collection: MaCallan whisky 1938, the oldest vintage known after the 1926. According to a catalogue sent to me by David Cox, Director of fine and rare MaCallan, *The Definitive Guide to*

'Directly from the barrel, it was bottled at 41.4° in the 1980s.'

Buying Vintage MaCallan, the 1926 is estimated at 50,000 pounds, and this 1938 at 6,000 pounds. Directly from the barrel, it was bottled at 41.4° in the 1980s. There are only about sixty bottles left.

The estimate in the catalogue is 1,000 euros, a bargain. I tell myself that it should not go too high, few people in France know that old whiskies are rare and expensive, and few people collect them. I will not have another opportunity. But two or three people speaking English are walking around the whisky showcase. So I quickly grab a friend (everybody knows everybody else at auctions), bring him to the showcase, and tell him: 'these bottles look bizarre, and that price! They must be counterfeits!' One of the Englishmen is listening, another one seems surprised, and gives me a furtive look. Victory! I have surely dissuaded them! The auction begins, and I discreetly sit in the back of the room so as to better observe. I am trembling for this whisky. Starting price of 600 euros. I bid 650... 700, 750, I let it go up... 1,050, then nothing. I wait, to sow doubt. The gavel is about to fall, and quickly I say 'One thousand one hundred!'; it bangs, it's mine, 'Do you want both?' asks the auctioneer. 'Take both, one will pay for the other', whispers my friend. I take both, it is an excellent bargain. Afterwards, there are the 1940 and 1945. They also sell for 1,100 euros, which is surprising since they are worth less than the 1938. I buy two of each. Total: 6,600 euros; I am broke, but six bottles for the price of one 1938 in England...

The auction continues. I have other lots in mind just in case. But there is no more 'just in case', I have the whiskey, that's enough! The Armagnac comes out, 1893, six bottles. Starting price 600 euros... 650, 800, 1000, 1150... no one goes higher, I announce 1,200, and bang! It's mine. Then the Rémy-Martin 1724-1974, the 250th anniversary bottle... 600 euros for the three bottles. Bang! This one is mine too. I thought I made a good bargain; I will learn later that I made an unbelievable bargain: the armagnacs, for one, belong to the Compte de Lamaëstre, sold for 10,000 francs per bottle ten years earlier. But I get it all for 12,000 euros, fees included! I have three weeks to pay. Where am I to find the money? I am not about to go unload fruit trucks at four o'clock in the morning in Rungis, like I did in 1987!

In the end, my mother lends me – yet again – 2,000 euros, a friend 500, I sell my collection of Roman coins: Trajan, Marcus-Aurelius..., my son gives me 500 euros. I finally have in my liquor collection the rarest whisky in one of the oldest vintages.

MaCallan's Whisky 1938

Highlands, Scotland, United Kingdom.

Small whisky pocket flask used by aristocrats and nobles in the 30s.

'You should come with us, you won't regret it, we are going to drink gold!' But to his great sorrow, Louis Renault, the famous automobile manufacturer, was unable to board on 10 April 1912 in Cherbourg for the maiden voyage of the extremely luxurious *Titanic*, for which he had in fact built the auxiliary engine. The gold in question was a special vintage of the liqueur Marie-Brizard containing gold flakes, only eight cases, ninety-six bottles, of which, we know not why, four stayed on land. How many were drunk by the privileged passengers, those ladies with their rivers of diamonds, under the flamboyant chandeliers in the salons of the liner, admiring the glittering golden flakes suspended in the smooth liqueur? And how many of those bottles still lie at the bottom of the Atlantic, along with a luxurious 25-horsepower Renault CC from 1912 and the rest of the cargo (including 202 cases of liquor, 26 casks and 230 cases of wine)? Louis Renault bought the last four bottles of Marie-Brizard. The family drank two, and the family auctioned the two others in 1988, at the Galerie des Chevau-Légers in Versailles, where I was able to buy them for 2,700 francs.

This liquor has been produced in Bordeaux since 1755, when Mademoiselle Marie Brizard treated an ill traveller from the Caribbean, who in turn gave her the recipe of an aniseed-flavoured elixir. Ten years later, the company was flourishing and developed a range of liquors: Parfait amour, Eau de cannelle, etc., served at the king's table. It was logical that it should be included on the list of liquors of this grand voyage to America. There remains the recipe of a cocktail, le 'Titanic':

Serves 4:
12 cl cognac
12 cl peach juice
2 cl grenadine syrup
2 teaspoons of Marie-Brizard
Champagne

Mix the first four ingredients in a shaker with ice. Pour into coupes, top off with champagne.

The practice of putting gold in liquor is ancient and known under the name of *Dantziger goldwasser*, Dantzig Liqueur, an anisette flavoured with cumin produced in that city (Gdansk today) since the 16th century. Gold was reputed to purify the blood, and there is no danger in ingesting it. Obviously alchemists were interested in this drink. Later, many companies produced this liquor, including Marie-Brizard for this Titanic vintage. When James Cameron filmed *Titanic*, the Maison Marie-Brizard offered me 100,000 francs to buy back one of the bottles. But I would not sell, not even to an American collector who offered me 50,000 dollars. In 1990, I met the last survivor of the Titanic, the philosopher Michel Navratil, who was three at the time of the tragedy. He gave me a few photos and a signed book. I learned the history of this Marie-Brizard shortly after buying it. The film *Titanic* had not yet been made.

'This liquor has been produced in Bordeaux since 1755, when Mademoiselle Marie Brizard treated an ill traveller from the Caribbean, who in turn gave her the recipe of am aniseed-flavoured elixir.'

Marie-Brizard from the *Titanic* 1912

Spirit, Marie-Brizard Company in Bordeaux, France.

'This liqueur has been produced since 1863 in the Neolithic palace that succeeded the former Benedictine abbey of Fécamp.'

This bottle comes from the auctioning of Maurice Chevalier's wine cellar on Sunday 17 December 1989 in Versailles. It is remarkable not for its complex flavours, but rather for its manufacture in special bottles, labelled D.O.M. for *Deo Optimo Maximo*, its cork sealed with a lead ring and red wax. This liqueur has been produced since 1863 in the Neolithic palace that succeeded the former Benedictine abbey of Fécamp

destroyed during the Revolution. Since the Renaissance, monks in that abbey manufactured a liqueur beloved by François I. In 1863, Alexandre Le Grand discovered the recipe in an old document; it uses twenty-seven plants and spices. The production process includes three distillations, one infusion and a year-long maceration before the assembly of different lots and the addition of syrup. Maurice Chevalier enjoyed Château-d'Yquem, and the Bénédictines that he bought in small bottles and drank in his armchair after the evening meal. Here is what Bernard Loiseau wrote in the preface of the catalogue: 'I am very moved to have the opportunity to introduce the sale of Maurice Chevalier's wine cellar. With the charm and style that were his alone, his good humour and his spirit, he became a legendary character. Still today, I find myself humming 'Ma pomme' or 'Valentine'. Maurice Chevalier loved wine, but his preference went towards the legendary wine Sauternes, so fit for ageing. May the sale of his marvel-

lous wine cellar make hearts throb one again.' Since then, Bernard Loiseau has passed away, joining Maurice Chevalier. At the auction, I purchased the two Bénédictines and the only bottle of Grande Fine Champagne Bisquit Dubouché 1858 cognac, one of the most renowned at that time. My heart indeed throbbed the day of the auction, given the prices: other wealthy and well-known artists also wanted to take home a souvenir of Monsieur Chevalier. But I have no regrets, except not to have purchased anything from the wine cellar of another artist, Claude François. I recently met Monsieur Perrin, a lover of great wines, who told me that he still had some bottles from the wine cellar of his good friend Claude François, so perhaps I still have the chance to get my hands on at least one bottle!
In winter, after a good meal, in a soft leather armchair, there is nothing like a Bénédictine or a Chartreuse from the beginning of the century to erase the stress of the day.

Bénédictine, early 20th century
Maurice Chevalier Collection
1900

Spirit, Bénédictine company in Fécampe, France.

Maurice Chevalier and his favourite cognac.

> **'Can you guarantee that what is in that bottle is still good? After all, it's been more than two centuries!'**

In 1987, in Versailles, impasse des Chevau-Légers, I attend an extraordinary auction of wines and spirits, with prestigious wines of the 19th century: Yquem 1864, Romanée-Conti 1894, Latour 1961... But what I absolutely need is a Hunt's Port 1735. This lot is at the end of the catalogue, which gives me a greater chance of getting it, since many buyers have already exhausted their budget and left before the end of the auction. Moreover, at that time, I was one of the only people to be interested in spirits! The port comes out. The auctioneer announces a port bottled before the war, and a starting price of 3,500 francs. I ask:

'Can you guarantee that what is in that bottle is still good? After all, it's been more than two centuries!'

'I cannot guarantee anything. More than likely it is no longer good, but the bottle is impeccable. 3,500 francs!'

But no one bids. I try my luck: 'For 1,500 francs, I'll take it, to put it in my collection.' Bang! The gavel falls, sold! An elderly gentleman cackles, saying that it's expensive for a tchotchke. Actually, it is an incredible bargain. I have already tasted ports from 1800, very good, and in his book *Vintage Wine*, the English expert Michael Broadbent cites ports from 1670, and gives five stars to an 1811.

There are three distinct types of port: tawny, LBV and vintages. Vintages always have a year. They come from a single harvest, only in the best years. They are stored horizontally and age like wine. Average years are used in the assembly of tawnies (10, 20, 30, 40 years...).

Hunt's Port 1735

Appellation: Porto, Portugal.

Coin with the head of Emperor Probus who, in the 3rd century, abolished the edict of Domitian prohibiting the planting of new vines outside of Italy, and thus permitted the replanting of vines in Roman Gaul.

Musigny Roumier | L'Extravagant de Doisy-Daëne | Les Sens du chenin, Patrick Baudouin | Screaming Eagle | Corton-Charlemagne, Coche-Dury | Champagne Krug | Harlan Estate | Ermitage Cathelin, Jean-Louis Chave | Penfold's Grange | Amarone, Quintarelli | Work, André Ostertag | Jéroboam Clos Windsbuhl, Olivier Humbrecht | Sassicaia | Impériale Château Mouton-Rothschild | Magnum Château Le Pin | Montrachet, Ramonet | Richebourg, Henri Jayer | La Mouline, Marcel Guigal | Trockenbeerenauslese, Egon Müller | Martha's Vineyard, Napa Valley | La Tâche | Magnum Château Lafleur | Magnum Château La Mission-Haut-Brion | Château Dassault | Barbaresco, Angelo Gaja | Hermitage La Chapelle, Jaboulet | Château l'Evangile | Château Lafite-Rothschild | Château Rayas | Grands Echezeaux, Leroy | Trockenbeerenauslese, Joh. Jos. Prüm | Brunello di Montalcino, Biondi-Santi | Château Musar | Grasevina | Tokay de Hongrie Eszencia | Magnum Château Cheval Blanc | Magnum Château Lafleur | Château Trotanoy | Magnum Petrus | Château Haut-Brion | Magnum Château Mouton-Rothschild | Muscat de Massandra | Châteauneuf-du-Pape, Célestins, Henri Bonneau | Vega Sicilia Unico | Clos des Lambrays | La Grande Rue | Muscat de Massandra | Cagore de Massandra | Chambertin Armand Rousseau | Quinta do Noval, Nacional | Château Latour à Pomerol | Salon blanc de blancs | Champagne Bollinger, V.V.F. | La Romanée | Muscat de Magaratch | Maury Mas Amiel | Château Ausone | Châteauneuf-du-Pape, Domaine Roger Sabon | Romanée-Conti | Petrus | Armagnac Laberdolive | Tokay 6 puttonyos, Otto de Habsbourg | Magnum Château Margaux | Cognac Rémy Martin Louis XIII | Château Coutet | Château d'Arche | Château Suduirau | Château Latour | Lacrima Christi, Massandra | Château-Chalon Bourdy | Vin de paille du Jura, Bouvret | Armagnac, Lamaëstre | Red Port, Massandra | Massandra, The Honey of Altea Pastures | Klein Constantia | Cognac Dudognon | Château Feytit-Clinet | Grenache | Château Gruaud-Larose | Vin de Zucco, duc d'Aumale | Cognac Hine | Louis-Philippe d'Orléans | Vinaigre balsamique, Leonardi | Syracuse | Château Bel-Air Marquis d'Aligre - Marquis de Pommereu - 1848 Vin de Louise | Muscat de Lunel | Porto King's Port | Château Palmer | Commanderia de Chypre | Pedro Ximénez, Toro Albala | Madère de Massandra | Madère Impérial, Nicolas | Marsala De Bartoli | Pommard Rugiens, Félix Clerget | Xérès, Nicolas | Château d'Yquem | Xérès de La Frontera, Trafalgar | Cognac Napoléon, Grande Fine Champagne Réserve d'Austerlitz | Malaga de la Marie-Thérèse | Cognac | Porto Hunt's | Whisky MaCallan | Marie-Brizard Titanic | Bénédictine début XXe siècle, collection Maurice Chevalier | Rhum Lameth | Calvados Huet | Chartreuse | Gouttes de Malte

I read in the *Guinness Book of World Records* that the oldest known and tasted rum in the world was the Lameth 1886. After meticulous research, I learn that Chantal Comte, specialist of the marketing of old rums, sells it at the Château de La Tuilerie, close to Nîmes. I find her at the Vinexpo. She explains to me that she has only one bottle left; the following year she agrees to give it to me

'The eye admires the amber and topaz nuances, the nose finds the smoothness of vanilla, the fire of spices, the fruity or roasted aromas.'

for my collection, in exchange for a few magnums of great vintages of my production of Château Feytit-Clinet in Pomerol. Here is the story of this rum: bottles from 1886 were found in a chateau in Burgundy, after having been brought back from South America by an ancestor. The daughter of the master of the house discovered, behind a tapestry, a crack in wall, then a hidden closet. Chantal Comte tasted this unre-

duced rum, which age had brought down to about 50°, and this was her enthusiastic reaction: 'The eye admires the amber and topaz nuances, the nose finds the smoothness of vanilla, the fire of spices, the fruity or roasted aromas. Finally, the mouth is dazzled by so much elegance, by the smoothness of the tannins, by the freshness of the aromas of this century-old liquor, exceptionally long in the mouth.' In a word, the perfection of old rum.

Going back in time, we find a certain Alfred Marie de Lameth, of an old family on Picardy, born in 1842 and died in 1916, captain in 1870, and proprietor of a chai of Martinique rums... in Charente! But it was in Paris that he registered his brand, on 6 July 1887. And he presented his rum at the 1889 World's Fair.

From Picardy to Paris, from Martinique to my wine cellar in La Chapelle-Bâton, through Charente, South America, Burgundy and Nîmes! This bottle has gone halfway around the world, like the buccaneers who invented this strange drink that figures among the greatest eaux-de-vie.

Lameth Rhum 1886

Rum, Martinique, French Antilles.
Sugar cane distillate.

Box in which the bottle was packed, made from several exotic woods representing the flavours of the rum.

1886

LIQUEUR
A LA Gᵈᵉ
Garnier

FABRIQUÉE
CHARTREUSE

Like many connoisseurs, I tasted Chartreuse in my youth, without paying any special attention. Perhaps it is an acquired taste. Then one day in 1995 in Drouot, I saw a Chartreuse Tarragone sell for 5,000 francs. I found that bizarre and did some research. I learned that Chartreuse called 'Tarragone', produced and aged in Spain from 1904 to 1989, were of rare quality. This is due to three factors:
- the liquor on which it is based was distilled from wines of Priorat in Tarragona, contrary to the French practice of using wines from Languedoc;
- the plants used, some indigenous, were not exactly the same as in France;
-the conditions of ageing were different: constant temperature in Fourvoirie or Voiron in France; change in temperatures conducive to a more complex taste in Tarragona, where the casks were placed in granaries.
I needed some bottles of Tarragona at any price, to complete my collection of great liquors. After a lunch at the *Bistro du Sommelier* where I had been invited by Philippe Faure-Brac, greatest sommelier in the world in 1992, I went across the street to the famous Augé wine cellar. I had the surprise of seeing some sixty bottles of Tarragona from 1961 to 1974, yellow and green, priced at 350 to 500 francs per bottle! I bought out the entire stock in front of the wide-eyed salesman, who must have been wondering what I was planning to do with it all. Then I bought two bottles from 1944 at the Taillevent cellars, and a hundred bottles from the period between the two World Wars at auction in Deauville, Paris, Toulouse... I was not buying to speculate, but because everything rare becomes impossible to find, and the heritage disappears like that of old rums or marsalas. In 2009, the price of old Chartreuse shot up to 2,000 or 3,000 euros per bottle.

Through the years, I have built a beautiful collection of old Chartreuse, from 1869 to 1989. And these are magnificent bottles. Here is a commentary by Olivier Poussier, greatest sommelier in the world in 2000, and fervent lover of this liqueur: 'Tarragona green 1910. The scent is a marvel: incense, wood wax, spices, green tea, peppermint. It is syrupy in the mouth, the balance of flavours is total, as a whole it is rich, flavourful, the persistence reaches an impressive level. It is an elixir.'
Indeed, this elixir, the recipe of which is a closely guarded secret, is composed of one hundred thirty plants. The best quality is the V.E.P. for 'Vieillissement Exceptionnellement Prolongé (Exceptionally Prolonged Ageing)', produced since 1963.

The recipe was given to the monks of the Chartreuse of Paris in 1605 by the Maréchal d'Estrée. In the 18th century, the Grande Chartreuse d'Isère markets the Élixir végétal, which still exists in small bottles and registers 71°, then green Chartreuse, 55°. The Revolution disperses the monks, but a copy of the recipe is saved. In 1838, yellow Chartreuse, 40°, is produced in the reopened monastery. In 1903, France having expelled

'This elixir, the recipe of which is a closely guarded secret, is composed of one hundred thirty plants.'

religious congregations, the Chartreuse monks are granted asylum in Tarragona, Spain (there is also a modest production of 'Tarragona' in Marseille). The monks resume production in France in 1929, in Fourvoirie, then in 1935 in Voiron where it is still based. I had the opportunity to visit the distillery in Voiron, as well as the Grande Chartreuse Monastery, where I had the privilege of meeting Don Benoît, representative of the Reverend Father of the Grande Chartreuse, and responsible for distillation. There I tasted ten varieties of Chartreuse from 1906 to 1971, unforgettable and majestically described by Antoine Munoz, director general.
My oldest Chartreuse dates from 1869. It is the only one from the 19th century, the bottle of which has the word 'Chartreuse' in relief. The circumstances of this acquisition are nothing short of miraculous and must remain secret. I meditate on the wisdom of the Chartreuse monks and keep in mind the last words of Don Benoît: 'Serenity, joy, peace.'
The history of this liqueur is the subject of a book published by Éditions Glénat.

Chartreuse 1869

Liqueur, Grande Chartreuse Monastery, Dauphiné, France.

In 1997, I owned half of the Château Feytit-Clinet in Pomerol and received cases of wine in payment under the vineyard rental system. My son bought the other half from the city of Bordeaux and, so that he could pay off his loan, I offered him my stock of fifteen thousand bottles. We had to sell them door to door and I visited antique dealers and gallery curators who were connoisseurs. One day, while I

'1865 is the oldest year of reference for old calvados.'

was hawking my wine in the Saint-Ouen flea market, I noticed a miniature wardrobe of Normand styling, finely decorated and very beautiful. It was no more than 50 centimetres tall. The dealer offered it to me for 1,000 francs, adding: 'What's more, you have a free bottle of calva inside'. For 800 francs, I took it. Inside, there was indeed a bottle wrapped in very old newspaper, dusty, tied with a little piece of twine made from twisted paper. And I continued selling my pomerol: Marché Biron, Malassis, etc. Back home, I discover that this old bottle is a calvados from the Huet Pierre estate in Cambremer, one of the most reputed producers. After carefully cleaning off the label, blackened by the years, I see the vintage: 1865. What a surprise!

The information I obtained from Cyril Marchand, of the Huet estate, is that this bottle by itself was worth half a dozen little Normand wardrobes! There have been no more bottles from this prestigious year for some time. Afterwards, I saw one sell at auction in Deauville for 700 euros. Although it is rather common to find armagnacs and cognacs from the 19th century, I have rarely seen calvados from that period and 1865 is the oldest year of reference for old calvados. The level of the bottle is perfect, and I have not heard of older bottles in my four years of research.

Huet Calvados 1865

Apple brandy.

Appellation: Calvados, Normandy, France.

Small pocket cask used to drink while travelling.

1865 • PASTEURISATION • JULES VERNE'S *FROM THE EARTH TO THE MOON* • FIRST ASCENT OF CERVIN BY WHYMPER

In 2001, a bon-vivant friend calls me from Marseille: 'Michel, why don't you come with us on the last Mediterranean cruise of the *France*?' It was a gourmet cruise, for which the Norway had reverted to its old name. I registered, to meet interesting people, but also to get the last bottle out of the cellar before the ship was sent to the junkyard.

Passing through Malta, we go ashore at La Valette. I notice small vineyards here and there. The wine is not very reputed, a little sweet muscat, but perhaps I could find a rare bottle. I go to see an elderly gentleman who I am told is a wine connoisseur. He has a bright and mischievous eye and immediately says: 'Vive Napoléon! You know, I never liked the English.' He has old bottles: marsala 1860, vino santo and Chartreuse from the early 20th century, etc. But I am intrigued by one bottle: Gouttes of Malta.

'That is a bottle I received from my great-grandfather, a fervent defender of the Sovereign Order of Malta. According to him, only the Knights of the Order knew the recipe, made from rare plants, and now it is gone. It must date from the 1850s, and I don't know how I came to have it. 'Goutte' means strong liquor.' The liquid, dark, seems as thick as oil. I could see it in my collection! Thinking of the price of old Chartreuse, I offer him 500 euros. But he tells me that it is not for sale. Discussion, more discussion, in vain. I meet up with the group, we visit the city, the churches where illustrious knights are buried under artistically decorated tombstones. My head was still with the old man. That bottle of Malta is historic, I must have it! But we leave in two hours! So I leave the group behind, and there I am diving into renewed negotiations. Come on, Grandpa, 1,000 euros! I

'The liquid, dark, seems as thick as oil.'

need the memory of Malta in my collection. 'You're more stubborn than a knight! I like you. I have no children, at eighty I don't know what I'm going to do with my collection. Take it!'

Wow! I have my relic. I will also have the last bottle from the *France*, given to me by the captain, with a piece of the ship – a piece of the hull that he used as a paperweight.

The level of this bottle is down to the shoulders, and I decide to change the cork. I take advantage to taste it with Andreas Larsson, current greatest sommelier in the world and great lover of Chartreuse. What aromatic potency! Fragrances of unknown perfumes, an extravagant complexity. We only have a few drops in our glass, but the syrupy liquor clings to the sides. Floral and medicinal aromas, the countryside, spices, oriental essences, cinnamon, ginger, resin, pine, an exotic garden after the rain... The liquor is very thick, smooth, and very strong: at least ten degrees more than an old Chartreuse. It becomes embedded in my taste buds; I remain captivated.

Gouttes de Malte 1850

Spirit

Here we are at the end of our journey through my one hundred mythical bottles. A surprising choice combining the greatest wines ever made with bottles historic or unknown, but essential for future generations. The tour is over; we close the door of the most beautiful wine cellar in the world. The most beautiful? It is not my word, but that of personalities such as Michael Broadbent or Andreas Larsson, the greatest sommelier in the world.

These thirty-five thousand bottles are merely exceptional bottles, in an impeccable state of preservation. I intend to live to be a hundred to drink Cheval Blanc 1947 with my grandchildren, and leave my wines to a foundation. Most people think of the week ahead; I think of humanity, of preserving the DNA of wines three hundred years old. Why not start a museum? Exactly, a museum, or a conservatory of great wines, with real, full bottles, this is my objective. For four decades I have been tracking down the last survivors of lost vineyards, during the not-so-distant period when these wines were sold in lots at the end of auctions for ridiculous prices. Like the art collectors who, in 1900, bought canvasses of the masters of the 18th century that no one wanted, I went against the fashion of the day. Then came the enlightened ones, experts like Michel Bettane, Michael Broadbent, Robert Parker, then the internet, diffusing information about exceptional bottles throughout the world. I could not reproduce this cellar today, wine has become a commodity for speculation, and the *nouveau riche* have drunk most rare wines.

One hundred fifty years ago, the big names were Tokaji, Syracuse, Madeira, Marsala, Constancia, Malaga... Some of these vineyards have disappeared, others are being reborn. And then wines change, and will always change: two hundred years ago burgundies were clarets, fifty years ago they were bitter, thirty years ago diluted, ten years ago over-extracted... In fifty years, perhaps we will have burgundies of grenache and cinsault, substituting the delicate pinot noir laid low by climate change. Anything can happen, but I will have saved some! Today, in newly-built houses, there is no cellar; in the past that would have been unthinkable. And yet it is a transmission that should be natural, the noblest product of agriculture. When a vine is planted, it is planted to last.

If my wine cellar contained only old wines, it would already be exceptional. But these great and old wines are merely the tip of the iceberg, the tip that appears in the press and on television. It is merely a glimpse of the whole of this collection, out of a list of two thousand references, where the greatest producers are represented by the greatest vintages of their best wines. One can see that there is a bit of everything in my collection. One can also see, and it might be surprising, that it is a cellar of memory, but also of the future: half of the wines referenced are less than twenty-five years old. Finally, one can see that this wine cellar is a loyal reflection of the evolution of the winemaking world: of the 19th century, it contains not only wines from France, or muted wines from Europe, but also all sorts of wines from around the world. For forty years, it has been incorporating wines from Italy and Spain, for twenty years wines from the New World, and recently wines from Eastern Europe have enriched it.

Standing on this fabulous stock of great and elusive bottles, one foot in the past, the other in the future, I am preparing the great wine cellar of tomorrow. With faith than can move mountains, I fill my underground museum as did the Russian Czars two centuries ago. And I suspect the wisdom of my choices will be confirmed by generations to come, as were those of art lovers in 1900. In that, I sincerely believe that my wine cellar is unequalled, for it is not the pleasure of one man, but a humanist and spiritual undertaking. Let us reopen the doors, and here is a livre de cave worthy of an encyclopaedia, and the content of which will one day constitute a conservatory of wines and spirits from around the world.

250 winemakers... (the perfect wine cellar)

My collection is composed of 35,000 bottles, 1,000 magnums and 100 jeroboams and imperials produced by the most prestigious winemakers in the world.

The appellations followed by an asterisk indicate the rarities.

ARGENTINA

Archaval Ferrer: *Altamira, malbec* 2002.
Chacayes: 2002
Bodega Catena Zapata: *Nicolas cabernet sauvignon* 2001, 2004, *Argentino malbec* 2004, *Alta cabernet* 1996, *malbec* 1997.

AUSTRALIA

Armagh: 1995, 1996, 1997, 2001.
Hardy: *Bastard Hill, chardonnay, pinot* 1994, 1997, *Eileen shiraz* 1993, 1994.
R. Blinder: *shiraz* 2004, 2005.
B. Bruthers: *S.G.N.* 1982.
Chambers Rosewood: *Rare muscadelle, Rare Muscat, special Tokay, S-G-N.*
Clarendon Hills: *Astralis* 1996, 2000, 2001, 2003.
D'Arembert: *Dead Arm* 1998.
De Bortoli: *Noble One* 1982, 1985, 1990, 1993, 1996, 2000, 2001. *Botritis.*
Glaetzer: *Amon-Ra* 2006.
Greenock Creek Vineyard & Cellars: *Roennfeld Road shiraz* 1998, 2001, *Roennfeld Road cabernet* 2003, *Creek Block shiraz* 2004, *Alice shiraz* 2006.
Henschke: *Hill of Grace* from 1992 to 2005. *Cyril* 2005.
Leewin Estate: *chardonnay Art Sevie* 1990.
Meshach: *shiraz* 1994.
Noon Winery: *Eclipse cabernet sauvignon* 2005, 2007, *shiraz réserve* 2006.
Penfold's: *Grange* 1983, 1985, 1988, 1989, 1990, 1991, 1992, 1993, 1994, 1995, 1996, 1997, 1998, 1999, 2000, 2001, 2002, 2003, 2004, 2005.
Petaluma: *chardonnay* 1997.
J. Ridooch: *cabernet* 1993.
Rosemount Estate: 1992, 1994, *cabernet* 1994.
Rusden: *Black Guts shiraz* 2003.
Taltarny: *cabernet* 1991.
Torbreck Vintners: *Run rig, descendant* 1997, 1998.
Veritas Winery: *Hanich shiraz* 2004, 2005.
Michael Wynns: *shiraz* 1994, 1998.
Wild Duck Creek: *Duck muck shiraz* 2002.
Yalumba: *Octavius* 1997.

AUSTRIA

F. Artinger: *essencia ruster Ausbruch* 1995, 1999.
Erbacher: *vendanges tardives* 1976.
Weigut Franz Hirtzberger: *riesling singeriedel* 2002, *grüner vetliner* 2003, *Riesling TBA* 2005, 2006.
Weingut Alois Kracher: 1991 *TBA*, 1992. *Cuvée* N° 9, 10, 11, 13.
Weingut Josef Nigl: *riesling* 2002.
Landauer: *welchriesling icewine* 1988, 1992, 1997, 2003.
H. Lunzer: 1997, 2000.
Nekowitsch: *schilfwein* 1998, 1999, 2000.
Opitz: *eiswein Sélection de grains nobles* 1992, 1993, 1994, 1998, 2002, 2003.
Weingut Franz Xavier Pichler: *Riesling kellerberg TBA*2003, *riesling Unendlich* 2005, *GR. Veltliner M.F F marag* 2005.
Weingut Prager: *riesling Smaragd* 2000.
Shandel: *Ruster rulander sélection de grains nobles* 1988, 1989.
Wenzel: *Ruster Ausbruch TBA* 1981, 1991, 1999.
Brundlmayer: *Grüner vetliner Kaferberg* 2004, 2005, *Alte Reben riesling* 2004.

CANADA

Inninskillin: *Icewine* 1989, 1991, 1995, 1996, 1997, 1998.
Château des Charmes: *Icewine Vidal* 1999.
Pillitteri: *chardonnay, riesling, icewine* 1995.
Colio: *Icewine Vidal* 1993.

CHILE

Alka: *Carmenère* 2003.
Alma-Viva: 1996, 1997, 1998, 2007.
Concha-Y-Toro: *Melchor* 1995, 1996, 1997.
Cousino Macul: *Finis Terrae* 1995, 1996.
Errazuriz: *Chadwick Sena, Kai, Don Maximiano,* 1996, 1997, 1999, 2006, 2007.
Lapostolle: *Clos Apalta* 1997, 1999, 2000, *merlot Alexandre* 1999, 2000.
Luigi Bosca: *verdot* 1997.
Montes: *Alpha M.* 1996, 1997.
Valdivieso: *'V'* 1998.
Tarapaca: *Millénium* 1997.

FRANCE

• CHAMPAGNE

Bollinger: *RD, vieilles vignes françaises,* 1928, 1981, 1985, 1988, 1989, 1990, 1995, 1996, 1999.
Egly-Ouriet: 1999, 2000.

Henriot: 1928.
Jacquesson: 1990, 1995, 1996.
Krug: *Clos du Mesnil et grande cuvée* 1982, 1983, 1985, 1990, 1995, 1996, *Clos d'Ambonnay* 1995, 1996.
Laurent Perrier: *Grand siècle* 1990.
Moët et Chandon: *Dom Pérignon* 1971, 1988, 1990.
Montebello: 1928.
Piper-Heidsick: 1933.
Pol Roger: *brut vintage, chardonnay vintage* 1961, 1996.
Roederer: *Cristal, blanc de blanc,* 1990, 1996, 2000, 2002.
Ruinart: *Dom Ruinart* 1990.
Salon: 1928, 1971, 1982, 1983, 1988, 1990, 1995, 1996.
Selosse: *Origine* 1990, *Substance* 1999.

• ALSACE

(SGN = sélection de grains nobles)
Marcel Deiss: *gewurztraminer, riesling, Bergheim* 1989, *Shonenburg* 1989, *tokay, riesling, gewurztraminer Quintessence* 1989, *grand cru Altenberg de Bergheim* 2005, *grand cru Schoenenbourg* 2005.
Hugel: 1976, 1989.
Kreydenweiss: *tokay, riesling, gewürztraminer SGN* 1989.
Kientzlere: *tokay, riesling SGN* 1988.
Seppi Landmann: *vin de glace* 1990, 1993, 2001, 2005, *gewurztraminer and riesling grand cru Zinnkoepflé SGN* 2007, *sylvaner Vallée Noble vin de glace* 2007.
Muré: Clos *Saint-Landelin vendanges tardives* 1997.
Ostertag: *sélection de grains nobles Work* 1989, *Barrique de Zelberg Work* 1992, *gewurztraminer Fronholz SGN* 1990, 2007, *riesling Heisenberg SGN* 1990, *Riesling Muenchberg SGN* 1990, 1995, *Riesling grand cru Muenchberg* 2007, *pinot gris grand cru Muenchberg.*
Schlumberger: *sélection de grains nobles* 1971, 1989.
Maison Trimbach: *Clos Saint-Hune* 1971, 1983, 1989, 1990, 2001, 2004.
Domaine Weinbach: *Quintessence et sélection de grains nobles* 1989, 1995, 2001, 2002.
Domaine Zind-Humbrecht: *tokay Clos Jebsal SGN* 1989, *Rotenberg* 1989, *Heimbourg* 1989, *Rangen* 1989, *Riesling Clos Windsbuhl SGN* 1989, *Gewurztraminer Schoenenbourg SGN* 1989. *Pinot gris Rangen de Thann Clos Saint-Urbain SGN* 1995. *Pinot gris Clos Windsbuhl SGN (trie spéciale)* 2005. *Jéroboam gewurztraminer Clos Windsbuhl* 1989, *Riesling Clos Saint-Urbain SGN* 1995. *Riesling sec Rangen de Thann Clos Saint-Urbain* 2005, 2007. *Gewurztraminer grand cru Hengst SGN* 2007.

• LOIRE VALLEY

Mark Angéli: 1989, 1990.
Patrick Baudoin: *Essence, Maria Juby, Après Minuit* 1997, 2002, 2005.

Domaine des Baumard: *Quart-de-chaume* 1989, 1990.
Château de Bellerive: *Quart-de-chaume* 1988, 1989, 1990.
Domaine Branchereau: 1990.
Clos de La Coulée de Serrant: 1983, 1988, 1989, 1990.
Didier Dagueneau: *Pouilly-Fumé Silex, Pur Sang, Astéroïde, Maudit* 1989, 1990, 1995, 2005, 2006.
Philippe Delesvaux: *Anthologie Carbonifera* 1990, 1996, 1997.
Philippe Foreau: *Goutte d'or, 1re trie, réserve,* 1947, 1989, 1990.
Château de Fesles: *Bonnezeaux* 1988, 1989, 1990, 1997.
Château de Fosse-Sèche: *Réserve du Pigeonnier* 2000, 2002, 2005, 2007.
Domaine Huet: *Le Haut-Lieu, Le Mont, Le Clos du Bourg, Cuvée Constance,* 1959, 1988, 1989, 1990, 1997, 2003.
Charles Joguet: *Chinon cuvée de la Dioterie* 1989.
Domaine du Landreau: *Coteaux du Layon Chaume* 1990.
Jo Pithon: *Ambroisie, Les Bonnes blanches, Quart-de-chaume,* 1994, 1995, 1996, 1997, 1999.
Clos Rougeard: *Le Bourg* 1990, 2005.
Vincent Ogereau: *Nectar* 1989, 1990.
Pinon: *Jasnières* 1989.

• RED BORDEAUX

Château Angélus: 1982, 1988, 1989, 1990.
Château Ausone*: 1921, 1937, 1959, 1961, 1970, 1971, 1982, 1983, 1988, 1989, 1990, 1995, 1996, 2000, 2001, 2003, 2004, 2005, 2006, 2008.
Château Beauregard: 1982, 1989, 1990.
Château Beau-Séjour Bécot: 1989, 1990.
Château Beauséjour-Duffau: 1988, 1990, 2000, 2005.
Château Belair: 1989, 1990.
Château Beychevelle: 1928, 1945, 1947, 1986.
Château Bourgneuf-Vayron: 1982, 1988, 1989, 2000.
Château Brane-Cantenac: 1928, 1989, 1990.
Château Canon: 1985, 1988, 1989, 1990, 2000.
Château Canon-La-Gaffelière: 1988, 1989, 1990.
Château Carbonnieux: 1928.
Château Certan de May: 1982, 1985, 1988, 1989, 1990, 2000, 2005.
Château Cheval-Blanc*: 1929, 1941, 1945, 1947, 1953, 1955, 1961, 1964, 1970, 1971, 1975, 1982, 1988, 1989, 1990, 1995, 1996, 1998, 2000, 2001, 2005.
Château Clinet: 1947, 1988, 1989, 1990, 1998, 2000, 2005, 2006.
Château Cos d'Estournel: 1928, 1955, 1970, 1982, 1989, 1990.
Château Dassault: 1959, 1961, 1962, 1971, 1982, 1988, 1989, 1990, 2005.
Château Ducru-Beaucaillou: 1961, 1982, 1988, 1989, 1990.

Église-Clinet: 1985, 1989, 1995, 1998, 2005, 2006, 2008.
Château Feytit-Clinet: 1870, 1893, 1911, 1928, 1929, 1945, 1947, 1949, 1952, 1959, 1961, 1964, 1975 and all vintages from 1976 to 2007 in 12-bottle cases.
Château de Fieuzal: 1988, 1989, 1990.
Château Figeac: 1941, 1982, 1988, 1989, 1990, 2000.
Château Gazin: 1982, 1988, 1989, 1990, 2000.
Château Gombaude-Guillot: 1989, 1990.
Château Gracia: 2000, 2001, 2005.
Château Gruaud-Larose: 1865, 1982.
Château Haut-Bailly: 1961, 1982, 1988, 1989, 1990.
Château Haut-Brion: 1926, 1945, 1947, 1961, 1964, 1970, 1971, 1975, 1982, 1985, 1988, 1989, 1990, 1997, 1998, 2000, 2001, 2003, 2005.
Château Haut-Tropchaud: 1982, 1988, 1989, 1990.
Château Hosanna: 2000, 2005, 2006.
Château La Conseillante: 1982, 1988, 1990.
Château La Croix de Gay: 1982, 1988.
Château La Dominique: 1945, 1946, 1988, 1989, 1990.
Château Lafite Rothschild*: 1878, 1891, 1918, 1959, 1961, 1970, 1971, 1975, 1976, 1982, 1985, 1986, 1994, 1995, 1998, 1999, 2000, 2001, 2003, 2005.
Château Lafleur*: 1947, 1950, 1955, 1959, 1961, 1966, 1971, and all vintages from 1975 to 2006 in 12-bottle cases.
Imperials 1985, 1988, 1989, 1990, 1995, 1998, 2000.
Les Pensées de Lafleur: 1998, 2001.
Château La Fleur de Gay: 1982, 1988.
Château La Fleur-Petrus: 1961, 1975, 1982, 1985, 1988, 1989, 1990, 1995, 1996, 1998, 1999, 2000, 2001, 2006.
Château La Gaffelière: 1988, 1989, 1990.
Château La Mission-Haut-Brion: 1959, 1961, 1975, 1981, 1982, 1989, 2000, 2001, 2005.
Château La Mondotte: 1996.
Château La Pointe: 1982, 1988, 1989, 1990.
Château Latour*: 1894, 1899, 1923, 1943, 1961, 1964, 1971, 1975, 1982, 1989, 1990, 1994, 1996, 1997, 1998, 1999, 2000, 2001, 2003, 2005.
Château Latour à Pomerol: 1961, 1982, 1988, 1989, 1990.
Château La Tour-Haut-Brion: 1982, 1988, 1989, 1990.
Château La Tour-Martillac: 1989.
Château La Violette: 1982, 1988, 1990, 2006, 2008.
Château Le Gay: 1982, 1988, 1989, 1990.
Château Le Bon Pasteur: 1982, 1988, 1989, 1990, 2000.
Château L'Eglise-Clinet: 1982, 1985, 1989, 1990, 1995, 2005, 2006, 2008.
Château Léoville-Barton: 1988, 1989, 1990, 2000, 2005.
Château Léoville-las-Cases: 1900, 1921, 1945, 1982, 1988.

ChâteauLéoville-Poyferré: 1870, 1988, 1989, 1990, 2000, 2005.
Château Le Pin*: 1982, 1988, 1989, 1990, 1993, 1995, 1996, 1997, 1998, 1999, 2000, 2001, 2002, 2004, 2005, 2006, 2007.
Château L'Evangile: 1961, 1982, 1985, 1989, 2000.
Château Lynch-Bages: 1970, 1982, 1985, 1989, 1990.
Château Magdelaine: 1989, 1990.
Château Margaux*: 1900, 1924, 1929, 1945, 1961, 1966, 1970, 1975, 1976, 1979, 1981, 1982, 1983, 1986, 1988, 1990, 1995, 1996, 2001, 2005.
Château Montrose: 1893, 1898, 1921, 1928, 1970, 1988, 1989, 1990.
Château Mouton-Rothschild: 1868, 1953, 1961, 1970, 1971, 1975, 1981, 1982, 1986, 1989, 1995, 1996, 1998, 2000, 2001, 2003, 2005.
Château Nénin: 1924, 1982, 1989, 1990.
Château Palmer: 1847, 1870, 1875, 1928, 1961, 1966, 1970, 1975, 1982, 1988, 1989, 1990.
Château Pape-Clément: 1989, 1990.
Château Pavie Macquin: 2000
Château Pavie: 1921, 1975, 1989, 1990, 2000, 2001, 2003, 2005.
Château Pavie Decesse: 2000, 2003, 2005.
Château Petit Village: 1982, 1989, 1990.
Château Pichon-Lalande Baron de Longueville: 1955, 1982, 1989, 1990.
Château Pichon-Lalande Comtesse de Lalande: 1970, 1989, 1990.
Château Rouget: 1928, 2000.
Château Talbot: 1989.
Château Tertre-Roteboeuf: 1989, 1990, 1995, 1996.
Château Troplong-Mondot: 1985, 1989.
Château Trotanoy*: 1945, 1947, 1961, 1966, 1970, 1971, 1975, 1976, 1978, 1979, 1980, 1982, 1985, 1988, 1989, 1990, 1993, 1994, 1995, 1996, 1998, 1999, 2000, 2001, 2006, 2008.
Château Trotte-Vieille: 1989.
Clos du Clocher: 1982, 1990.
Clos Fourtet: 1988, 1989, 1990, 2000.
Clos L'Eglise: 1989, 1990.
Clos René: 1982.
Domaine de Chevalier: 1982, 1988, 1989, 1990, 2000, 2005.
Petrus*: 1914, 1924, 1928, 1934, 1939, and all vintages up to 1969 in doubles and from 1970 to 2006 in 12-bottle cases.
Imperials 1985, 1988, 1989, 1995, 2005, 2006, 2007.
Vieux Château Certan: 1961, 1982, 1985, 1988, 1989, 1990, 2006.

• WHITE BORDEAUX GRAVES

Château de Fieuzal: 1989, 1990.
Château Haut-Brion: 1989, 2003, 2004.
Château Laville-Haut-Brion: 1982, 1990.
Château Pape-Clément: 2000, 2005.
Château Smith-Haut-Laffite: 2000.
Domaine de Chevalier: 1975, 1983, 2001, 2006.
Y de Yquem: 1983.

• BORDEAUX DESSERT WINES

Château d'Arche: 1893, 1906, 1983, 1988, 1989, 1990.
Château Bastor-Lamontagne: 1988, 1989, 1990.
Château Caillou: 1921, 1937, 1947, 1961, 1967, 1975, 1983, 1988, 1989, 1990.
Château de Cérons: 1989, 1990.
Château Climens: 1921, 1928, 1929, 1953, 1961, 1971, 1976, 1983, 1986, 1988, 1989, 1990, 2001, 2003, 2005.
Château Clos Haut-Peraguey: 1983, 1988, 1989, 2001.
Château Coutet: 1899, 1900, 1928, 1934, 1947, 1953, 1955, 1959, 1983, 2003, 2005, *Cuvée Madame* 1971, 1981, 1986, 1988, 1989, 1990.
Château Doisy-Daëne: 1924, 1953, 1959, 1970, 1983, 1988, 1989, 1990, 2003, *L'Extravagant* 1990, 1996, 1997, 2001, 2003.
Château de Fargues: 1975, 1988, 1989, 1995, 2003, 2005.
Château Filhot: 1921, 1928, 1929, 1934, 1937, 1953, 1971, 1983, 1988, 1989, 2001, 2003.
Château Gilette: 1921, 1949, 1955, 1961.
Château Grillon: 1947, 1949.
Château Guiraud: 1959, 1961, 1967, 1983, 1988, 1989, 1990, 2003, 2005.
Château Haut-Bergeron: 1983, 1989, 1990, 1997, 2001.
Château Lafaurie-Peyraguey: 1959, 1983, 1986, 1988, 1989, 1990, 2001, 2003, 2005.
Château La Rame: 1988, 1989, 1990.
Château La Tour Blanche: 1921, 1957, 1967, 1983, 1988, 1989, 1990, 2001, 2003, 2005.
Château Les Justices: 1990.
Château de Malle: 1988, 1989, 1990, 2001, 2003.
Château Raymond-Lafon: 1983, 1988, 1989, 1990, 1997, 2003.
Château de Rayne-Vigneau: 1900, 1929, 1941, 1988, 1989, 2001, 2003.
Château Nairac: 1988, 1989, 1990.
Château Rabaud-Promis: 1906, 1926, 1988, 1989, 1990.
Château Rieussec: 1926, 1937, 1947, 1975, 1983, 1986, 1988, 1989, 1990, 2001, 2003, 2005.
Château Sigalas-Rabaud: 1961, 1962.
Château Suduiraut: 1899, 1900, 1928, 1937, 1947, 1949, 1962, 1970, 1971, 1983, 1988, 1989, 1990, 2001, 2003, 2005, *Crème de Tête* 1982, 1989.
Château d'Yquem*: 1811, 1821, 1865, 1885, 1894, 1895, all vintages from 1900 to 2007 in doubles, and since 1970 in 12-bottle cases. Imperials 1986, 1988, 1989, 1990, 2005, 2007.

• RED BURGUNDIES

Domaine des ducs d'Angerville: *Volnay Clos des Ducs, Champans,* 1990, 2002, 2005, 2006.
Domaine du comte Armand: *Pommard Clos des Epeneaux* 1990, 1999, 2000, 2002, 2005, 2006.
Domaine Jean-Marc Boillot: *Pommard* 1990.
Bouchard Père et Fils: *La Romanée* 1999, 2003, 2005.

Domaine Charlopin: *Chambertin* 1990.
Domaine Bruno Clair: *Chambertin* 1988.
Clos des Lambrays: 1937, 1989, 1990, 1999, 2000, 2002, 2003, 2005, 2006.
Clos de Tart: 1990, 1999, 2000, 2001, 2002, 2003, 2005, 2006.
Domaine Jean-Jacques Confuron: *Romanée-Saint-Vivant, Clos de Vougeot,* 1999, 2002, 2005.
Domaine Cathiard: *Romanée-Saint-Vivant, Vosne-Romanée Les Malconsorts,* 1999, 2003, 2005, 2006.
Domaine Drouhin-Larose: *Bonnes-Mares* 1990.
Domaine Claude Dugat: *Griotte-Chambertin, Chapelle-Chambertin, Charmes-Chambertin,* 2004, 2006, 2007.
Domaine Dugat-Py: *Chambertin, Mazy-Chambertin, Charmes-Chambertin,* 2002, 2003, 2004, 2005.
Domaine Dujac: *Clos Saint-Denis* 1988, 1990.
Domaine Engel: *Clos de Vougeot* 1999.
Domaine Sylvie Esmonin: *Gevrey-Chambertin Clos Saint-Jacques* 2005.
Domaine Faiveley: *Corton Clos des Cortons-Faiveley* 1990, 1999, 2002.
Domaine Henri Gouges: *Nuits-Saint-Georges Clos des Porrets Saint-Georges,* 1999, 2000.
Domaine Groffier: *Chambolle-Musigny Les Amoureuses, Bonnes-Mares,* 2005.
Domaine Anne Gros: *Echezeaux et Richebourg* 2000, 2002, 2005, 2006.
Domaine Grivot: *Richebourg* 1988, 1989, 1990.
Louis Jadot: *Chapelle-Chambertin, Echezeaux, Charmes-Chambertin, Clos Saint-Jacques,* 1979, 1985, 2000, 2002, 2005
Domaine Henri Jayer: *Richebourg, Echezeaux, Vosne-Romanée Cros Parentoux,* 1978, 1990, 1993, 1995
Domaine des comtes Lafon: *Volnay-Santenots* 1990.
Domaine Lamarche: *La Grande Rue* 1934, 1988, 1990, 1999, 2000, 2005, 2006.
Domaine de La Pousse d'Or: *Volnay Clos des Soixante Ouvrées* 1990.
Domaine de La Romanée-Conti*: 1870, 1904, 1915, 1921, 1929, 1944, 1945, 1959, 1966, 1971, 1976, 1978, 1985, 1989, 1990, 1991, 1995, 1996, 1998, 1999, 2000, 2001, 2002, 2003, 2005, 2006, *jeroboam La Tâche* 1996, *jeroboam Romanée-Conti* 2000.
Domaine Hubert Lignier: *Clos de La Roche, Charmes-Chambertin,* 1999, 2000, 2003, 2005, 2006.
Domaine Liger-Bélair: *La Romanée* 1926, 1947, 2002, 2003, 2004, 2005, 2006.
Domaine Leroy: *Grands-Echezeaux* 1959, *Romanée-Saint-Vivant, Corton-Renardes, Clos de la Roche, Richebourg, Vosne Aux-Brûlées, Nuits-Saint-Georges Aux Boudot,* 2000, 2002.
Domaine Méo-Camuzet: *Richebourg, Vosne-Romanée Cros Parentoux, Corton, Clos Vougeot,* 1988, 1989, 1990, 1999, 2000, 2003, 2005, 2006.
Domaine Mongeard-Mugneret: *Grands-Echezeaux, Richebourg,* 1988, 1989, 1990, 1993, 1996, 1999, 2005.

Domaine Denis Mortet: *Chambertin* 1999, 2002, 2004, 2005.

Domaine Mugnier: *Chambolle-Musigny Les Amoureuses, Musigny,* 1990, 2003, 2004, 2006.

Domaine Pacalet: *Charmes-Chambertin, Ruchottes-Chambertin, Gevrey-Chambertin Lavaux Saint-Jacques,* 2005, 2006.

Domaine Perrot-Minot: *Chambertin Clos de Bèze, Charmes-Chambertin, Mazoyères-Chambertin,* 2002, 2003, 2005, 2006, 2007.

Domaine Ponsot: *Clos de La Roche, Clos Saint-Denis, Griottes-Chambertin,* 1989, 1999, 2001, 2002, 2005, 2006.

Domaine Emmanuel Rouget: *Vosne-Romanée Cros Parantoux* 1999, 2000, 2002, 2003, 2005, 2006.

Domaine Roumier: *Bonnes-Mares, Musigny,* 1988, 1989, 1990, 1998, 2004, 2005, 2006, 2007.

Domaine Armand Rousseau: *Chambertin* 1933, *Chambertin, Clos de Bèze, Clos des Ruchottes, Mazis-Chambertin, Clos de la Roche, Clos Saint-Jacques,* 1988, 1989, 1990, 1999, 2000, 2002, 2003, 2005, 2006, 2007.

Domaine Serafin: *Charmes-Chambertin, Gevrey-Chambertin Les Cazetiers,* 2002, 2005, 2006.

Domaine de Vogüé: *Musigny* 1989, 1990, 1999, 2000, 2002, 2003, 2005, 2006.

• WHITE BURGUNDIES

Domaine Henri Boillot: *Corton-Charlemagne* 2006.

Domaine Bonneau du Martray: *Corton-Charlemagne* 2006.

Bouchard Père et Fils: *Montrachet* 1990, 2000.

Domaine Coche-Dury: *Meursault-Perrieres, Corton-Charlemagne,* 1996, 1998, 1999, 2000, 2001, 2002, 2003, 2005, 2006, 2007.

Domaine Marc Colin: *Montrachet* 1989, 1990, 1996, 1998, 1999.

Domaine Dauvissat: *Chablis Les Clos, Les Preuses,* 1989, 1990, 2005.

Louis Jadot: *Chevalier-Montrachet Les Demoiselles,* 1978.

Domaine des comtes Lafon: *Meursault Perrières, Montrachet,* 1983, 1989, 1990, 2000, 2005.

Marquis de Laguiche: *Montrachet* 1989, 1990.

Domaine Anne Leflaive: *Montrachet, Bâtard-Montrachet, Chevalier-Montrachet,* 1983, 2000, 2002, 2005, 2006.

Domaine Niellon: *Bâtard-Montrachet et Chevalier-Montrachet,* 1990, 1999, 2006.

Domaine Ramonet: *Montrachet* 1979, 1983, 1989, 1990, 1999.

Domaine Raveneau: *Chablis Les Clos, Montée de Tonnerre,* 1989, 1990, 2005, 2006.

Domaine Roulot: *Meursault Perrières et Charmes,* 2005, 2007.

Domaine Etienne Sauzet: *Montrachet, Bâtard-Montrachet,* 1990, 1999, 2000, 2002, 2005, 2006.

Domaine du baron Thénard: *Montrachet* 1986, 1989, 1990, 1995, 1999.

• RED RHÔNE

Château de Beaucastel: 1995, 1999, 2000, 2003, 2005, 2006, 2007.

Domaine Henri Bonneau: *Réserve des Célestins* 1942, 1989, 1990, 1995, 1998, 1999, 2000, 2001, 2003, 2005.

Chapoutier: *Hermitage, L'Ermite, Le Méal, Le Pavillon, Côte-Rôtie La Mordorée,* 1945, 1988, 1989, 1990, 1999, 2003, 2005, 2007.

Les Cailloux: *Châteauneuf-du-Pape* 2005, 2006, 2007.

Domaine Charvin: *Chateauneuf-du-Pape* 2005, 2006, 2007.

Domaine Chave: *(including Hermitage Cuvée Cathelin):* 1988, 1989, 1990, 1998, 1999, 2000, 2003, 2005, 2006, 2007, *straw wine* 1989, 1990, 2003.

Domaine Clape: *Cornas* 1978, 1990, 1999, 2001, 2005.

Delas Frères: *Côte-Rôtie, Hermitage Les Bessards, La Landonne,* 1999, 2003, 2005, 2006.

Jean-Michel Gérin: *Côte-Rôtie Les Grandes Places, La Landonne,* 2003, 2005, 2007.

Marcel Guigal*: *Côte-Rôtie, La Mouline, La Landonne, La Turque,* 1976, and all vintages from 1978 to 2006 in 12-bottle cases.

Paul Jaboulet Aîné: *Hermitage La Chapelle* 1945, 1961, 1983, 1988, 1989, 1990, 1995, 2000, 2003, 2005.

Domaine de La Janasse: *Châteauneuf-du-Pape, Cuvée Chaupin, Vieilles vignes,* 2003, 2004, 2005, 2006, 2007.

Domaine de La Mordorée: *Châteauneuf-du-Pape, La Plume du peintre, Reine des bois,* 2000, 2001, 2003, 2005, 2006, 2007.

Château La Nerthe: *Châteauneuf-du-Pape, Cuvée des Cadettes,* 1989, 2005.

Domaine de La Vieille Julienne: *Châteauneuf-du-Pape* 2000, 2003, 2005.

Domaine Les Cailloux: *Châteauneuf-du-Pape, cantenial vintage,* 1998, 2000, 2001, 2003, 2005, 2006, 2007.

Le Vieux Donjon: *Châteauneuf-du-Pape* 1998, 2003, 2005, 2007.

Domaine de Marcoux: 2001, 2003, 2004, 2005, 2007, *Châteauneuf-du-Pape vieilles vignes.*

Clos du Mont-Olivet: *Châteauneuf-du-Pape, cuvée du Papet,* 1990, 1998, 2003, 2004, 2005, 2006, 2007.

Michel Ogier: *Côte-Rôtie Belle Hélène* 2005, 2006.

Clos des Papes: *Châteauneuf-du-Pape* 2000, 2003, 2004, 2005, 2006, 2007.

Domaine du Pégau: *Châteauneuf-du-Pape, cuvée Da Capo,* 1990, 1998, 2000, 2003, 2005, 2007.

Château Rayas: *Châteauneuf-du-Pape* 1959, 1978, 1988, 1989, 1990, 1995, 1996, 1997, 1998, 1999, 2000, 2001, 2003, 2005.

Domaine René Rostaing: *Côte-Rôtie, Côte Blonde, La Landonne,* 1999, 2001, 2003, 2005.

Domaine Roger Sabon: *Châteauneuf-du-Pape, Le Secret des Sabon,* 1921, 1959, 2000, 2001, 2003, 2005, 2006, 2007.

Clos Saint-Jean: *Châteauneuf-du-Pape, Deus ex-Machina, La Combe des Fous,* 2005, 2006, 2007.

Domaine Santa-Duc: 1995, 2001, 2003, 2005.

Domaine Pierre Usseglio: *Châteauneuf-du-Pape, Réserve des Deux Frères, cuvée Mon Aïeul,* 2001, 2003, 2005, 2006, 2007.

Domaine du Vieux Télégraphe: *Châteauneuf-du-Pape* 1976, 1998, 2001, 2003, 2005.

• WHITE RHÔNE

Domaine Chave: 2005, 2006.

Beaucastel: *Roussane V.V* 1990.

Château Grillet: 1988, 1990, 1996, 2005, 2006, 2007.

Marcel Guigal: *ex-Voto,* 2003, 2005.

• JURA

Château-Chalon: *Bourdy* 1895, 1911, 1921, 1928, 1942, 1947, 1964, **Macle** 1983, 1988, 1990, 1997, **Bouvret** 1964, 1967, 1975, 1976, **Rolet** 1990.

• SOUTH-WEST, LANGUEDOC AND PROVENCE

Mas Bruguières: 1998.

Alain Brumont: *Château Montus* 1988, 1998, *2000 jours* 1994, *cuvée XL* 1995, *Cuvée des Cimes* 1987, *Bouscassé* 1988, 1989, 1998; *Pacherenc Frimaire* 1996, *décembre* 1990.

Domaine Cauhapé: *Jurançon, Quintessence du petit manseng, Folie de janvier,* 1988, 1989, 1990, 1998, 1999, 2000, 2001, 2005.

Château du Cèdre: *Cahors Cuvée G.C.* 2001.

Domaine du Clos des Fées: *La Petite Sibérie* 1999, 2000, 2002.

Clos des Truffiers: 2000.

Coume del Mas: *Banyuls Quintessence* 2001, 2003, 2005, 2007.

Château de Crémat: 1988, 1989.

De Volonta: *Maury* 1925, 1932, 1939.

Domaine Gauby: *La Muntada* 1998, 1999, 2000, 2007.

Domaine de L'Aiguelière: 1998, 2000.

Domaine de La Grange des Pères: 1999, 2000, 2002.

Château de La Négly: *La Porte du Ciel* 2000, 2001.

Château Lagrézette: *cuvée Le Pigeonnier* 2000, 2001, 2005.

Mas Amiel: *Maury* 1924, 1941, 1954.

Mas de Daumas Gassac: 1982, 1985, 1989, 2005, 2006.

Château de Pibarnon: 1989, 1998.

Domaine Plageoles: *Gaillac Vin d'Autan* 1983, 1988, 1989, 1990, 1997, 2001, 2002, 2005, *vin de voile* 1981, 1983, 1987, 1998.

Producteur de Plaimont: *Pacherenc Saint-Sylvestre* 1992, 1994, 1995, 1996, 1997, 1998, 2000, *Madiran plénitude* 2001, *Fête de Saint-Mont* 2005.

Château Pradaux: 1989, 1990, 2001.

Puig Parahy: *Rivesalte* 1875, 1890, 1898, 1900, 1910, 1930, 1936, 1940, 1945, 1971.

Château Simone: 1990.

Domaine Tempier: 1989, 1990, 2007.

Château Tirecul-La-Gravière: *Cuvée Madame* 1995, 1997.
Domaine de Trévallon: 1988, 1990, 1998.

• ARMAGNAC

Domaine de Boingnères: 1955, 1959, 1964, 1971, 1974, 1978, 1984, 1988.
Castarède: 1893, 1900, 1924.
Corcelet: 1907.
Gelas: 1941.
Domaine de Jouanda: 1914, 1919, 1920, 1929.
Laberdolive: 1904, 1911, 1923, 1929, 1935, 1942, 1954, 1970, 1976.
Lamaëstre: 1893.
De Maillac: 1928.
Renaud: 1904.
Samalens: 1891, 1904.

• COGNAC

Baulon: 1976.
Bisquit-Dubouché: 1904, 1918, 1958.
Brillet: 1900.
Camus: 1878.
Courvoisier: 1864.
Croizet: 1870.
Delamain: 1930, *Réserve Familiale.*
A.E. Dor: *N° 9.*
Dudognon: 1874, *Ancêtre, Héritage Henri IV centenaire.*
Frapin: 1893, *Rabelais, Extra.*
Paul Giraud: 1959.
Goury: 1780.
Hennessy: N° 1.
Hine: 1863, 1914, *Family Reserve.*
Landes: 1859.
La Peyrouse: 1900.
Clos de L'Aumônerie: 1893, 1896.
Lozay: 1790.
Monet: 1865.
Morton: 1893.
Moyet: 1823-1923, 1848, 1880-1920.
Napoléon: 1805, 1811.
Nicolas: 1855.
Château Paulet: 1811.
Pinet Castillon: 1918, 1920.
Premier Empire: 1909.
Rémy-Martin: 1900, 1924, 1974.
Reynard: 1893.
Robin: 1865.
Sainte-Marie: 1867
Tuileries: 1905.
Varaize: 1859.
Vidal: 1906, 1910.

• CALVADOS

Camut: 1873, 1878, 1929.
Chort-Mutel: 1905.
Groult: 1865, *Ancestral, Doyen d'Âge.*
Huet: 1865, 1893, 1900, 1924, 1929, 1945.
Lemorton: 1926, 1944.
Morin: 1895.

• CHARTREUSE

Fourvoirie 1853, 1868, 1878, 1904, 1932. *Voiron* 1936, 1940, 1941, 1944, 1951, 1956, 1964, 1966, 1975. *Tarragone*1904, 1921, 1945, 1960, 1965, 1967, 1968, 1969, 1970, 1971, 1972, 1973, 1974, 1975, 1976, 1977.

• RHUM

Bally: 1900, 1924, 1929, 1939, 1947, 1950, 1957, 1966, 1987, 1990.
Clément: 1956, 1976.
Eldorado: 25-year collector's edition.
JM: 1984, 1986, 1987, 1992.
Lameth: 1886.
Madinina: 1895.
Saint-Benoît: 1830.

GERMANY

(TBA= *trockenbeerenauslese*,
BA = *beerenauslese*)
Burkling Wolf: *TBA* 1990.
Hermann Dünnhoff: *BA Hermannshöhle* 2006, *eiswein oberhaüser Brüke* 2007.
Weingut Fritz Haag: *Riesling brauneberger Juffer Sonnenuhr TBA* 1994, 2000.
Johannisberg: *TBA* 1971, 1991, 1996, 2003, 2005, *auslese* 1997, *spätlese* 1998, *eiswein* 1999.
Weingut Egon-Müller: *Scharzhofberger auslese* 1959, *Scharzhof riesling TBA* 1975, 1994, 2005, 2007, *Scharzhofberger cabinet* 2007, *auslese* 2007, *spätlese* 2007.
Weingut Müller-Catoir: *Kult-Breumel Riesling TBA* 2007.
Weingut Joh. Jos. Prum: *Wehlener Sonnenuhr TBA* 1959, *Graacher Himmelreich L-G-K auslese* 2005, 2007.
Weingut Willi Schaefer: *Graacher Domprobst Riesling BA*2005, *Riesling auslese N°14*2006, *Riesling auslese* 2007.
Weingut Selbach-Oster: *Zeltinger Sonnenuhr Riesling TBA* 2006.
Weingut Robert Weil: Kiedrich *Gr*

GREECE

Samos: *muscat* 1993.
Santorin: *vino santo* 1982, 2000.
Skourias: *Mega oenos* 1997, Labyrinth '9903'

HUNGARY

Aszu Eszencia: 1906, 1957, 1959, 1963.
Eszencia: 1947.
Hetszolo: *5 puttonyos* 1993, *late harvest* 1996.
Oremus: *6 puttonyos* 1972.
Nyulaszo Royal: *6 puttonyos* 1993.
Pazos: *eszencia* 1993, 1997, *5 puttonyos* 1988.

Samorodni: 1963.
Sarospatak: *6 puttonyios* 1901, 1972, 1988.

ITALY

Elio Altare: *Barolo Brunate, Arborina* 2001.
Marchesi Antinori: *Solaia, Tignarello*, 1995, 1997.
Castello dei Rampolla: *Vigna d'Alceo* 1999, 2001.
Brunetto Ceretto: *Barbaresco Bricco Asili, Barolo Bricco Rocche,* 1988, 1989, 1990, 1995, 1996.
Dal Formo Romano: *Amarone della Valpolicella* 1996, 1997, 2003.
Domenico Clerico: *Barolo Mosconi Percristina et Pajana* 2000.
Giacomo Conterno: *Barolo riserva Monfortino* 1990, 2001.
Falesco: *Montiano-Macillano* 1999.
Angelo Gaja: *Barbaresco, Sori San Lorenzo, Costa Russi, Sorri Tildin,* 1961, 1990, 1995, 1997.
Galardi (Terra di Lavoro): 2003.
Bruno Giacosa: *Barolo Falletto* 2000, *Barbaresco Asili* 2000.
Le Macchiole: *Massorio* 2004.
Montevetrano: 2000.
Luciano Sandrone: *Barolo Cannubi Boschis et Le Vigne,* 1989, 1990, 1995.
Livio Sassetti (Pertimali): *Brunello di Montalcino Riserva* 1997, 2001.
Paolo Scavino: *Barolo Rocche dell' Annunziata* 1997, 1998, 2000.
Quintareli: *Amarone* 1985, 1988, 1990, 1997, 2003.
Soldera: *Brunello di Montalcino Case Basse* 1999, 2001.
Tenuta dell'Ornellaia: *Masseto* 1999, 2001, 2004, 2006.
Tenuta di Argiano: *Solengo*1995, 1996, 1997.
Tenuta San Guido: *Sassicaia* 1977, 1985, 1987, 1988, 1989, 1990, 1991, 1992, 1993, 1994, 1995, 1996, 1997, 1998, 1999, 2000, 2001, 2002, 2003, 2004, 2005, 2006.
Tua Rita: *Nostri* 2004, *syrah* 2006, *Redigafi* 2004.
Roberto Voerzio: *Barolo Brunate, Cerequio, La Serra,* 1995, 1996, 2006.

• MARSALA

De Bortoli: *Riversa* 1830, 1860, 1900, 1935, 1945, 1955, 1966, 1986.
Florio: 1939, 1944, 1963, 1964.

LEBANON

Kefraya: *Comte de 'M'* 2002.
Massaya: 2003.
Château Musar: 1954, 1959, 1981, 1982, 1983, 1985, 1988, 1989, 1990, 1991, 1994, special vinatge 2000.

MEXICO

La Cetto: 2000 (1928-2003).

MOLDAVIA

Cojusna: *aouriou* 1979, *marsala* 1979.
Crivova: *ayriou* 1975, 1979, *cahors* 1987.
Miceski-Mici: *ayriou* 1970, *iratiesti* 1970, *frondafir* 1970, *cahor* 1975, *riesling* 1979, *cadrou* 1975, *cabernet* 1975.
Murtaflar: 1970.

NEW ZEALAND

Stonyridge: *Larose* 1997, *cabernet* 1999.
Te Mata: *Coleraine* 1994, *1997, 1998.*
Te Motu: *cabernet merlot* 1996, 1997, 1998.
Matua: *riesling Botrytis* 1991.

PORTUGAL

Barca Velha: 1983, 1985, 1991.
Buçaco Palace: 1990 red and white
Setubal: *muscat* 1900, 1934, 1965, *old Muscat 20 years.*
Vale Meao: 2000, 2001, 2004, 2006.

• PORT

Croft: 1945.
Dow's: 1977, 1985, 2000.
Fonseca: 1948, 1963, 1977, 1985, 1997, 2000, 2003.
Graham's: 1948, 1985, 1994, 2000, 2007.
Quinta do Crasto: 2000.
Quinta do Noval national: 1931, 1932, 1963, 1966, 1985, 1994, 1997, 2000, 2001, 2003, 2007.
Ramos Pinto: 1911, 1937, 1985.
Taylor's: 1927, 1945, 1977, 1985, 1992, 1994, 2000, 2003, 2007.

• MADEIRA

Barbeito: *bual* 1860, 1863, 1885, 1908, 1910, 1912, 1978, *malvasia* 1860, 1875, 1916, 1954, *sercial* 1925.
Funchal: *old sercial* 1835.
Nicolas: *Brown Imperial* 1835, 1875.
Madère: *Sercial* 1830.

ROMANIA

Cotnati: *Grassa sélection de grains nobles* 1977, 1988.

SLOVENIA

Kraski: Teran 1997.
Jagodni Isbor: pinot 1999.

Kerner Isbor: 2003.
Kogl: *Laski Riesling sélection de grains nobles* 2003, *icewine* 2001.
Ledeno: 1992, 1993, 1999.
Radgonski: 1997.
Renski: *riesling* 1961.
Simcic: *chardonnay* 1999, *Leonardo* 1999, *merlot* 2003, *riboulot* 2002, *Theodor* 2001, 2004,
Suhi Jagodni Izbor: *trockenbeerenauslese* 1999.
Teraton: 1987.
Traminer: 1960.
Vrunsko vino: 1999.

SOUTH AFRICA

De Weltreve: Edel Laatoes, *sélection de grains nobles* 1988.
B. Finlayson: *pinot* 1997.
Fleur du Cap: 1990.
Groot Constancia: 1991.
Kanonkop: *pinotage* 1995.
Klein Constancia: 1989, 1991, 1995, 2001, 2004.
K.W.V.: *Noble harvest* 1988.
Seneja: 1998, 2000.
Steleryk: *Bergkelder* 1989.
Stellenzicht: *syrah* 1997, 1998.
Sadie Family: *columella* 2005.

SPAIN

Alto: *Ps* 2003, 2004, 2005, 2006.
Allende: *Aurus* 2004, 2005.
Artadi: *El Pison* 1996, 1998, 2001, 2004, 2005.
Casa Cisca: *Castano* 2003.
Cims Porrera: 1996, 1998, 2001, 2004, 2005.
El Nido: *Jumila* 2006.
Dominio de Pingus: 2000, 2004.
Enate: 1995, 2001.
Clos Erasmus: 2000, 2001, 2003, 2004.
Marques de Riscal: 1925.
Clos Mogador: 1995, 1999, 2000, 2001, 2003, 2006, *Espectacle* 2006.
Alvaro Palacios: *L'Ermita* 1994, 1998, 1999, 2001, 2004.
Hermanos Sastre: *Pesus* 2005.
Tinto Pesquera: *Janus* 1986, 1989, 1991, 1994, 1996, 2002.
Thermentia: 2003, 2005.
Torrès: *Reserva Real* 1989, 1994, 1996, 1998, 2001, 2003, *Grans Muraille.*
Bodegas Vega Sicilia: 1942, 1968, 1979, 1981, 1985, 1986, 1990, 1994, 1998.

• SHERRY

Barbadillo: *Relique* 1921.
Friedner: 1870.
Garvey: *Sacristia, Palo Cordado, Brandy Conde de Garvey* 1780.

Gonzalez Byass: *Brandy* 1886, 1940; 30 ans.
Lustau: 20 ans, 30 ans, *cordado*, 1996.
Nicolas: *Nelson* 1805, *Impérial* 1811.
Pezez Baquero: 1805.
Pilar Arenda: *Cavebar* 1946.
Xérès roux: 1870.
PEDRO XIMENEZ
Toro Albala: *Montilla Moriles* 1844, 1897, 1910, 1947, 1950, 1960, 1971, 1976. *P.X.* 1971, 1972. *Cuvée Don PX-Bacchus* 1939, *cuvée Marques de Poley* 1945.

• MALAGA

Enriques: 1986, 1996.
Lopez Hermanos: *25* ans.
'Marie-Thérèse': 1800.

SWITZERLAND

Castagnoud: *Avigne flétrie* 2005.
Chappaz: *Marie-Thérèse grains nobles* 2002, 2003, 2004.
Corbassières: *Noble* 2000, *Cornulus, cornalin cornulus and coeur de clos Grains nobles.*
S. Maye: *syrah* 2003.
Rouvirez: *sélection de grains nobles* 2000.

UKRAINE

(CRIMEA, MASSANDRA)
Aï-Danil: *Madeira* 1837, 1892, *pinot gris* 1929, 1938 1945, *red Port* 1893, 1899, 1901, *tokaj* 1929, 1937.
Alupka: *rose muscat* 1937, *white Port* 1937, *Madeira* 1947, *white Port* 1947, 1948.
Ayu-Dag: *Cahors* 1933.
Crimea: *Madeira* 1969, 1975, *red Port* 1947, 1969, 1975, *white Port* 1945, 1969, 1975.
Dessert rose muscat: 1945, 1975.
Dessert white muscat: 1946.
Gurzuf: *rose muscat* 1937, *tokaj* 1924, *white muscat* 1931.
Honey of Altea Pastures: 1886.
Kastel: white muscat 1943, 1947.
Kotkebel: *Madeira* 1947.
Kron Brothere: *Madeira* 1913.
Kuchuk Usen: *Madeira* 1923.
Kutchuk Lambat: black muscat 1923, 1932.
Lacrima Christi: 1894, 1896, 1897.
Liqueur white muscat: 1944, 1945.
Livadia: red Port: 1891, 1903, 1930, 1938, 1972, **rose muscat:** 1895, 1905, 1929, *white muscat* 1905, 1928, 1947, 1950, 1959, 1975, 1994, *white Port* 1891, 1892.
Madeira N°83: 1915.
Massandra: black muscat 1966, 1975, Madeira 1900, 1903, 1905, 1906, 1909, Malaga 1918, pinot gris 1888, white muscat 1910, 1923, 1929, red Port 1897, 1900, 1903, 1923, 1975, riesling 1929, Sherry 1969, 1972, 1975, white Port 1916.

Muscat N° 35 Golitzin: 1907.
Pedro Ximenez Liqueur Malaga: 1913, 1914, 1945.
Red stone white muscat: 1947, 1948, 1975.
Rose muscat dessert: 1975.
Selected Sherry: 1840.
Selected Tokay: 1945.
South Coast: red Port 1945, 1964, 1975, rose muscat 1945, 1975, tokay 1957, 1968, 1975, white muscat 1945, 1975, white Port 1945.
Su-Dag: white Port 1940.
Sunlit Valley: 1975.
Surozh: Kokour 1965, 1975, white Port 1944, 1975.
Tavrida: black muscat 1937, 1938, red Port 1944.

UNITED STATES

Abreu Vineyard: *Madrona Ranch cabernet sauvignon* 1993, 2005.
Alban Vineyards: *Reva syrah, Lorraine syrah, Seymour's syrah, grenache, roussane, viog-*

nier 2004, 2005, 2006, 2007.
Araujo Estate Wines: *Eisele, cabernet and syrah*1995, 2002, 2003, 2004, 2005, 2006.
Beringer Vineyards: *cabernet-sauvignon* 1991.
Bond: *Vecina, Eden, Matriarch, Melbury, Pluribus* 2005.
Bryant Family Vineyard: *cabernet-sauvignon* 1992, 1995, 1998, 2000, 2004, 2005, 2006.
Cayuse: *syrah, chamberlin, bionic, frogcabernet Widowmaker* 2005.
Colgin Cellars: *Herb Lamb cabernet-sauvignon, Tychson Hill cabernet-sauvignon, Cariad IX estate* 1999, 2000, 2001, 2002, 2003, 2004, 2005, 2006.
Dalla Valle Vineyards: *Maya* 1995.
Dominus Estate: *cabernet, merlot, verdot* 1989, 1990, 1991, 1994, 1998.
Dunn Vineyards: *cabernet-sauvignon Howell Mountain* 2004.
Grace Family: *cabernet-sauvignon* 2000, 2001, 2002, 2005, 2006, 2007.
Harlan Estate: *cabernet-sauvignon, merlot, verdot* 1990, 1994, 2006, 2007.

Kistler Vineyards: *chardonnay, Cathleen, Durell, Wine Hill* 1994, 1997, 1998.
Marcassin: *chardonnay* 1993, 1995.
Robert Mondavi Winery: *cabernet-sauvignon Opus One* 1985, 1990.
Château Montelena: *cabernet-sauvignon* 1992, 1997, 2002.
Newton Vineyards: *cabernet-sauvignon* 2002.
Ridge Vineyards: *cabernet-sauvignon, Monte Bello, Geyserville, Lytton Spring* 1992, 1994, 1995, 1996, 1997, 1999, 2001, 2002, 2005.
Rochioli: *West Block, River Block* 1997, 1999, 2000, 2001, 2002.
Saxum: *James Berry, Bone Rock* 2006.
Screaming Eagle: *cabernet-sauvignon* 1997, 1999, 2001, 2002, 2003, 2004, 2005, 2006.
Shafer Vineyards: *cabernet-sauvignon Hill Side Select* 1995, 1996, 1997, 1999, 2001, 2002.
Sine Qua Non: *grenache, rouanne, TBA, syrah, viognier* 2002, 2004, 2005.
Philip Togni Vineyard: *cabernet-sauvignon* 2006.
Quilceda Creek (Washington): *cabernet-sauvignon Reserve* 2004, 2005.

Jeroboam Romanée-Conti 2000.

Musigny Roumier | L'Extravagant de Doisy-Daëne | Les Sens du chenin, Patrick Baudouin | Screaming Eagle | Corton-Charlemagne, Coche-Dury | Champagne Krug | Harlan Estate | Ermitage Cathelin, Jean-Louis Chave | Penfold's Grange | Amarone, Quintarelli | Work, André Ostertag | Jéroboam Clos Windsbuhl, Olivier Humbrecht | Sassicaia | Impériale Château Mouton-Rothschild | Magnum Château Le Pin | Montrachet, Ramonet | Richebourg, Henri Jayer | La Mouline, Marcel Guigal | Trockenbeerenauslese, Egon Müller | Martha's Vineyard, Napa Valley | La Tâche | Magnum Château Lafleur | Magnum Château La Mission-Haut-Brion | Château Dassault | Barbaresco, Angelo Gaja | Hermitage La Chapelle, Jaboulet | Château l'Evangile | Château Lafite-Rothschild | Château Rayas | Grands Echezeaux, Leroy | Trockenbeerenauslese, Joh. Jos. Prüm | Brunello di Montalcino, Biondi-Santi | Château Musar | Grasevina | Tokay de Hongrie Eszencia | Magnum Château Cheval Blanc | Magnum Château Lafleur | Château Trotanoy | Magnum Petrus | Château Haut-Brion | Magnum Château Mouton-Rothschild | Muscat de Massandra | Châteauneuf-du-Pape, Célestins, Henri Bonneau | Vega Sicilia Unico | Clos des Lambrays | La Grande Rue | Muscat de Massandra | Cagore de Massandra | Chambertin, Armand Rousseau | Quinta do Noval, Nacional | Château Latour à Pomerol | Salon blanc de blancs | Champagne Bollinger, V.V.F. | La Romanée | Muscat de Magaratch | Maury Mas Amiel | Château Ausone | Châteauneuf-du-Pape, Domaine Roger Sabon | Romanée-Conti | Petrus | Armagnac Laberdolive | Tokay 6 puttonyos, Otto de Habsbourg | Magnum Château Margaux | Cognac Rémy Martin Louis XIII | Château Coutet | Château d'Arche | Château Suduiraut | Château Latour | Lacrima Christi, Massandra | Château-Chalon, Bourdy | Vin de paille du Jura, Bouvret | Armagnac, Lamaëstre | Red Port, Massandra | Massandra, The Honey of Altea Pastures | Klein Constantia | Cognac Dudognon | Château Feytit-Clinet | Grenache | Château Gruaud-Larose | Vin de Zucco, duc d'Aumale | Cognac Hine | Louis-Philippe d'Orléans | Vinaigre balsamique, Leonardi | Syracuse | Château Bel-Air Marquis d'Aligre - Marquis de Pommereu - 1848 Vin de Louise | Muscat de Lunel | Porto King's Port | Château Palmer | Commanderia de Chypre | Pedro Ximénez, Toro Albala | Madère de Massandra | Madère Impérial, Nicolas | Marsala De Bartoli | Pommard Rugiens, Félix Clerget | Xérès, Nicolas | Château d'Yquem | Xérès de La Frontera, Trafalgar | Cognac Napoléon, Grande Fine Champagne Réserve d'Austerlitz | Malaga de la Marie-Thérèse | Cognac | Porto Hunt's | Whisky MaCallan | Marie-Brizard du Titanic | Bénédictine début XXᵉ siècle, collection Maurice Chevalier | Rhum Lameth | Calvados Huet | Chartreuse | Gouttes de Malte

| Musigny Roumier | L'Extravagant de Doisy-Daëne | Les Sens du chenin, Patrick Baudouin | Screaming Eagle | Corton-Charlemagne Coche-Dury | Champagne Krug | Harlan Estate | Ermitage Cathelin, Jean-Louis Chave | Penfold's Grange | Amarone, Quintarelli | Work, André Ostertag | Jéroboam Clos Windsbuhl, Olivier Humbrecht | Sassicaia | Impériale Château Mouton-Rothschild | Magnum Château Le Pin | Montrachet, Ramonet | Richebourg, Henri Jayer | La Mouline, Marcel Guigal | Trockenbeerenauslese, Egon Müller | Martha's Vineyard, Napa Valley | La Tâche | Magnum Château Lafleur | Magnum Château La Mission-Haut-Brion | Château Dassault | Barbaresco, Angelo Gaja | Hermitage La Chapelle, Jaboulet | Château l'Evangile | Château Lafite-Rothschild | Château Rayas | Grands Echezeaux, Leroy | Trockenbeerenauslese, Joh. Jos. Prüm | Brunello di Montalcino, Biondi-Santi | Château Musar | Grasevina | Tokay de Hongrie Eszencia | Magnum Château Cheval Blanc | Magnum Château Lafleur | Château Trotanoy | Magnum Petrus | Château Haut-Brion | Magnum Château Mouton-Rothschild | Muscat de Massandra | Châteauneuf-du-Pape, Célestins, Henri Bonneau | Vega Sicilia Unico | Clos des Lambrays | La Grande Rue | Muscat de Massandra | Cagore de Massandra | Chambertin, Armand Rousseau | Quinta do Noval, Nacional | Château Latour à Pomerol | Salon blanc de blancs | Champagne Bollinger, V.V.F. | La Romanée | Muscat de Magaratch | Maury Mas Amiel | Château Ausone | Châteauneuf-du-Pape, Domaine Roger Sabon | Romanée-Conti | Petrus | Armagnac Laberdolive | Tokay 6 puttonyos, Otto de Habsbourg | Magnum Château Margaux | Cognac Rémy Martin Louis XIII | Château Coutet | Château d'Arche | Château Suduiraut | Château Latour | Lacrima Christi, Massandra | Château-Chalon, Bourdy | Vin de paille du Jura, Bouvret | Armagnac, Lamaëstre | Red Port, Massandra | Massandra, The Honey of Altea Pastures | Klein Constantia | Cognac Dudognon | Château Feytit-Clinet | Grenache | Château Gruaud-Larose | Vin de Zucco, duc d'Aumale | Cognac Hine | Louis-Philippe d'Orléans | Vinaigre balsamique, Leonardi | Syracuse | Château Bel-Air Marquis d'Aligre – Marquis de Pommereu – 1848 Vin de Louise | Muscat de Lunel | Porto King's Port | Château Palmer | Commanderia de Chypre | Pedro Ximénez, Toro Albala | Madère de Massandra | Madère Impérial, Nicolas | Marsala De Bartoli | Pommard Rugiens, Félix Clerget | Xérès, Nicolas | Château d'Yquem | Xérès de La Frontera, Trafalgar | Cognac Napoléon, Grande Fine Champagne Réserve d'Austerlitz | Malaga de la Marie-Thérèse | Cognac | Porto Hunt's | Whisky MaCallan | Marie-Brizard du Titanic | Bénédictine début XXᵉ siècle, collection Maurice Chevalier | Rhum Lameth | Calvados Huet | Chartreuse | Gouttes de Malte